As never before in our nation's history, formerly marrieds are remarrying to form blended families. Most of these well-intentioned couples have no idea of the potential conflicts and hurt they may be opening to themselves, their children and other loved ones. As a counselor, I have longed for effective ways to help couples better anticipate the impact of their remarriage, as well as assist those who are currently struggling with blended families. Maxine Marsolini's new book *Blended Families* should be required reading for couples considering remarriage. In her book, Maxine reveals the journey she and her husband Charlie have taken since joining their families over twenty years ago. In a transparent way, she reveals how God turned shock and confusion into faith and family blessing. Do not get remarried without reading this book!

DON MEREDITH

Many factors complicate life for remarried people. Any really helpful book on the subject has to recognize and address a range of subjects.

Maxine Marsolini's book does not disappoint. It offers much of value from her own personal experience as well as from research and the experiences of other remarrieds.

"Who's in Charge?" the chapter on sticky issues involving discipline of each other's children, gives great insights. This chapter alone is worth the price of the book. I found myself wishing all couples—remarried or not—could read it.

I could say the same with regard to other chapters, such as "The Influence of Guilt and Shame."

Blended Families can help those who are remarried to become truly blended and not just mixed up.

STANLEY C. BALDWIN

Blended Families is a comprehensive book that covers every topic that blended families will face. Though I am not in a blended family, I found Maxine Marsolini's book practical, inspiring, and Biblically based. Her book will be helpful for *every* family and marriage. I particularly appreciated her chapter on coping with anger. I'm sure you'll find this book refreshing and stimulating. After reading it, you'll think, "Yes, we can love each other—even as a blended family."

KATHY COLLARD MILLER

D0018140

BLENDED FAMILIES

CREATING HARMONY AS YOU BUILD A NEW HOME LIFE

MAXINE MARSOLINI

MOODY PRESS

CHICAGO

Moody Press, a ministry of Moody Bible Institute,
is designed for education, evangelization, and edification.
If we may assist you in knowing more about Christ
and the Christian life, please write us without obligation:
Moody Press, c/o MLM, Chicago, Illinois 60610.

© 2000 by
MAXINE MARSOLINI

The characters you find in the pages of this book are real. In some cases the names and
certain details have been changed to protect the privacy of the individuals involved.

All Scripture quotations, unless indicated, are taken from the *Holy Bible: New International Version®*. NIV®. Copyright © 1973, 1978, 1984 by International Bible Society.
Used by permission of Zondervan Publishing House. All rights reserved.

The "NIV" and "New International Version" trademarks are registered in the United
States Patent and Trademark Office by International Bible Society. Use of either trademark requires permission of International Bible Society.

Scripture quotations marked (KJV) are taken from the King James Version.

Scripture quotations marked (NASB) are taken from the *New American Standard Bible®*,
Copyright © 1960, 1962, 1963, 1968, 1971, 1973, 1975, 1977, 1995 by The Lockman
Foundation. Used by permission.

Scripture quotations marked (TLB) are taken from the *Living Bible* © 1971. Used by permission of Tyndale House Publishers, Inc., Wheaton, IL 60189. All rights reserved.

ISBN: 0-8024-3056-2

5 7 9 10 8 6 4

Printed in the United States of America

With thanks to my husband, Charlie,
and to our many friends for their encouragement.
I dedicate this book, with love, to our children—
Andrea, Mike, Felicia,
Grace, Charles, Sabrina,
and Deborah,
acknowledging the pain divorce
has inflicted upon their lives.

CONTENTS

INTRODUCTION

Twenty-four years ago I found myself caught off guard by the uniqueness of the blended home. Divorced and raising two children, I again stood in a chapel repeating lifelong vows before a clergyman. I was linking my life to a man who was already the father of three children. His prior marriage, like mine, had ended in divorce. We both thought this new marriage would be different. After all, we were in love.

At that time the emotional high of fresh romance kept us from realizing the complexity of the journey we were embarking upon as we uttered the simple words "I do." Within days we were facing reality with a clearer vision. Not only did we as newlyweds face transition in every arena of life, but so did every member of our family. Unwanted change paid frequent visits, clothed in unexpected emotional pain, too often causing victory in our home to seem unattainable. It wasn't long before we were struggling with rejection, blame, rage, and jealousy, as well as alcohol to deaden the pain, competition between siblings, and surprises from ex-spouses.

Blended families—families formed as the result of divorce and remarriage, with children to nurture—represent the most difficult form of family life people attempt to live out today. And our numbers are increasing.

More than half of Americans today have been, are now, or will eventually be in one or more step-situations during their lives.[1] Why should this statistic alarm us? Because the stepfamily population is growing each year. The National Institute of Child Health and Human Development's (NICHHD) newest demographic projections show that by the year 2000 more Americans will be living in stepfamilies than in nuclear family structures.[2]

The Institute enlisted Dr. James Bray to begin an extensive study of the stepfamily. In 1984 he and his group launched what became a nine-year study of families living with a stepparent, in particular a stepfather. One of the findings of his research was the high incidence of divorce in second marriages. Nearly 60 percent of these unions were not surviving. Many failed to make it past the first two years.[3]

The September 1997 issue of *Journal of Family Issues* reported that "for recent cohorts, one half of all marriages have involved at least one previously married partner."[4]

What had happened to this second chance at "happily ever after"? Why didn't these couples' dreams come true? Why were husbands and wives throwing in the towel—again? Does it really matter to the overall population how these individuals learn to manage family life? Let's explore that thought further.

In June 1998 the ABC News program *20/20* aired a special on stepfamilies. Hugh Downs noted that "it's projected that in just seven years, more Americans will be living in stepfamilies than in traditional families, which makes our next report critically important." A significant portion of our population is "the *new* American family," Hugh continued, "better defined as the *blended family*. It is ludicrous to believe our lives won't be touched by blended families. We need to take their needs seriously. They are in our workplaces, our churches, and our neighborhoods. They are our friends. The natural result of life exhibited in the blended home is its trickle-down effect to the children of divorce and remarriage—tomorrow's adults. These are the people who will teach the next generation, lead the nation, and be an integral factor influencing the job force, the military, and the church of the future. Their moral fiber matters to all of us."[5]

The blended families addressed within this book fall into one of six formations:

1. Both the husband and wife have divorce histories. At least one has young children to nurture. Most often both have children in formative stages.

2. One spouse has been divorced and has children, and the other spouse has not previously been married.

3. The marriage of a divorced man or woman (with or without children) to an individual who has broken off a cohabiting relationship, having never been married, yet parenting children. This man or woman is feeling the emotional upheaval of a severed relationship but is without legal documents. The child still has a nonresident birth parent imposing influence on the family.

4. A divorced individual (with or without children) remarries a previously unwed mother or father. Perhaps parenting is the result of a teen pregnancy, abandonment of the child, or excessive promiscuity where the parentage of the child is perhaps unknown.

5. The remarriage of a parenting, previously divorced husband or wife to a partner who has lost a mate to death and is still rearing children.

6. The blended family brought about by a spouse becoming involved in an extramarital affair. This particular couple perhaps had no original history of divorce or remarriage,

but suddenly found themselves in the midst of blended family issues as the result of promiscuous actions resulting in the birth of a child belonging to one of the spouses. The couple feels the tug on their heartstrings and feels responsible as parent figures.

In all but one of these blended family formations are two common threads. There is at least one personal history of divorce and remarriage, and there are already children to care for. As these two family units come together they often find a collision course rather than a rose-strewn path. It is crucial to the survival of these families that they learn how to bring union out of diversity. Each family member needs to feel respected, loved, and included. By using effective life management skills, the couple can put their new marriage on the path to a happy ending.

When the wedding bells stop ringing and day-to-day living begins in the ready-made family, the impact of two separate family structures begins to occur. As the differences are exposed short tempers often follow. The parents' prior intimate relational histories suggest that children in stepfamilies have a much higher risk of exposure to conflict, both predivorce and postdivorce, than do children of traditional nuclear families.

Our own marriage occurred at a time when many outsiders looked down on divorced and remarried individuals. Little information was available to us about this particular type of family. We faced an attitude of self-righteousness: "You made your bed; now lie in it." Many friends fell by the wayside, no longer pursuing active involvement in our lives. We were in uncharted territory and quickly becoming prey to many adversaries intending to tear our family asunder.

Eight difficult years later, in my desperation for either answers or escape, I found a relationship with Jesus Christ. Life began to change. Things began to get better. We were finally meeting the issues with a new perspective. It was so refreshing to discover God had another plan—a plan for healing our family.

I know many remarried families whose struggles mirror those we faced. Often their battles are such reflections of our own family's past conflicts that I can feel the pain within their homes. Their joy has been sapped. These precious people are as surprised by the dynamics of blended living as we were. Without solid answers and a glimmer of hope, their stress can finally become so heavy the family breaks apart . . . again.

This would set the stage for a life symbolic of Elizabeth Taylor's —the multiple marriage syndrome. When this pattern emerges it puts into motion a succession of ever-changing stepparents for our children. Rather than life becoming easier with each breakup, it becomes more complex. The self-image of the adults lessens with each failed relationship, and the children learn there is no stability in marriage.

Yet, most divorced individuals remarry. People still feel drawn to try again. Each new beginning sparkles with hope. No one goes to the altar with a long face. But what is there to sustain the joy after the wedding? How can we help couples find answers to stop the revolving door of marriage? How do men and women, boys and girls, process the difficult changes? One person may use anger, another silence. Many choose denial, live with ghosts from the past, or refuse to build relationships within the stepfamily. There is an attempt to conceal or escape what is really happening, while the tumult continues to boil beneath the surface. A lifeline is needed. These families need a functional knowledge of God's promise of hope. I love the way God describes His plan for our lives in the book of Jeremiah.

> "For I know the plans I have for you," declares the Lord, "plans to prosper you and not to harm you, plans to give you hope and a future." (Jeremiah 29:11)

This single promise—given from God to us—offers a solid direction for family life. It is a plan to prosper our family, not harm it. A plan to give us a future full of hope. It is time for adults and children to take God's promises seriously. We are not destined to a pathetic life. God's kids walk a path of victory.

I was delighted to read of a remarkable discovery Dr. Bray made that is contrary to preconceived thinking about remarriages:

"A strong, stable stepfamily is as capable of nurturing healthy development as a nuclear family. It can imbue values, affirm limits and boundaries, and provide a structure in which rules for living a moral and productive life are made, transmitted, tested, rebelled against, and ultimately affirmed."[6]

The blended family isn't just an ordinary family times two. It's a special kind of family with special needs. The goal of this book is to address areas of conflict found repeatedly in divorce and remarriage and describe solutions to those problems. In the next twelve chapters and epilogue, I intend to give you a glimpse of our family and several other families who are on this same journey. This journey into blended lives has been one of expressing unconditional love and forgiveness, learning to become one in marriage, identifying generational sins, understanding birth order among children, the effect of our attitudes on those we love, and much more. Some issues we are still working on. Stepsibling relationships with one another as brother and sister remain incomplete—but they are getting better.

This book is intended as a tool for personal growth and a guide for small group studies or Christian counseling. The "Growth and Application" questions at the end of each chapter can be applied to all these settings to aid the family's blending process. This book will work well within a church's thirteen-week format for Sunday school classes.

One thing for sure—blending doesn't just happen. We purposely journey into it. And it takes years. I hope knowing that God has a plan for family victory will spur you on to meet these challenges God's way and see them result in a happy family. As you explore the pages of *Blended Families* ask yourself the question: What is the goal I would like to achieve for my family? You may want to write your goal down to chart your progress as you begin to explore the pages of this book.

NOTES

1. J. Larson, "Understanding Stepfamilies," *American Demographics* 14 (1992): 37–51.

2. James H. Bray and John Kelly, *Stepfamilies: Love, Marriage, and Parenting in the First Decade* (New York: Bantam Doubleday Dell, Broadway, 1998). Research supported by The National Institute of Child Health and Human Development (NICHHD).

3. Ibid., 8.

4. Megan M. Sweeney, "The Role of Women and Men After Divorce: The Role of Socio-economic Prospects," *The Journal of Family Issues* 18, no. 5 (1997): 479, quoting National Center for Health Statistics, 1990.

5. "One Big Happy Family," *20/20 Friday,* American Broadcasting Company, 19 June 1998.

6. Bray and Kelly, *Stepfamilies,* 12.

Chapter One

AND THERE CAME A LION

We've had so much fun with you the past three weeks," Charlie said to his children before getting out of the car. "I'll miss seeing you every day, but I know Mom is waiting for you. Remember —I love you. We'll talk soon."

"See you in two weeks," they chimed. One by one they hugged us both good-bye and ran to Mom's open arms.

We left, reminiscing over the good times we had shared with our blended family. Our first extended visitation had gone better than we expected. The next two weeks passed quickly. We arrived at the door ready to pick up the children.

This time something was different. It was unusually quiet. The children ordinarily ran out to meet us, but there was no sight of them. We rang the doorbell—but no one answered. We saw a real estate sign on the front lawn. The sign in itself wasn't alarming, but we still wondered why no one was home. This was very peculiar. Charlie and I peered through the windows.

"There's no furniture!" I said in alarm. "Nothing is left!"

"Oh no! She's taken them!" Charlie's voice rose in panic. "My children are gone! How will I find them?"

Minds reeling, hearts pounding, we hurried back to our house. Charlie began a series of frantic phone calls in an attempt to find some answers. He called every friend or acquaintance of his ex-wife that he could think of. He called the neighbors and the parents of the children's schoolmates. He even contacted the real estate agency that listed the house. It was fruitless. Those who knew where she had moved were not going to betray her confidence, and she had covered her tracks well. She had left no forwarding telephone number or change of address.

We did discover that the house had been sold nearly a month before, giving ample time for the children and their mother to be *anywhere*. It occurred to us that when we took Grace, Charles, and Sabrina back after our last visitation they had probably returned to an empty house and left town the same day. But now, two weeks later, there were no leads as to where the children were living.

At the time we were married, my husband's ex-wife had custody of their three children, ages nine, seven, and five. The court granted Charlie a visitation schedule. My two children, eight and six years old, lived with us and regularly visited their birth father. These were typical judicial decisions of the early 1970s, where the mother was most often given custody of the children and the father received visitation privileges void of custodial rights, yet full of financial responsibility. Joint custody wasn't common practice.

A blended home involves so much adjustment. We didn't have a clue the effort it would require to feel like one family instead of two single-parent families. Yet, despite these new challenges, the children, Charlie, and I were learning how to cope with visitation schedules and the unforeseen realities of family life when this startling change was thrust upon us. Charlie plummeted to the brink of desperation.

"Do you really think you should have another drink?" I ventured as he reached for the bottle of whiskey sitting beside the kitchen sink.

"I know what I'm doing. Do we have any more cherries?"

"No. I'm sorry. Guess we ran out," I said, with a growing concern for the rest of our evening together. "You know that won't really make anything better. You've already had three."

"Just leave me alone," Charlie said, agitation growing in his voice. Lifting the glass to his lips, he sullenly walked to the stereo and began playing (for the hundredth time) *My Way*. I grew to hate that song.

We were devastated by the children's disappearance. Our emotions took an incredible downward spiral into mourning, fear, and extreme frustration. Every waking hour was consumed with the thought of locating the children . . . or the dread that we might not be able to.

I felt like Dorothy in the *Wizard of Oz*—suddenly transported to a world I knew nothing about. Lions and tigers and bears were everywhere. How could I find the yellow brick road? I knew I wouldn't wake up like Dorothy and find out it was only a bad dream. This was a nightmare not limited to the darkness. Its length could not be known. Morning's light would not take away its fears.

I had no ability as a private detective and no training helpful to sort through my husband's incredible anger and mood swings. I felt trapped. How could our newly formed family survive such a devastating crisis? Blending our families was now a moot issue. We were consumed with the circumstances and emotions surrounding the loss of the children. Charles Swindoll, in his book *Active Spirituality*, describes well the tone of our home those days.

> For many folks, the struggle to keep things in balance is not an annual conflict, but more like a daily struggle. . . . When things are adverse, life gets simple; survival becomes our primary goal. Adversity is a test on our resiliency, our creativity. Up against it, we reach down deep into our inner character and we "gut it out."[1]

These were truly days filled with tests of our resiliency. Bouncing back was getting harder and harder. Each day we grasped for new creativity that would lead to answers, and each dead end was a drain on our emotions. Each morning was a new challenge threatening our family's survival. By bedtime, exhaustion from the constant concern for the missing children overtook me—the continual lack of time and energy for healthy interaction with my two children and maintaining our marriage was taking its toll. We were drowning. Who would throw us a lifeline?

A DISCOVERY

I realize that for many this particular heartache lasts for years. Perhaps it never ends. Today, many parents are kidnapping their own children in the aftermath of divorce. The anguish is overwhelming for the parent left behind and frightening for the children who are taken into a world of hide-and-seek, often told to change their names for fear of being found.

Jane Pauley reported the amazing story of Barbara Kurth and her missing daughters on *Dateline NBC* in May of 1998.

> It was a story that made headlines across the country—18 years after two little girls had disappeared, they were found. For all those years, they believed their mother to be dead. Now they know the truth, that their father had lied about that. He'd been lying about a lot of things over the years. Accused of kidnapping now, he says it's just a story about a father's love. What about the mother?[2]

As the documentary unfolded, we learned of a father who had brazenly orchestrated an ingenious plot. He simply didn't return his children from their weekend visitation. Within days, he had set up an entirely new identity for himself and the girls. A new city and new names. Their mother's searching, and even money spent on private detectives, was to no avail. Even more devastating to Barbara was the way her ex-husband succeeded in motivating the girls to want no relationship with her. He led them to believe that his deception (rather than a kidnapping, he labeled it a rescue) was for their ultimate good. So even after Barbara found her daughters, she didn't find consolation.

Urged on by the aftermath of unresolved conflicts, divorced moms and dads throughout our culture devise ways to avoid contact with an ex-spouse and maintain a controlling interest in the children's lives. One parent is willing to live on the run, even risk years in jail, to avoid the influence of the other birth parent in the lives of their children. This ploy will never remove the estranged parent from the child's thoughts—which is precisely why Barbara's husband took his deception to a higher level, creating a dead mother in the minds of his girls. Through this particular lie he found a way of settling the issue—of guaranteeing his daughters wouldn't look for their mother.

TRUTH AND TRUST

Proverbs 22:6 tells us to train up our children in the way they should go. God admonishes us to give our youngsters a wholesome standard to follow. For me, that means a truthful model. We cannot do that unless we live it ourselves. The truth must be an important factor to the parent before the child will value the concept. If we live a lie we teach a lie. Barbara Kurth's former husband construed a network of lies for his children to live with. Today those lies are being exposed. There will be many feelings for the girls to sort through in the years ahead.

Trust is a precious thing to violate. Truth may not always be easy to accept, but living on the basis of truth develops a perception of life based on how things really are. Maybe things aren't perfect, but at least you're dealing with reality. Living truthfully improves mutual trust. A life of changing identities is a life of fear and uncertainty and traumatizes our children. The parent who lives a lie places himself in a house of cards. No one benefits when it tumbles.

> Therefore each of you must put off falsehood and speak truthfully to his neighbor, for we are all members of one body. (Ephesians 4:25)

> Because you are a Christian, your life ought to be permeated with truth. When you were born again, God put the spirit of truth in

you. ([see] John 16:13). The Spirit's role is to guide you into all truth. . . . If you allow the Spirit to fill you with God's truth, you will be truthful in your actions and in your relationships.[3]

A REBUFF

We know we are one of the fortunate families. We finally located our children. Several months after we drove up to that empty house, and after digging daily for clues and following deductive thinking and gut instincts, we finally hit pay dirt. For whatever reason, God allowed us to make a discovery.

Using the name of the children's stepfather, we learned that they were enrolled in a school three hundred miles north of our home. They lived in the same neighborhood and near a couple we had previously contacted in our desperate search for answers. That couple had repeatedly lied to us and was a party to the mother's successful disappearance with the children. By now we knew we could not trust others with our newfound information. We decided to visit the children's new school unannounced.

"Could you direct us to our daughter's classroom?" Charlie asked as we stood in the elementary school office that morning.

The secretary was very helpful, and we were soon on our way to a classroom. Grace, our fifth-grade daughter, looked surprised yet happy to see us. Suddenly she acted like something was wrong.

"Does Mom know you are here?" she asked.

We truthfully told her "No" and began to explain what had happened and our long search to find her and her brother and sister.

The other side of the story began to unfold. The school officials had been instructed to contact the mother and the police if the children's father ever tried to find them.

The children's mother arrived soon and the police a few minutes later. Now we saw the children inside a locked automobile across the parking lot, their faces filled with fear and sadness. We weren't even allowed to speak with them or give them a hug. An angry verbal exchange followed between my husband and his ex-wife. She filed a complaint against him, claiming harassment, and he was banned from Washington County, in northwestern Oregon. Rather than fight her desire to escape and risk having her take the children even farther away, my husband backed off. We returned home . . . defeated.

MOURNING

Never again did we have scheduled visitations with Charlie's three children. They did contact us periodically. Perhaps once a year, on their own and sneaking behind their mother's back, they phoned us. We didn't have the liberty to call the children, since their communication with us was carried out in secret. On those rare occasions when their mother gave in to their desire to see us, it always seemed there was a mountain to climb—an uphill battle in an attempt to restart relationships.

Our newly formed family had to find a way to adjust. Andrea, Mike, and I could not fully realize the depth of pain simmering inside of Charlie as he went from day to day. Depression would have possibly been the clinical description. He was in a state of mourning, yet there were no physical deaths to relate to. We discovered that the death of a personal relationship with your children is often worse than a physical death. There is never really closure, and yet there is no closeness because the children live beyond your reach. So hope springs up each morning and dwindles away each night.

Every morning Charlie wondered if this would be the day for a phone call or letter from his children. By night we faced the reality that we were no better off than the day before. Did the children think of their father? Did they still know he loved them? Did they know he still wanted to be an important part of their lives? We hoped so.

HOPE AND PAIN

Life is bearable because an eternal spark of hope somehow simmers deep in the human spirit, refusing to burn out.

(And for this we labor and strive), that we have put our hope in the living God, who is the Savior of all men, and especially of those who believe. (1 Timothy 4:10)

Both of us knew God existed. But in those days we were not walking in fellowship with God and didn't know how to find peace in godly hope. So we were unable to appropriate God's comfort to our lives. We simply understood our state of powerlessness to make these three children an active part of our family life.

Yet for some reason, a spark of hope kept burning in our hearts. Hope must be a gift from the Lord, a reflection of His love for each of us. Because we loved Grace, Charles, and Sabrina we could not accept the permanency of never being a part of their lives. They were an important part of our family picture. (I wonder if God experiences this same pain as He hopes, in love, for us to come to Him?)

Charlie's pain was obviously greater than was mine. As the birth parent, he would forever feel a tug at the heartstrings by these children. But he was also the head of our home. Whatever he felt on the inside set the tone for our family life. Because he couldn't come to grips with his loss but chose to rehearse it daily, the air was often pretty thick at our house. Hope mingled with despair is a difficult lifestyle to balance. My husband's misery controlled our daily lives, holding us fast in its grip.

Life in our home centered on three people who were not even there. Everything surrounding Charlie verified his loss of parental influence with his children. He saw no way to turn back the hands of time and create a lifescape more pleasing to his emotions. As he began living out this conclusion and feeling the full weight of his own prior decisions, Charlie wouldn't allow himself to become a healthy stepparent to my two children. He was too focused on what he had lost to appreciate what he had gained. Andrea and Mike were a constant reminder of the relationship he couldn't have with his own flesh and blood. He had traded fatherhood with his children for confinement with mine—a role he was unwilling to accept. Suddenly I found a hardness in his heart I had not expected.

"I didn't marry your children. I married you."

"That is very unfair. You knew I had children all along. Our wedding meant you accepted coming into their lives as well as mine."

This tension sent the message that I could not count on my husband to nurture my children. I began an awkward attempt to cover for the love he wouldn't give them, often trying to play both mom and dad. I became a Brownie leader for Andrea and a Cub Scout leader for Mike. Their lives wouldn't be put on hold because of their stepfather's inability to participate.

It was hard to balance raising two children with living successfully with a man whose inner struggles I could not soothe. What would happen to our family? The plans we made before our marriage seemed to be shattering. The bedrooms lovingly prepared for Grace, Charles, and Sabrina sat shrine-like as empty reminders of what could have been.

It was as if lions were crouching at our door, awaiting every opportunity to pounce. I felt the children and I had become their prey—and began having second thoughts about this marriage and blaming myself for unwise decisions. Yet I felt locked into the marriage.

DEFINING LIONS

"Lion attacks"—those aggressive and injurious assaults that take place in our lives—can originate with the choices we as individuals make or they can originate in sudden life events, such as the termination of a job, an automobile accident, or the diagnosis of a terminal illness.

A lionlike attack can be premeditated, devised by someone to catch us off guard, or it could be thrown upon us from out of the blue. One sunny day life is defined for us by one set of family boundaries. The next day the family unit we cherished is in total disarray. We had no warning of the change and so we didn't have time to avert the attack.

Why do lion attacks occur? Perhaps the person attacking us is acting out of self-preservation, or out of the fear of suffering his own emotional attack, or even because he harbors a vengeful spirit. There are as many reasons for attacks as there are circumstances. We may not be privileged to know the answers.

The temperament of the lion is to be the predator. He stalks his prey, plans to gain the upper hand, and at just the right moment pounces on his intended victim. The swiftness of the lion is to be feared.

Perhaps this is why, when we encounter a lion in life, our body sends a wave of fear, shock, anger, even grief, over us. Physically we experience an immediate adrenaline surge to cope with the surprise event. In a split second we jump into action, often in the form of panic.

That's exactly what happened to us. When we realized our children were missing, fear struck. We jumped into the car, brainstorming as we sped through the streets toward our home. Fear made search for quick answers.

DAVID

Looking back, we now see this particular lion attack as the beginning of a long journey, one God would use to draw us to Him. That is why hindsight is so valuable. It allows us to gain an entirely new perspective. However, at this crucial time in our lives, we could only see the road blocked at every turn. To make matters worse, it was such a bumpy road. It led to no pleasurable destination.

How could the loss of a relationship with three children possibly be building character in us? Why would God allow such a cruel event to take place? We have since discovered a man in the Bible named David, whom God prepared for bigger life purposes through the lions he encountered as a shepherd.

At a young age he was given the responsibility of tending his family's flock of sheep. This teenaged boy's job description was— day and night—to defend those helpless sheep from the wild animals who roamed the grazing fields of Israel. God was grooming him. It wouldn't be easy, but David was learning how to have victory over the lions.

David knew that physical strength alone wasn't sufficient to overcome the prowess of the beasts. What was his most powerful weapon? He would find that answer as he learned to rely on the protection of the mighty God he loved. But learning to trust in God's deliverance meant that a time of testing would come. And it did.

And there came a lion.(1 Samuel 17:34 KJV)

The Bible tells us that God enabled David to triumph over that lion. As David's confidence grew, his fears were transformed into valor. All the years of grooming in the fields of Israel had a purpose. Because of David's experience with lions as a young man, he was ready to face the Philistine challenger Goliath without fear, triumphing over him and going on to survive many attacks against his life by King Saul. When David went to Saul to ask permission to face Goliath, he said:

> "Your servant has killed both the lion and the bear; this uncircumcised Philistine will be like one of them, because he has defied the armies of the living God. The Lord who delivered me from the paw of the lion and the paw of the bear will deliver me from the hand of this Philistine." (1 Samuel 17:36–37)

David had a confident mind-set. The Philistines described Goliath as the largest and most feared man in all the land. Yet David likened him to the lion in the field—and appropriated the same victory over Goliath he had gained over the lion. He had seen the Lord's deliverance in the past. He did not doubt it in this new circumstance.

Later David faced other challenges.

> [King] Saul tried to pin him to the wall with his spear, but David eluded him as Saul drove the spear into the wall. That night David made good his escape. Saul sent men to David's house to watch it and to kill him in the morning. But Michal, David's wife, warned him, "If you don't run for your life tonight, tomorrow you'll be killed." (1 Samuel 19:10–11)

27

David had a multitude of adversaries. Yet, over and over, David escaped the plots of a jealous and angry Saul and the attacks of other foes. His inner assurance was in the Lord's deliverance. That was where he found his strength.

We could have used confidence like David's on the day we went to pick up our children. We discovered that kind of assurance only after years of sleepless nights and far too many angry days trying to fight the battle in our own strength.

PAUL

Lest we think David's life was representative of the way things were like in the Old Testament but not applicable to life today, we find the same lion-sized struggles in the New Testament in the life of another faithful man of God, the apostle Paul. His life was hard. He was beaten, shipwrecked, thrown in prison, persecuted, and deserted by those he once thought were his friends. Yet Paul testified to deliverance from life's lions (even *literal* lions) —just as David had.

> At my first defense, no one came to my support, but everyone deserted me. May it not be held against them. But the Lord stood at my side and gave me strength. . . . And I was delivered from the lion's mouth. The Lord will rescue me from every evil attack and will bring me safely to his heavenly kingdom. To him be glory for ever and ever. Amen. (2 Timothy 4:16–18)

Even though everyone deserted him, Paul had this to say: "May it not be held against them." Why could he say such a thing? Read on. "The Lord stood at my side . . . " He knew a better Friend, One closer than any of his fleshly brothers and completely able to deliver him. His name was Jesus.

With both the Old and the New Testaments speaking to us of the lion's attack, we should expect to experience extreme events in our own lives. Our circumstances will be different from David's and Paul's, but these men have given us a pattern to follow. Our strength, hope, and victory lie in the same place—in calling on the Lord.

Growth and Application

Commit to memory 1 Timothy 4:10.

1. Are you facing a lionlike event in your family? If so, how are you coping? Try to define the event and your emotions.

2. Read the Scripture passages from 1 Samuel 17 and 19 again, and express how these verses help you understand the assurance David had. Do you have that same assurance of God's deliverance? Why or why not? What difference could it make in your own struggle?

3. What concept from chapter 1 was most valuable to you? Why? How could these new thoughts impact your family today?

Prayer of Application

Lord, You know the lions we have met thus far on our blended journey, and only You know the ones yet to come. Help us to see Your hope and gain confidence in Your deliverance. We pray for strength to go beyond the heartache of disappointments and the challenges of blending our family. Let us discover Your forming hand upon our lives. Create in us a desire to overcome, and not succumb, to the adversities of blending that we might be a family reflecting a confident faith in a God who is able to bring us the victory. We do not serve the God of hopelessness but the God of all hope. Amen.

NOTES

1. *Active Spirituality: A Non-Devotional Guide,* by Charles R. Swindoll © 1994, Word Publishers, Nashville, Tennessee. All rights reserved.
2. *Dateline NBC,* National Broadcasting Company, 18 May 1998, page 2 of transcript.
3. Henry Blackaby and Richard Blackaby, *Experiencing God Day-by-Day* (Nashville: Broadman & Holman, 1997), 209.

Chapter Two

FROM NAÏVETÉ
TO REALITY

Huge drops of snow fell quietly on the windshield. Our sedan's blue hood lay hidden beneath a beautiful white blanket. The pavement had long since ceased to be the cushion under our tires as we slowly journeyed on, driving deeper into a winter wonderland, not knowing what another mile would bring. This was one of the worst storms I'd ever driven in, and Donner Pass still lay several miles ahead of us. Looking at the drifts of snow steadily growing beside the road, I felt a shiver of apprehension.

"Do you think we can make it through?" Charlie asked. "Maybe we should turn around."

"We're doing OK," I answered. "The snow is powdery and the tires are still grabbing well. Besides, we've come so far already it will be as difficult to turn back as to continue on."

Many might say we were very adventurous that wintry weekend twenty-four years ago. Others might believe the storm we braved that day was a precursor to the stormy life we were about to discover. But on that day we had a goal. We were eloping

—and not even our children knew. This was to be our wedding night. Hence our expectations ran high despite the extreme weather.

By eleven o'clock that night (twelve hours after we'd set out on our six-hour journey) we were married in a discreet, yet tasteful, ceremony in Reno, Nevada, by a minister and before witnesses we'd never seen before in our lives. We purchased a picture package, audiotape, and corsage to create memories. Within thirty minutes our wedding nuptial drew to a close and we exited the chapel, mission accomplished. Two days later we were home—announcing our news.

The children readily accepted the surprise of our marriage. For mine, it meant that Mom would no longer be dating, so life should become more normal. Charlie and I looked ahead with blind anticipation, jumped in with both feet, and began to forge a family cohesiveness with our combined children. In reality we didn't have a clue what two families becoming one family would really be like. It wouldn't take long for our naïveté to become evident to all.

The term *blended family* wasn't even a popular phrase at the time we were married. The midseventies introduced a trendy attitude that permeated our minds. "If it feels good—do it." So, naively, we began our life together. Full of romantic optimism. Believing everything would work itself out.

We even bought a four-bedroom house and, with careful attention to detail, prepared space to accommodate our five children —canopy beds for the girls, bunk beds for the boys. Next we tackled the yard project. Hours of tedious labor, often questioning who really writes the how-to instructions, finally resulted in a wooden backyard gym set complete with blue swings, shiny steel bars, a climbing rope, and a slide. As the last bolt was screwed into place, we breathed a sigh of triumphant relief.

"And they said it couldn't be done," I said, as our hands touched in a high-five tribute. "Guess we really can get the upper hand on those instruction manuals."

"I'm sure glad that's over," Charlie replied. "It even looks like it will be sturdy enough not to tip over when they all play on it at the same time."

We envisioned the hours of fun our children would have swinging, climbing, and sliding on their new toy the following Saturday. We assumed they would learn to like each other, given time to adjust to life with additional brothers and sisters. We thought we could get through any stepsibling or stepparenting rivalries that might come our way.

WHAT IS BLENDING?

According to Webster, *blending* is "fitting or relating harmoniously, to have no perceptible separation." Applying that concept to the blended family led me to believe that our two family units would be able to relate harmoniously and not feel fragmented.

Webster's definition may have worked for blending milk, fruit, and ice cream into a milk shake, but we soon found that blending families was much more difficult. The children were not as amicable, the parents not as lenient with the spouse's child as with their own, and ex-spouses often threw a glitch into plans.

Bringing two families together doesn't necessarily result in a sweet strawberry shake. Sometimes the results are more like vinegar and oil. The two don't naturally mix and they have to be shaken up often to combine the flavors into a palatable experience.

As I speak with many blended families, I continue to hear the same old laments. "My husband (wife) doesn't love my child." "Your child doesn't respect me." "Is it OK to buy new jeans for my child when his father hasn't sent the child-support check?" "Why can't my stepchild accept me?" "You're not my mom (or dad). I don't have to listen to you." "I have more chores than your son does. Just because he doesn't live here all the time doesn't make that fair." "I'm blamed for everything." "She gets away with everything." The statements are as numerous as the individuals. Most family members discover early on that harmony is not doled out in as abundant a measure as competition and conflict.

If this sounds familiar to you, know that you are in the majority of families who are starting over after divorce and remarriage. All family members are building a new lifestyle not necessarily as comfortable to them as the one they left behind. Our new spouse may not be a welcome addition to our children. They were not shopping for another dad or more brothers and sisters. Compatibility of family personalities often seems an elusive dream for blended families. It is, without a doubt, a difficult task—a labor of love requiring a great deal of perseverance to develop the family feeling we as marriage partners expect to achieve.

MAKING THINGS BETTER

The difficulty of making blending a pleasant experience forced us to seek new solutions. One avenue we chose was to have another child. Perhaps this would lessen the sense of lost fatherhood for Charlie. Maybe he would feel a closer bond with our family, and the new baby would tie all the children together, linking them by a common bond to both of us. In January of 1977, two months shy of our second anniversary, Felicia was born. This birth experience was different for Charlie than the births of his other children. Times had changed. Now fathers could be in the delivery room.

"Take these," Dr. Moore said, as he held the scissors in his outstretched hand, "if you'd like you can cut your daughter's umbilical cord."

"Really?" Charlie asked, a bit afraid of doing something wrong. "You really want me to cut her cord?"

"Sure. I'll show you where," the doctor said with encouragement as he directed the procedure, freeing Felicia from the lifeline that had fed her so well during the past months.

As he took the scissors, a new sense of fatherly participation entered Charlie's heart. He was bonding with Felicia from the moment of her birth. He looked proudly at his new baby, then bent down to give me a kiss. "She's so beautiful. You did a great job. I love you."

Meanwhile, we were getting nowhere in our attempts to reinstate visitation with Charlie's three children. Each phone call to their mother ended in more anguish. Charlie's role as the children's father was devalued by their mother as a mere biological occurrence, not to be mistaken for a genuine father-child relationship. At the same time, the children's stepfather was being heralded as a superdad. This provoked jealousy and anger for a while, but eventually made Charlie think of himself as an even greater failure as a father figure.

He was continually agitated in his spirit. After-work cocktails became a nightly habit, heightening the unrest within his soul. And there were his friends—the ones who were all too eager to stew in his misery with him, thinking they could offer cheer as they tipped one more round together at a local lounge. All these attempts to escape sadness only gave Charlie more time to relive the pain he was trying to escape. He never came home feeling better, only more bitter, and with a terrible headache.

With Charlie's use of alcohol and anger escalating, our arguments were increasing. We needed some form of release. If his ex-wife's new husband was deemed a better dad than he, then perhaps he should be allowed to adopt the children. Conceding failure and denied interaction as a dad, Charlie chose this solution. His ex agreed

My two children continued to visit their birth father for a considerable length of time. This visitation concept was hard on our delicate new family life. On paper it sounded reasonable, but in reality it seemed to provoke anger in my husband and set up nervousness in me. He didn't want the neighbors to see the children leave with someone else, nor did he want to be reminded of my past relationship with another man on a regular basis.

His own past was difficult enough to make sense of, but my past marriage presented a greater emotional challenge and threat to his masculinity. He wanted to look at me as his alone, as if I had not had intimacy with another man. Jealousy was a factor. There was no way to wipe out my former relationship and pretend it didn't exist. This caused me great distress. It seemed impossible to find a balance between my past life and my present life.

Bottom line, we didn't have the maturity to share the children with another household, even though it was good for the children not to sever those relationships. Within three and a half years we began talking with my children's birth father. It was decided that

Charlie would adopt Andrea and Mike. We, the adults, were searching for the optimum solution to create a "normal" nuclear structure to a blended family framework we did not fully understand. The impetus was to recreate the familiar family unit.

Beyond the legal paperwork surrounding Charlie's adoption of Andrea and Mike, none of us, including my ex, ever really intended to bow out of the children's lives. The adoption of Andrea and Mike would only take away the rigid concern about visitations, stop bad attitudes concerning the regularity of child-support payments and unmet expectations, and remove the embarrassment of a household with two last names. It wouldn't repair all the wounds.

Let me take a minute to clarify our own selfish actions. Visitation problems, child-support payments, and embarrassment are not valid reasons to decide to make our adult lives more convenient. They demonstrate our inability to cope maturely in the blended home. The children's well-being should be the real focus. The children's need for a secure identity is fulfilled when they continue to feel love from both birth parents. A stepparent's love is a great asset, providing wonderful encouragement, but it cannot replace the love or natural attachment of a birth parent. This is not the place for competition among adults.

In an underlying, perhaps subconscious way, Charlie's adoption of Andrea and Mike was a cover-up for Charlie's shame over his divorce—and mine. This was detected years later. Yet, at this time in our lives, Charlie convinced us his reasons were sincere. He felt that if he followed through in making my children his children, the father feelings for them would come. Naively persuaded of his genuineness, the three of us believed him. In our hearts we so badly wanted this to be true.

In 1979 Andrea and Mike legally became Charlie's children. They now bore his name. The reality of the adoption offered a more convenient home life, but the legal formalities didn't bring about the heart change we had hoped for. Although my husband didn't know how to verbalize it—or didn't choose to—it was evident by his actions that he still had not found it in his heart to love my children.

Oh, he agreed to provide for Andrea and Mike, but that is different from love. He would excuse his lack of involvement and love by saying, "After all, blood is thicker than water." I couldn't understand this statement. From the beginning I had chosen to love his children as my own. Where was the fair play? I was angry with him and impatient with his lack of fatherly affection toward two of the children in our home. For me, fatherly affection was a core element necessary to family formation.

As a father, Charlie had many discussions with Andrea and Mike regarding values, integrity being a high priority. He included them in vacation plans and painting the fence outside the house. He has always been a good negotiator when he has a goal to accomplish, but he seldom participated with Andrea and Mike in the joys of childhood. It was easier for him to keep them occupied than to interact with them on a closer relational level. I knew the children needed more. They wanted him to respond to their love. They could feel things weren't as they should be in their relationship with him. After their little sister was born his lack of involvement became even more noticeable. He could show *her* love, but he wouldn't express the same fatherly feelings toward them.

Things hadn't changed a lot for me either. I was still trying to provide the missing-dad side of home life for them. Often I was excusing his ill moods by telling the children he'd just had a bad day.

We should have anticipated the future far more than we did. One day these children would be teenagers and then adults. How would they view their own identity then? Would they want their "real" name back? Would they feel abandoned . . . cheated?

It all seemed so innocent then. Hindsight has shown that adoption really didn't make things better from the broader family perspective. A few years later the man who adopted Charlie's three children divorced their mother and she remarried again. In adulthood, two of those children chose to petition the court to regain their birth surname. The other daughter married prior to doing that.

The spring of last year found Charlie apologizing to Andrea

—first, for denying her a relationship with her birth father, and second, for failing to be the father she really needed. All those years he had harbored the feeling that he had stolen her and her brother from their father. For twenty years he lived with silent uneasiness over his actions surrounding the adoption.

DISCOVERING NEEDS

While preparing this chapter I came across a quote from Mother Teresa. We can learn from her wisdom. The lives she touched in India brought her a great realization.

"I have come more and more to realize that it is being unwanted that is the worst disease that any human being can ever experience. Nowadays we have found medicine for leprosy and lepers can be cured. There's medicine for TB and consumption can be cured. For all kinds of diseases there are medicines and cures. But for being unwanted, except there are willing hands to serve and there's a loving heart to love, I don't think this terrible disease can be cured."[1]

Every blended family member needs to adjust to losses and new beginnings. Because of this it's so easy for us to fall into a space of feeling unwanted. All of us hunger for the assurance of loving relationships. Love needs to flow in a greater measure in our homes. Then we will have eyes to identify the needs of our children and ourselves and have the energy to meet those essential components of healthy relationships.

If we think of love as an active noun and solid substance, not an isolated feeling, we will discover its full potential—and it *is* powerful. Love is a growing thing. It means growth in knowledge and in depth. It means opening our minds to the process of learning how to love as God intends. This is the love necessary to overcome the insecurities naturally found in the blended home.

And this is my prayer: that your love may abound more and more in knowledge and depth of insight, so that you may be able to discern what is best and may be pure and blameless until the day of Christ. (Philippians 1:9–10)

Love takes time to evaluate the needs, both emotional and physical, of family members. Making a list is helpful. This exercise opens our eyes to see the uniqueness of those we live with. What we discover brings us out of self-focus into family focus. We walk for a while in the shoes of our spouse and our children.

While compiling your list remember that you are an important person too. We must find the balance between meeting the needs of others and satisfying the needs within ourselves that are necessary to healthy living. I find it easy to overlook my own needs, sacrificing them to cover the necessities of other family members. I usually put myself at the bottom of the priority list. One day I realized it was OK to tend to me. By not caring for myself I was cheating my family. I lacked the necessary enthusiasm to be effective in the lives of my husband and children. So I dared to write my list. There were lots of items.

- I need to pursue personal interests.
- I need time to nurture my marriage.
- I need to be an effective mother.
- I need to know that my children feel loved.
- I need my stepchildren's acceptance.
- I need romance and honest companionship with my husband.
- I can never be completely satisfied without a peaceful home.
- I need to feel secure financially.
- I need time to reflect.

Being a wife and a mom is full-time work, but I found it necessary to develop my own areas of personal interest outside the home. My talents needed expression.

To satisfy my outside interests I began to volunteer a few hours a week at our local hospital. I felt a broader personhood emerge. My scope of being was stretching beyond family interests and family problems. It was like a breath of fresh air. My attitudes lifted immediately, and I came home rejuvenated.

When we start writing down our family's individual needs, we are amazed to find out the variety of simple things important to family blending. Come together as a family and discuss personal needs. Don't assume you know what is important in the life of another family member. Talk about it. Then put pen and paper to work as you record what is said. An easy format to follow would be:

Name: *Charlie*
Relationship to me: *Second husband*
Needs: *Companionship, worth as a father, praise,
        understanding, sex*

Name: *Mike*
Relationship to me: *My son from my first marriage*
Needs: *Love, relationship with Dad (and stepdad), encouragement, sports, fun, animals*

Remember to do this exercise on more than one occasion. As we move through time, our needs change. Once the needs are identified, like Mike's need to have pets, the next step will be to creatively find ways to enter into the world of our family members and begin to meet their needs.

In our city we have an animal shelter where we can select pets that would otherwise be destroyed. Pets are a responsibility, but weigh the joy they can give and the burden becomes light. Mike had a lot of fun with his dogs and kittens. If family members demonstrate love by their actions, it won't be long before everyone in the family feels special.

THREE PARTS—NOT ONE

Blending is a long-term learning experience. Our first major breakthrough was in accepting the fact that, as a blended family, we could never be a model copy of an original nuclear family unit. At first, this thought gave us a great deal of sadness. But the time came when grieving over this loss came to an end. We had to move from what we did not have to what we had in order to create a healthy family.

One day we opened our eyes and freely decided we—the yours . . . the mine . . . and the ours—were in this thing together. We had a unique family environment. Accepting this different family configuration as an OK way to live lifted the burden.

Our expectations are now more realistic. We are now able to bring a more compassionate understanding to those within the present family. So what if the outside world reminds us of our familial differences more often than we would like. Our friends don't mean anything malicious; they are just curious—and we are a novelty. But after twenty-some years the questions still take us by surprise.

A few months ago we were out to dinner with friends relating all the exciting details of our fourth granddaughter's arrival.

"She's so tiny, only six pounds, but very snuggly," I said, with full grandmotherly pride. "We now have four granddaughters, all so different and all so delightful. This grandparenting thing is so much fun."

"I can see you are both enjoying this family growth, but whose daughter had the baby, yours or Charlie's?" asked our friend.

We looked at each other as if to say, "Not again." Once more we began to explain our family structure and unravel its details for our friends.

"Ours," Charlie began. "Well, Maxine's birth daughter . . . but my adopted daughter. Katie is Andrea's second baby."

We acknowledge that our family mystifies a certain portion of the population. That is, unless they are like us. As long as others know of our family history, curious questions will arise, reminding us afresh we are a different kind of family. Being gracious while helping others to become comfortable with our blended family is sometimes inconvenient, but also is a reminder of where we have grown as a family. Defining bloodlines is no longer our focus, but theirs. That is very refreshing.

FAMILY DEFINITION

Let's look at how our blended families are defined. When entering remarriage, it is not just myself, my spouse, and the children. There are satellite family units to be considered. These are the two secondary families that will forever impact our primary family. They consist of both ex-spouses and the extended relationships therein. We are actually a three-part family.

Primary Family Unit You, your spouse, and your combined children

Satellite Family	Satellite Family
A	B
Husband's ex + relatives related to his children	Wife's ex + relatives related to her children

After looking at this diagram, make a chart listing the members of *your* extended satellite groupings. Beside each name list the relationship that person represents to your child. Deem if the relationship is valuable enough to your child to encourage it to develop. Try not to think of your convenience but the child's greater family tree. What we interrupt in their childhood may be difficult to piece back together later on. We cannot turn back the hands of time and re-create missing memories. For my children a portion of the chart would look like this:

Child's (children's) name: *Andrea and Mike*
    Satellite family member: *Phil*
    Relationship to consider: *Birth father*
    Reasons to continue: *Heritage, father's love, honor divorce decree*
 	
    Satellite family member: *Mary Jane*
    Relationship to consider: *Grandmother*
    Reasons to continue: *Grandmother's love*

> Satellite family member: *Paul*
> Relationship to consider: *Uncle*
> Reasons to continue: *Paternal family connections*
>
> Satellite family member: *Mark*
> Relationship to consider: *Cousin*
> Reasons to continue: *To be included in extended family*

All of these people are caught up in the aftermath of my divorce. Their relationships with my children were put on hold. Andrea and Mike would have enjoyed knowing these family members during their childhood years. I regret that loss for them today.

If you are already in more than a second marriage, you will have multiple satellite families. Since it is common for remarriages to fail within the first two years, many men and women today are experiencing third, fourth, or even fifth marriages. With so many extended relationships, it is harder to manage communication with satellite families.

For the sake of the following illustration we will assume the husband has been married twice before, giving him satellite families A and A1, and the wife has had three prior relationships, giving her satellite families B, B1, and B2. If there are children from differing parentage because of these multiple relationships, your family unit could look like the following diagram, with several satellite individuals still in the children's lives.

> **Primary Family Unit**
> You, your spouse, and your combined children
>
> Satellite Family   Satellite Family
>
> A + A1   B + B1 + B2
>
> Husband's 2 exes + relatives   Wife's 3 exes + relatives
> related to his children   related to her children

The dynamics of additional individuals has escalated dramatically. With the ever-widening picture comes added emotional stress.

Since the satellite families are ordinarily a very important part of the children's lives, they become a continual part of our lives as well. For family harmony to exist, dignity and respect must be given to the role of the satellite family members. How can we diminish stress and come to workable relationships with these members of our children's extended family? Sometimes these people do things we have difficulty accepting. They even think very differently than we do and can instill value systems we can't embrace and give gifts we can't notice without feeling hostility. Consider the following true-life drama.

"Look! It's Jason," Faye said in disbelief.

"It can't be," replied her husband Frank. "He doesn't have a car."

"Well, he's behind the wheel of *that* car," Faye continued, "and he's turning into our driveway."

Anger began to rise in Frank's voice. "His father's done it again! I'm sick and tired of not being consulted in decisions that affect us all. How will Jason ever understand our rules while your ex continues to do these things?"

Meanwhile, Jason—totally delighted—proudly parked his shiny black car in the driveway and emerged with a big grin. "Look what Dad got me. Isn't it great? He even paid for the insurance."

This could have been a positive experience for all had both sets of parents been included in the decision. Or, at the very least, Jason's dad could have given his ex and her husband time to adjust to the gift he intended to give his son. Instead we see a classic case of interhousehold tension. Rather than sharing in Jason's joy, stepdad Frank turned angrily and walked away, leaving Faye to make sense of the differing emotions surfacing in her son and her husband. Now we witness the emergence of intrahousehold conflict as well. Faye suddenly found herself a sounding board, caught between her son's enthusiasm and her husband's disgust.

"I'm sick of doing this," Faye said, weariness in her voice.

"Where can I go to resign? There is no way I can control the gifts Jason's father chooses to give him."

CREATING POSITIVE ENCOUNTERS

There will be negative encounters with satellite family members. Count on it. Looking back, we realize that divorce didn't stop us from dealing with the persons to whom we were once married. This is part of the "till death do us part" portion of the wedding ceremony. It will be better if we *other* parents, even though we may have primary custodial rights, can find a way to teach responsibility and thankfulness to our children at the same time we enjoy their happiness with the gifts given by the other parent. There are ways to allow the child to enjoy the best of both worlds. After all, the generosity of a birth parent can free us from having to fund many high-ticket items.

Last summer my grown daughter told me, "I thought as a child I had to agree with what you felt about my dad, even if I didn't want to." If I, as her mother, was unhappy about something he had done she felt she had to take on the same feelings. I didn't realize that my angry moments were having that effect on her. My problem was simple. I had not forgiven my ex-husband, so I was not over my feelings of resentment toward him. As Christians we are to set a different standard. John MacArthur helps us understand the idea of forgiveness:

> When Christ did speak in those final hours before He gave up His life, it was clear that His mind was not on revenge—not even on self-defense. Forgiveness was the predominant theme of His thoughts throughout the whole ordeal of His crucifixion. . . . At the very moment when most victims of crucifixion might scream out in fury with a curse, He prayed for forgiveness for His tormentors: "Father, forgive them, for they do not know what they are doing" (Luke 23:34). . . . Do you see the glory of that? Although Christ is the sovereign, eternal, omnipotent God, He did not threaten, He did not condemn, He did not pronounce doom on His crucifiers. Instead of lashing out against them, He prayed for them.[2]

"Love your enemies and pray for those who persecute you."
(Matthew 5:44)

Forgiveness is an act of love. Once, again, we find love means more than feelings. After a divorce the thought of loving actions toward an ex-partner won't often be our mind-set. Somehow we have to move beyond negative feelings to a godly perspective.

To please the Lord, Charlie and I concluded that reconciliation with past relationships represented the judicious path to workable association with satellite family members. That involved letting go of past offenses and even of present expectations for the good of the family unit. The word *forgiveness* took center stage. (Yes, I do realize some of us have ex-spouses who want no part of reconciliation.)

Our desire to have reconciliation is not dependent on whether the other party accepts our offer. We do it simply because it is the right thing to do. God knows our hearts and the intent of our actions. We don't have to invite satellite family members over for a barbecue, but we are responsible to do our part in giving respect to these people. We can find a way to understand that those other parent figures want to express their love to the children as much as we do. They just have a differing perspective on how it should be done. Unless there is potential danger, we must make space for satellite family members to demonstrate their love to the children. Once again, we are not competing—we are trying to blend successfully.

Remember our trip to Reno through the snow? Can we make it through? Would it be easier to turn back? The same questions apply to blending—and the answers are the same. It is as difficult to turn back from the blending process as it is to continue on to our destination—in this case binding up the wounds of two families and becoming an extended family where we embrace one another despite the bonds of blood. It will take a determined effort to create positive encounters with satellite family members. But quitting will only testify to the inability of adults to be mature enough to meet blended family issues with compassion and sound reasoning. We are capable. Are we willing?

We have seen both sides of reconciliation. On one side we have seen congenial acceptance and on the other side we have experienced vicious verbal attacks from those who had no intention of entering into any concept of reconciliation.

Where reconciliation has been successful, our children have greatly benefited. Where those efforts have been rebuffed, our children still live in confusion. We have made peace with my ex-husband and found ourselves visiting and praying together as Andrea gave birth to our grandchild. It was a beautiful time to share.

Sadly, it has not been possible to reconcile fully with the mother of my husband's children. Her refusal to let go of past hurts, complicated by the years of missing contact, has made Grace, Charles, and Sabrina unable to trust that Dad really loves them and enter into a complete father-child relationship. If not resolved, this heartbreak easily passes into the next generation when grandchildren are born. We are at that point now with Sabrina's two girls. In six years we have only seen our granddaughters on half a dozen occasions because the past is not fully reconciled.

Growth and Application

Commit to memory Philippians 1:9–10.

1. Considering your expectations for blending families when you married your spouse, how have naïveté . . . and reality . . . been evident?

2. Take time to write down the needs of your family members. How could this benefit you? How could it benefit family members? List several creative ways to meet those needs.

3. Does love play a significant role in your blended family? How have you evidenced your love growing?

4. Consider satellite family relationships. How could they be improved? Attempt to make out a family satellite member chart.

Prayer of Application

Lord, please forgive us for the times we have lacked sensitivity and tried to make our lives more convenient without thinking of the long-term effects on others. Show us how to understand the needs of our family members and in love try to fill those needs. Give us a heart to reconcile with and understand those satellite family members that are important to our children. For us, this all sounds so difficult, but as we follow You, these things are all possible. Amen.

NOTES

1. Mother Teresa, interview by Malcolm Muggeridge, in *Something Beautiful for God: Mother Teresa of Calcutta*, by Malcolm Muggeridge (New York: Harper & Row, 1971), 98–99.
2. John F. MacArthur, *The Freedom and Power of Forgiveness* (Wheaton, Ill.: Crossway, 1998), 38.

Chapter Three

BUILDING A STRONG PRIMARY FAMILY UNIT

It was Christmas, and tradition brought back the production of Handel's *Messiah* to our church. Performers dressed in formal black and white filled the entire platform. Shiny instruments were raised and happy faces readied themselves to entertain the rapidly growing crowd assembling in the soft orange pews. As the clock struck seven, the conductor stepped up, took a courteous bow, turned, and with arms raised, motioned to the orchestra. Silence fell over the audience as remembered melodies filled the air. Within minutes, a deep sense of tranquillity settled over me. What a great feeling. Like a refugee from the storms of life, I wished I could linger in those moments forever.

Something in the way the orchestra blended seemed so awesome. Each instrument added its cohesive touch of beauty to the pieces. The instruments were almost alive, as if playing without the skilled fingers of the musicians. Some instruments didn't have as big a part to play as others. But together—as each one answered the appropriate cue—they produced a delightful unity of sound.

Each oboe, violin, clarinet, and drum had a significant part to play. By themselves their sound could never be so sweet. The violin didn't try to play the part of the clarinet. The drum didn't do what the oboe was intended to do. Instead, each instrument did the job best suited to its makeup. Their blending made the sound so enjoyable, so powerful. The air resonated with notes of celestial harmony, carrying its listeners to hidden places of the soul.

A fresh sense of God's presence rested on me. This became a turning point in my life, a graphic illustration of what could happen if as a couple we could find this type of harmony in our marriage. It was imperative to our future that we identify why our marriage didn't reflect this same blended quality. I felt we both wanted to find the unity the musicians expressed, but for some reason long-lasting unity continually eluded us.

Questions filled my mind. What was preventing our relationship from taking on this quality? Why weren't we experiencing the beauty of blending? Could remarriage really overcome the chaotic aftermath of divorce? Was disharmony somehow a natural consequence or even a punishment for those who remarry? Would our lives ever stop reflecting discordant notes screaming, "Yours, mine, and ours"? Did God have answers we had not yet discovered? I needed to know.

Maybe it would take lots of practice, as it did for the musicians. Or maybe we just didn't know how to properly read the lyrical composition of marriage. After all, we didn't find this kind of harmony in our last relationship. This could be the key. To reach an optimum potential in any concert takes an accurate reading of the music. Middle C must not be misread for a B flat. That would result in a pitiful sound.

Not one of the musicians in the orchestra played whatever notes seemed right to him. Each musician followed the score, worked with the other players, and paid close attention to the conductor. Nor was there a spirit of competition. Instead, the musicians concentrated on teamwork.

I decided that Charlie and I could learn a lot from this orchestra. If we could somehow make an accurate reading of the notes composing the sonata of matrimonial bliss, I felt we could successfully blend our two distinct sounds into a pleasing duet. Discord really could become a thing of the past.

A HEAVENLY CONDUCTOR

First things first. To make it through the struggles of remarriage, a couple must first find a way to form a successful, strong primary unit as husband and wife. Without the couple's strong marriage bond, there will be no family unity.

For Mike and Tina, blending was a challenge early on. Mike had been married before and was the father of a preschool son. Tina, although never married, had experienced multiple long-term relationships before marrying Mike, but had no children.

Mike and Tina are definitely different in their basic makeup. Mike loves to look at life through humor and satire—and a splash of the nonchalant. Tina is far more serious, goal oriented, and assertive. She angers easily.

Both have similar histories of substance abuse. Together they bring a lot of excitement to their marriage—but also the potential for dysfunction. Within a few months of their wedding, they were polarizing one another.

"Tina and I have been in so much counseling," Mike said, throwing up his hands in exasperation. "It didn't seem to work for us. When we got angry and dissatisfied with one another, we couldn't remember how the counselor wanted us to react or what he wanted us to say to get over the problem. We both just wanted to escape and even went back to some of our old habits to ease our unhappiness.

"But the old habits weren't helping either. We became even more miserable. Finally we realized we couldn't heal our marriage the clinical way, but we *could* do what God wanted us to do. We saw incredible success when we put God first and lived like He says. It's the only way that works for us. We are happier now than we ever thought possible."

God is the Author of marriage. He personally ushered it into existence. That makes Him our heavenly Conductor—the One from whom we should take our cues. He is the expert on marriage. That makes the Bible our music book. Within its pages we find the notes we need to create a harmonious husband-wife melody.

> Then the Lord God made a woman from the rib he had taken out of the man, and he brought her to the man. The man said, "This is now bone of my bones and flesh of my flesh; she shall be called 'woman,' for she was taken out of man." For this reason a man will leave his father and mother and be united to his wife, and they will become one flesh. (Genesis 2:22–24)

Here we see God's ideal for marriage. But how do we put this pattern into action? The scriptural statement "they will become one flesh" (familiar words used in many marriage ceremonies) nagged at our spirits. How was it possible for two very different people to think and live as one? Did that mean we would lose our individual identities and one of us fade into a clone of the other? What an appalling thought! Thankfully, God didn't have that in mind when He spoke of marriage as composed of one man and one woman who become one.

DIFFERENT BY DESIGN

So—what did God really mean when He said, "They will become one flesh"? It may surprise you, as it did us, to discover the beauty God intended for this special union between a husband and wife. Let me take you back to the creation story found in Genesis 1: "God created man in his own image, in the image of God he created him; male and female he created them" (v. 27).

There is a significant substance to pluck from internalizing the implications of creation's story. God is one with Himself, yet in passing His likeness on to mankind, He created male and female, two separate human gender forms, to display His totality. In doing this, God created within each human likeness the need for companionship.

The Lord God said, "It is not good for the man to be alone. I will make a helper suitable for him." (Genesis 2:18)

If the man could satisfy all of his needs alone, God would not have had to say this or make provision for two genders. Both the male and the female natures are needed to more closely experience the fullness of the diverse characteristics found in God's multifaceted nature. It makes sense that in marriage each spouse encounters a more elaborate display of personality traits than he had by himself, thus giving the couple the ability to see a bigger picture of God.

A suitable helper brings to the marriage things we can't find in ourselves. It is so important we see this to understand why oneness with our mate really matters. We came into being as needy people—people in need of companionship and in need of what others have to offer. God never intended us to be self-contained units able to satisfy our every requirement.

GOD'S PROTOTYPE

God molded man from the dust of the earth. But woman's origin was very different. She was formed from the rib of the man—that part of the body forming a covering for the heart. In fact, she is the *only* living being formed in such a unique way. It's fascinating to see how God made the man and the woman part of one another from the moment the woman came into being.

Because the woman was taken out of the man and brought by God to stand beside him, Adam (the first created man) felt an immediate closeness to her. He eagerly received her as a gift. Finally there was a companion "with skin on" for him to communicate with. Unlike the animals, she was like him, yet in a wonderful way not like him.

Her physical appearance was different in several ways. She was more delicate, her breasts were larger, her genitalia very different, and she had no hair on her face or chest. When the man and the woman embraced, they fit well together, as if strength and tenderness had found common ground.

The man found the woman's emotional differences refreshing. Whereas he looked after the upkeep of the garden, she noticed the garden in a more descriptive way, taking full note of its beauty in every blossom, every bird of the air. She had a more sensitive concern for the things she saw. Together, the couple had complete enjoyment of one another, as God intended.

ONE FLESH

I sense no competition between Adam and his wife. She was not a foe. A husband who competes with his wife wages battle against himself. The Bible says that the woman was "bone of [his] bones and flesh of [his] flesh," making her an extension of Adam's very own body. I can only surmise (being a woman) that this feeling Adam experienced could have been similar to the attachment a woman feels toward the child to whom she has just given birth. A part of her is forever formed in her offspring and her goal is not to compete with the child, but to nurture him to attain his full potential. A good marriage needs the same nurturing.

Adam was as emotionally charged as a new mom by the attachment he felt toward Eve. It felt good to know that she was part of him. He had no hesitation in accepting God's gift. There was no whining, "God, why did you give me *this* woman?" The man and the woman began their life together with a strong feeling of attachment both in the bodily sense and on the emotional level. Both welcomed their unique origins—his from the dust of the earth, hers from the rib of man, but both by the hand of God.

This concept seemed a bit overwhelming when Charlie and I first encountered it. It was fine and dandy for Adam and Eve, but how could we put into practice what God meant for our marriage in this Scripture passage? I wasn't sure how Charlie, my husband groomed by this modern age of worldliness, would understand this flesh-and-bone concept. Could he ever feel this kind of closeness toward me? Would I be able to feel like a part of his body beyond a stubbed toe?

For sure, we would have to move out in faith onto this arena. I'm glad we did. We joined a neighborhood church, one that honored the holiness message of the Bible, and began attending God-centered classes on relationships. We found books. We read. We took courses on godly marital growth. For us, learning has never ceased. In fact, it's been a fun part of our life together.

One of the most influential small-group studies we had the privilege of participating in was called *Becoming One* (now available as *Two . . . Becoming One* from Moody Press). In chapter 6 of this study guide we found a wonderfully freeing insight regarding oneness as it applies to remarriage. If a couple can grasp this concept it will propel them forward, bringing them nearer to a true one-flesh relationship.

> With the advent of sin, natural oneness was destroyed. Today, couples can find marital oneness only through faith in God, and then in understanding His principles of marriage. Each of us desires to be loved unconditionally. However, that will not happen on this earth unless someone chooses to love you by faith.
>
> If you were formerly divorced, or not a Christian when you married, or just cannot be sure your spouse is your Eve or Adam, the principle of oneness still works for you. Scripture tells us that God hates divorce (see Malachi 2:16), and He desires for you to stay married. Therefore, the principle of leaving and cleaving and becoming "one flesh" is still God's desire for your marriage. If you leave and cleave by faith, God indicates oneness will result!
>
> We also know from Scripture that God forgives past failures when they are confessed to Him. He gives us a new beginning and tells us not to look back. No matter what our past was, God's plan for marriage works today. Do not let Satan confuse you or rob you of a wonderfully satisfying marriage. Become one and move ahead to reflect, reproduce and reign. God is honored each time a couple commits to His plan for marriage.[1]

Because we chose to believe this truth we found the ability to begin our journey to oneness. God has honored our faith. His Word is so practical. It's not to be read as any other book, but instead read to plant godliness into our lives. Adam and Eve were a prototype (a pattern to follow) for our own relationships. The verses in Genesis were given to us as a clear, beautiful, godly look at a one-flesh union. With this first couple we see the artistry of our Creator as He sculpts the gift of marriage into its final crescendo. The moment the bride is presented to the bridegroom, they begin a journey into one flesh as husband and wife.

Becoming one flesh is an active decision, and a continual journey, not a final destination like going cross-country from California to New York. Along the road we will continually make choices to honor God and our mate as we share in the ups and downs of life. Trials will come and conflicts will arise, but we can get through it together because the goal of one-flesh relationships is unity.

Our mate's strengths will become a wonderful resource for family life. We will come to understand how nice it is to share our days together, not having to do it all, be it all, or have every answer. Compassion for our spouse grows in times of weakness if we are attentive to becoming one flesh. Our thoughts will not turn to put-downs, and we will feel sheltered in the arms of our mate.

Year after year, as oneness evolves, we become more and more amazed at the unique nature and incredible creativity of our God. He is God Almighty, the Composer of masculinity and femininity. Together they are a terrific blend.

CHERISH THE BLUEPRINT

I am thankful that God wrote a blueprint for marriage. History has carried the written word through the centuries to our place in time. From this pattern we can glean elements that lead to successful one-flesh marriages.

1. The husband accepts the wife as part of his own body.

2. The husband loves his bride in the *same* measure as he loves himself.

3. The wife is a gift.

4. The woman is a suitable helper-nurturer, not a competitor.

5. The man and woman *together* bring completion to their individuality.

6. The one-flesh union, marriage, is God's plan.

7. The word *united* indicates "united together in purpose."

8. The couple is forging a new life apart from their homes of origin.

Women often get caught up in the Cinderella, happily-ever-after syndrome. There is so much preparation before the marriage. There are dresses and colors and flowers to pick out, bridesmaids and groomsmen to select, a church to reserve, and a reception to plan. An enormous amount of attention is given to the bride's appearance. She is the one all eyes will soon be on. She must be presented a radiant bride to the groom.

Excitement builds as she envisions sharing her entire self with her soon-to-be husband, the man God has given to her. But how well does she understand what a helpmate is to look like? Is she really prepared to become his helpmate, for better or for worse, trusting he will cherish what she is giving to him?

At some level I think every bride envisions being the perfect wife, but does she know God wants her to be a suitable helpmate, not a competitor to her husband? In all the excitement, unrealistic expectations set in. A few months later these unfulfilled expectations can result in postmarital disappointment. This is especially true in remarriage, where there is no time for the after-the-honeymoon, eyes-only-for-you stage of marriage. Family life already awaits the couple.

When my husband and I first read this Scripture passage we were far from being one flesh. We were each vying for control of the marriage relationship and far from feeling cherished, let alone suitable helpers to one another. Quite often we were a duel, not a duet.

Thankfully, our eyes began to open as we explored Scripture.

For the first time in our lives we were discovering an immovable source of truth, one we could both respect. I don't know about you, but when I discover that God has said something about a particular subject, such as marriage, it takes on new significance. There is a sense of final authority given. It is no longer my husband's opinions versus mine, but the voice of truth. God's Word gave us direction, exposed our distorted thoughts, and opened a new door for us to enter.

After eight years of battling cyclical struggles, we were both hungry enough for change to occur. We were determined to open new doors. We realized change couldn't happen unless we swallowed our pride and took advantage of the "open door" moments God was bringing about.

TURNING DIFFERENCES INTO POTENTIAL

We spend a great deal of time wondering, in exasperation, why our spouse can't think or act like we do. Well, they were not made to be the same as us. God created us different enough to be attracted to the opposite sex. In courtship we are drawn close to one another by the strengths we see in our beloved. None of us possess all the qualities of every personality. We need each other to find life interesting and to ease the burdens. This is a fabulous on-purpose teamwork design by our Creator.

It is fun to see science come alongside creation. God made us male and female. Laboratory results have proven the gender differences God already breathed into existence. Male chromosomes are always X and Y, whereas female chromosomes are X and X. When we think of men and hormones, we think in terms of testosterone. And when we think of women and hormones, we talk about estrogen and progesterone levels. Today there is a tremendous concern over hormone replacement therapy to keep moods and body functions in check for both sexes.

With God and science supporting the gender differences, it is obvious that from the time of conception men and women are very different. Something physiological takes place in the womb that equips us to specialize as either male or female. It is intended to be a thing of beauty. I like to think of this natural difference as God's way of saying, *You don't have to do it all.* But knowing that doesn't always make it easier to communicate with the "opposite" one we are married to.

Dr. John Gray is most often associated with the book *Men Are from Mars, Women Are from Venus.* Men from the fiery planet of Mars; women from the romantic atmosphere of Venus. The message given is that before marriage we acted as whole individuals with distinct differences, whereas after marriage we often look at one another as though we arrived from a very foreign planet. In another book, *Men, Women and Relationships,* Dr. Gray continues in this same vein. Only now the Martians and the Venusians suffer from a strange form of amnesia.

> They forgot that they were from different planets. . . . In one night, they lost the awareness necessary to respect each other's unique qualities; differences were now interpreted as flaws and afflictions—temporary manifestations of stupidity, sickness, craziness, meanness, immaturity, stubbornness, selfishness, weakness, or badness. Immediately, a host of problems arose. Differences between the Martians and the Venusians had become a source of conflict instead of joy, appreciation, and wonder.[2]

I can surely relate to Dr. Gray's analogy. My husband and I fell into this amnesia scenario. Our differences had become thorns of conflict. We lost sight of the joy!

To bring back the joy we had to learn about our differences. It is natural for our male and female life roles to look different and for men and women to think and act differently. We are not the same, but both are in the same degree expressive of God's creativity. In the context of Scripture, there is no one-upmanship, no valuing one over the other. One is a complement to the other.

Appreciating and embracing the male-female differences brings the necessary elements to the family unit. Men have long been seen as the protectors and providers, fortifying the home from peril; the warriors out on the front lines. Through the ages women have kept the home fires burning. They are most often visualized as the nurturing, stabilizing, nest-building, childbearing caregivers of the home. When a husband and wife demonstrate qualities like this, their home becomes a refuge from the outside world, a safe haven for the family to come to for comfort.

As we allow our mate to become the full expression of his or her God-intended design, we forge a one-flesh relationship. I don't take on my husband's role; he doesn't take on mine. The mystery of healthy primary family units is that each partner knows that their togetherness combines gifts that are much greater in total than the simple sum of their single abilities.

My husband's male qualities hold an ancillary benefit for me. By marriage they are now a part of me. I can draw on them in time of need. I can count on them in daily living. In the same way, my female qualities bring completion to him. We are one. When we live this way as husband and wife, appreciating and implementing the total personalities of each spouse, power is released within the home. We are able to reach our fullest marital potential.

LEAVING AND CLEAVING
TO FORM A NEW SUPPORT BASE

Because my husband and I had experienced multiple "bones and flesh" encounters, we had to sort through a lot of confusing thoughts and emotions regarding forming oneness. As divorced individuals, we brought baggage into our marriage. To succeed this time would require us to understand more of the inner workings of a one-flesh marriage. We took another look at Genesis 2:24.

> For this reason a man will leave his father and mother and be united to his wife, and they will become one flesh.

We have already talked about this verse in reference to the "one-flesh" aspect of marriage. But there remains another valuable truth to apply. When a couple marries there are two action steps: *leaving* and *uniting* (cleaving). God speaks of the man and woman saying good-bye to former support relationships and uniting to each other, thus forming a new relational attachment with their spouse.

Leaving involves letting go of something familiar on which we have depended. It's like an old pair of shoes—the fit is so comfortable we often balk at breaking in a new pair. They just don't feel the same. It's human nature to want to continue living inside our comfort zone.

As the wedding ceremony unfolds, the bride walks down the aisle arm in arm with her father. Moments later, she is letting go of her father's arm and placing her hand in the open hand of the groom, symbolic of leaving behind the familiar parental relationship and accepting the new attachment to her husband—for better or for worse. This isn't always easy to live out after the ceremony. There are many unknowns to discover after saying "I do."

When we marry for the first time, God expects us to let go of parental control. For some, even this basic step is not effectively enacted. Some parents continue to exert a controlling influence over the marriage relationships of their children.

Multiple marriages create a need for a more extraordinary leaving process to be put in place. Remarrieds not only have parents who may refuse to let go, but also ex-spouses from whom to separate.

We are not always aware of the strong attachment we have to our ex-spouse. After all, didn't the divorce settle all that? Not necessarily. If we have an excessive interest in controlling what is happening in the other household, if bitter thoughts persist, or if we find ourselves melancholy most of the time, we have not emotionally let go of the past marriage. This includes feelings of ill-spent anger, which represent a strong emotional attachment fueling a negative environment for your new family.

After choosing to remarry, we need to come to a place where we no longer see ourselves as part of the old marriage. Until then, we will be unable to biblically unite as a couple in the new marriage. Remaining emotionally scattered will bring hardship into your new marriage because your marriage partner cannot consciously feel he has all of you emotionally. The environment will be one of competing for spousal position with an ex-spouse. Cleaving is not effectual in this setting. What you will find is disenchantment with the marriage.

Cleaving is creating a bond, being stuck together, as with glue. We come first to our spouse rather than to others for comfort and expression of needs. Together we seek solutions to the storms of life. Together we share in the joys of life. As a synchronized team we forge workable boundaries for our blended home. We cling together in the good and the bad. We draw near to one another and understand the meaning of contentment and goal setting as a couple. The "I wants" don't supersede the greater picture of "we."

Larry and Lagene have been married for thirteen years. Larry's first wife died, leaving him to raise their two sons. Lagene was divorced and had two boys of her own when she and Larry began dating. Although Larry's sons didn't want a new mother, Larry and Lagene's friendship blossomed into marriage.

"Blending our families hasn't been easy," Lagene remarks, "but I think it worked well because Larry made it clear to the boys that they were not to be disrespectful to me."

"Did he just demand that of them without following through himself," I asked, "or did he set an example for them to follow?"

"Yes, his example made all the difference. He has always treated me with high regard. When the boys are out of sorts with me Larry reminds them they are not just speaking to their stepmother or mother, but to *his* wife. I began this marriage with an incredible assurance of Larry's love. This was very different than what my boys witnessed when I was with their father. In that relationship I was often belittled in front of them and felt devalued."

The boys came to respect their parents because of the unity their parents displayed. There was an assurance of order in the home because Larry and Lagene's primary unit as a couple got off to a good start.

CORPORATE BONDS AND CORPORATE ASSETS

A great way to make a break in emotional ties to a former spouse and household is to consider them in a different light—as separate entities bound to us in a business relationship rather than a marriage union.

Imagine that a new corporation has been formed. Legally a corporation is treated as an entity with its own personal identity. It even files its own tax return. Bylaws are drawn up to govern the corporation.

Our divorces were similar to this. The judge gave us a set of documents by which we could exercise reasonable control over our lives after the divorce. Those documents constituted the divorce decree, or, to extend the comparison to a business corporation, the corporate bylaws. This contractual paperwork legally bound us to a set of standards that caused the past marriage to take a businesslike position in relation to the new marriage unit.

Corporations retain assets that give them a net worth, an intrinsic value. In a corporate atmosphere with our ex-spouses, the most valuable assets of the blended entity are the children, who are a part of both families. As the parents and executive officers of the corporation, the former husband and wife each hold a percentage of common stock reflective of their legal claim to those assets.

In the business world, management makes the difference. For a couple of years Charlie and I held shares of stock in a locally owned Northwest bank. Because the operations were handled with care, management made good decisions, and personal interest was shown in development of the entity, it was successful. When the bank prospered so did we, the shareholders.

We doubled our money in a fairly short period of time. The common stock's value had increased because the assets grew. Why did we see positive growth? Because the bank made good loans, bought another company, and hired men and women who were growth oriented. In the end, the bank's net worth was worth far more than when we first purchased the stock.

Just like a bank's corporate assets, our children, the assets of our corporation, should experience positive growth. When growth is healthy it always adds value to the assets held. As the assets increase the liabilities decrease. It will be up to us to set a high business standard for this newly formed entity. If we honor agreed-upon boundaries, turmoil should be kept to a minimum and growth to a maximum. With this mind-set there can be a secure emotional atmosphere within the new marriage that nurtures oneness between you and your new spouse while at the same time honoring your contractual agreement with your ex-spouse.

A business viewpoint allows new boundaries to be formed, ones that honor while not manipulating or becoming a pawn of the ex-spouse. Most of us struggle with attitudes after divorce. And we've not gone down this road of new negotiations before. So it feels foreign. That's because it is. But if we can look at the issues factually, keeping emotions at bay, we will be able to look with integrity at the one piece of paper that really matters now— the divorce decree. We have agreed in writing to carry out particular responsibilities as the result of divorce. Our decision to respect the decree will be the beginning of responsible, healthy growth in our corporately held assets—our children.

We should ask ourselves a couple of simple questions. Will the stock of our corporation increase or decrease in value as a result of our honoring the agreements we have made? Will our actions nurture the corporate assets or bring more liabilities? It is critically important for the children—our combined assets determining our net worth—to see adult maturity exhibited in the way we handle this difficult business arrangement. That will give them the freedom to grow well in a difficult soil. When *they* succeed, we succeed as a family.

Our child-assets sense added value as each day passes when we make a conscious effort to put the good of the corporate entity above selfish interests. Even though our children come from a fragmented family, they can grow up emotionally whole if we handle our "business affairs" wisely. This will be the true measure of our success.

BECOMING LOVE-RELATED

Awkward beginnings are common for blended families. Reality brings us a complicated sense of family from the start. Immediately each member of the family has emotional, physical, and monetary needs that won't wait.

It takes a far greater measure of *deliberate* love choices to build a blended family unit than an original first-time family. The new home front is engulfed in a climate of uncertainty. We feel certain we can unite to our spouse, but what about uniting to our stepchildren? What about our stepchildren uniting with each other and with their stepparent? In most first-time families, individuals take it as a given that they are loved, even in times of conflict, simply because there is a genetic connection. So there isn't nearly as much work to be done to make everyone feel loved. They already do.

That's not so for the blended family. As competitive natures surface, the fact that we are not all equally related by blood brings out irritation and choosing sides. It's a "*your* family, *my* family thing" trying to coexist under one roof.

The goal is to take the *yours* and the *mine* and turn them into *ours*. This can only be done with love. We need to make each combined family member feel *love-related*. This can be done as we make a conscious and deliberate decision to love, transform that to our hearts, and express it by our actions.

Andrea and Mike never questioned my love for them, but my stepdaughter Sabrina needed more convincing. I often told her, "Even if you don't choose to love me, I am choosing to love you. I would like you to love me, but that is your choice. However, nothing you can do will change the fact that I intend to love you . . . not only in my mind . . . but in my heart as well." Eventually she was able to accept my love, and sometimes she even gives hers in return.

HARMONIZING PARENTING STYLES

Within weeks after our marriage, we were asked to care for the neighbor's yard while she was away. Nine-year-old Grace was with me as I watered the plants. She began to play with the hose, squashing it so the water wouldn't flow and interrupting the work needing to be done. Initially it was kind of cute, but it soon became annoying. Four or five times I politely asked Grace to stop being mischievous. I was definitely tiring of the activity.

"Grace, if you stand on the hose one more time, I'm going to spray you with water," I said in a more serious tone of voice. "Please believe me!"

Once again she cut off the water supply. I followed through, exactly as I had said I would. I sprayed her with the water.

"Dad, Dad!" Grace cried, running off. "Maxine got me soaking wet."

Grace didn't tell Charlie the whole story. And my husband instantly chose sides—against me. I was so hurt and so angry. Suddenly I was the enemy. Guilty without a trial. I felt a lynching was in the air.

I had not treated Grace any differently than I would have treated my own children. In my newness at stepparenting, I had not given any thought to different parenting styles. I figured one size fit all. Wrong. What would have worked well for my children had not worked with Grace.

At that moment I felt devalued as a stepparent. I was being looked upon as a careless baby-sitter, not a significant person in the life of my stepdaughter. The rest of the day was ruined, the night was ruined, our family plans were curtailed, and it was evident there was a wall of distrust forming between my husband and me.

God gave each of us a deep protective mechanism that causes us to jump into action if we sense our children are threatened. It is intended to be a good thing, and we are right to be guarded when it comes to our little ones. But we must also be willing to listen. There are always two sides to the story. My parenting style and Charlie's were obviously different. I always follow through with the actions I have stated. I feel it is less confusing to children. So my actions toward Grace were consistent with the way I was already raising my own children.

Sometimes tension occurs because a parent treats his own children with a different set of standards and portion of love than he allows his stepchildren. So emotional wounding can begin early on. Favoritism does not go unnoticed. There is validity—and sad truth—to the story of Cinderella and the unloving stepmother and stepsisters. Life wasn't fair for Cinderella. She got all the yucky chores, verbal abuse, and tattered clothing, while her stepsisters were pampered.

Today many stepchildren live out a Cinderella lifestyle as a result of remarriage. This places incredible stress on the unity of the marriage relationship. It is also a poor example of becoming love-related in a blended home. Rather than expressing love, these parents are closing their hearts to some family members. Yet God gave us the ability to stretch our hearts to meet each child's need for love.

Marital love blossoms when we open our hearts and become sensitive to the parental heart of our spouse. Remarrieds don't just marry a partner, but a parent. Love allows parenting roles to be appropriately enacted within the family. A confident spouse accepts that he or she may not be as successful as his or her partner in certain parent-child discussions. Love intuitively knows when to back off, not feeling threatened, and let our mate deal with a particular problem. Then we receive additional blessings. We gain a greater admiration from our mate, a probable resolution to the problem, new respect from a child, and a new depth of intimacy in our marital relationship.

Even those family members who do their best to be unlovable will most often respond, in time, when touched by love. This can be challenging, but also rewarding to the family unit.

A TIME TO REFLECT

Sometimes old, hurtful ways and hidden fears and pain thwart the unity we desire in our marriage. My husband and I found ourselves seeing past cycles repeat themselves. Sometimes we thought about the "D" word—again. We were in the throes of cyclical dysfunction. Why did Charlie's anger flare up so easily? Why did I experience so many instances of self-pity and the desire to escape? Why weren't we able to confront the issues of daily living without fear of rejection?

What was it that brought us to have the lifestyles we each possessed? Why were we so *different?* What were the driving forces behind our emotional responses? There had to be more to this madness than just the strain of a blended family.

We found the boldness to begin charting our individual histories. By digging deep we found an unusual appreciation for who we were as people. None of us chooses the family we were born into or where we will spend our childhood. We must attribute those circumstances to the decision of the Lord. Courage to look back came when we recognized God played a significant role not only in the past but also in the present.

We asked God to search our hearts, expose hurtful ways, and uncover hidden fears and pain. Through Bible study, we again found David to be our model of a God-centered man. He was a king—and a sinner—and a man after God's own heart! He sinned big-time just like we had. But after adultery, deceit, and even murder, David knew he needed to seek the Maker of his soul. He was intensely burdened. His peace was gone. He asked God to search his heart and to clean him up.

> Surely you desire truth in the inner parts; you teach me wisdom in the inmost place. Cleanse me with hyssop, and I will be clean; wash me, and I will be whiter than snow. Let me hear joy and gladness; let the bones you have crushed rejoice. Hide your face from my sins and blot out all my iniquity. Create in me a pure heart, O God, and renew a steadfast spirit within me. (Psalm 51:6–10)

Our desire was to be clean like David. We wanted to be honest with God and honestly know who we were. So we came to the Lord, sought His forgiveness, and began applying His grace. In the end we discovered the same peace and restoration David did. God's desire was to give us a new beginning. Assurance of God's forgiveness readied us to face the challenges of our life together. If God Almighty, the most Supreme Authority ever to exist, has chosen to set us free, we are free indeed. The approval of others now took a lesser position to the approval of God.

A GLIMPSE OF HEAVEN

It's incredible to know that God designed the marriage union to be the closest earthly example we have of Christ's bridegroom relationship to His bride, the church.

> Jesus spoke to them again in parables, saying: "The kingdom of heaven is like a king who prepared a wedding banquet for his son. He sent his servants to those who had been invited to the banquet
>
> to tell them to come, but they refused to come. Then he sent some more servants and said, 'Tell those who have been invited that I have prepared my dinner: My oxen and fattened cattle have been butchered, and everything is ready. Come to the wedding banquet.'" (Matthew 22:1–4)

There is preparation going on in the heavenly realm. A glorious preparation for lovers—lovers of Christ. (Those who love Christ also love one another.) The strange thing is, it has to do with a wedding. Marriage is the vehicle God has chosen to give us a glimpse of our future as the bride of Christ. Each of us, male and female, who personally chooses to accept Jesus as Lord and Savior will one day be a part of the marriage feast of the Lamb now being prepared in heaven. This will be a feast beyond comparison to our wildest imagination, the celebration of all celebrations! We believers, as the bride of Christ, will finally see our heavenly Bridegroom face-to-face. We will be welcomed into His loving arms forevermore.

Rest assured, no greater joy will be found than to sit at His banqueting table . . . on the day prepared for us in heaven . . . in the glorious realm of eternal life. In fact, the Bible reveals we will be called "blessed."

> Then the angel said to me, "Write: 'Blessed are those who are invited to the wedding supper of the Lamb!'" And he added, "These are the true words of God." (Revelation 19:9)

I love the way this verse ends with the powerful declarative, "These are the *true* words of God." By making this statement the angel declared emphatically that God was the originator of these words, not crediting himself, and removed any doubt regarding their accuracy. By personal invitation we are given assurance that the wedding supper of the Lamb will one day take place.

This picture is of a marriage union free of combative attitudes and full of incredible joy, pleasure, and peace. It is *blessed*. This raises questions concerning our earthly marriage covenants. It would behoove all of us to consider the seriousness of our personal attitude toward our marriage covenants. How would you answer this question: Does the relationship I have with my spouse reflect the oneness Christ has with His church?

As was true when we sat listening to the orchestra that Christmas night marveling at the loveliness of their harmony, God holds the key to beauty in our lives. Charlie and I are still different. But now we know this is God's intention to bring completion to our lives, not competition. We often have differing views on the same subject, but now we share the same goals. We are no longer threatened by the differences. We know we need them to give us balance in decision-making times. Today we can say with thankful hearts that we are no longer a duel—but a duet. We are a symphony of oneness that most often we know reflects harmoniously back to the very ears of God. What a great feeling!

Growth and Application

Commit to memory Genesis 2:22–24.

1. How have you and your spouse begun to build a primary family unit that is strong and truly "blended"?

2. Why is it important to our family that we understand God's meaning of one flesh?

3. Do you see your unique male/female differences as a completion or a competition to your marriage? In what way?

4. Considering the corporate structure with your household and that of ex-spouses, is there a determined effort being made to increase the net worth of your common assets (the children)? What still needs to be done to achieve success?

Prayer of Application

Lord, we have been so shortsighted in our understanding of marital oneness. Please forgive us. We now know You have created one-flesh relationships to be a beautiful part of our intimacy as a couple, to bring completion, and to offer greater portions of wisdom to our lives. Our desire is to achieve a relationship with our spouse that reflects the truth of Your Word. As we do this, give us courage to admit our wrongs and embrace new thoughts from You—thoughts meant to draw our family into a closer relationship with one another. Help us, as parents and business partners with our ex-spouses, to bring healthy growth to our children, the true assets of our heritage. Thank You for opening our hearts and minds to Your truth. Amen.

NOTES

1. Don Meredith and Sally Meredith, *Becoming One* (Charlotte, N.C.: Christian Family Life, 1997), 88. This book is now out of print. Please see page 74 of *Two . . . Becoming One* (Chicago: Moody, 1999).
2. John Gray, *Men, Women and Relationships* (New York: Harper, 1993), 19.

Chapter Four

LET'S
LOOK BACK

As a child, I thought of the lazy months of summer as a time for riding horseback, picking blackberries, and gathering black caterpillars with yellow-and-white stripes from the fields around our house. I loved finding these and placing their wiggly bodies in a big glass jar. After adding a stalk of milkweed, I took a nail and poked several holes in the lid.

Within a couple of days the caterpillar would attach itself upside down to the milkweed and fun changes began to occur. A leaf green cocoon, studded with golden drops, soon encased the small creature's body. I must have looked at that jar a hundred times a day, not wanting to miss a thing. As the chrysalis darkened with each passing day, my anticipation grew. I knew the big event was nearing. Finally enough time had passed and a monarch butterfly—as if from an artist's paintbrush with shades of black, brown, orange, and white—sat drying its wings in my jar. Totally awesome!

To this day I don't understand how God can bring such magnificence out of a belly-crawling worm. Not only is it notable for splendid colors, but delicate wings give this once earthbound creature the freedom to fly. Beyond the long antennae, I saw no resemblance to the caterpillar I'd placed in the jar.

As I dwelt on these memories, the butterfly pictured the metamorphosis God had brought about in my life. It was a beautiful picture of what the Bible calls a born-again life. God's transforming power works a similar change in the life of every Christian.

> Therefore, if anyone is in Christ, he is a new creation; the old has gone, the new has come! (2 Corinthians 5:17)

Something amazing takes place in our souls. Our heart of stone is removed and replaced with a heart of flesh—one that is sensitive to the things of God. This new heart is more powerful than the old. When we lay down the old life, with its worldly belief system, we begin to fly in the freedom of the newfound life in Christ.

I no longer live or think as I did before I knew Christ. I was once like the caterpillar, crawling through the maze of life, bound by the dictates of our culture. I actually believed man had answers to life's deepest issues. As morality within society slipped, I became desensitized to its impact on my family. I bought into the ever-widening looser values of our society. Being happy took the place of fulfilling vows of commitment.

But I continually searched for what being happy meant and found myself still lacking the peace I wanted. Only when I took Christ into my heart did I encounter the assurance man was never able to give me. I found I had been living a life inconsistent with God's plan. In asking for forgiveness I found the freeing experience of the butterfly. With my past forgiven, I found the courage to look at myself with honest eyes. I could face the foul-ups and even look further back to see my own history. Life's journey became interesting, not threatening.

REVISITING THE PAST

The world inside you is as real as the outside world, but because it is harder to see, hear and understand, many people do not take the time to learn from it.

Your inside world determines what your outside world will look like. Should you not pay attention to it? . . . There are many states of mind within you—fear, worry, sadness—or if you choose —love, happiness, well-being. Where are you?[1]

Revisiting the past—even unpleasant memories and discoveries —is a privilege. When we look at it as a healthy thing we are able to appreciate what it has to offer. It brings defining insight to the present. Insight, when aptly applied, stares at the truth, slays the giants, and gathers wisdom. Wisdom, in its fullness, gives birth to healthy choices, empowers us to destroy ungodly strongholds, and settles our purpose.

Early childhood memories are like threads woven together to form the fabric of self-understanding. The equation is simple: the more early childhood memories, the more threads; the more threads, the stronger the fabric; the stronger the fabric, the more personal insight.[2]

Memories have affected our feelings, attitudes, and chosen reactions to the moments of life. All of us began forming our personalities out of those things written in the annals of our minds from our earliest years. If we experienced a lot of criticism we may have fears to look back upon. If we were praised for doing a job well we may possess an air of confidence as a consistent part of our personality. As we examine the past, we can learn how we processed disappointment and how we comforted others.

Like my butterflies, some reflections give me pleasure as I fondly remember people and happy times gone by. Other memories cause me to relive painful moments, some trivial, like the time I caught my finger in the back door and needed to go to the doctor, and some serious, like the time my mother decided to divorce my father and moved far away. Either way, I believe God allows us to see snapshots of ourselves for many reasons:

- So that we will know that both joy and pain add value to life's journey
- For personal reflection to evaluate the choices we've made
- To understand how the choices others made affected our life
- To learn our strengths and our weaknesses
- To see how the hand of God has been with us all along
- To keep pride at bay and to keep us humble, pliable, and open to seek the Lord

We are safe in presuming that no child is created with feelings of anger, rejection, hate or depression. God was well pleased with His creation when He created us. He did allow us to have personality strengths and weaknesses, light hair or dark hair, even physical difficulties or disabilities.

There is no evidence, however, to suggest we were created with those dark emotions. They were put into us later. The way we were treated, the things that happened to us, the acts that were done to us—all had their impact upon our childhood feelings. Our bodies grew and matured, but for many of us those emotions never did.

The hurts of childhood may still be hurting you today. They may be affecting your adult behavior far more than you might have believed.[3]

I understood myself about as much as Peter understood himself in the gospel of Luke. I professed to be loyal to family and friends and fully intended to live out that attribute. Most of the time I did just fine. But what about the really important times? Did I really know myself? Would I fall away the way Peter did after he professed that he would die for the Lord?

But he replied, "Lord, I am ready to go with you to prison and to death." (Luke 22:33)

Yeah, right! What Jesus said next tells us He knew Peter better than Peter knew himself.

> Jesus answered, "I tell you, Peter, before the rooster crows today, you will deny three times that you know me." (Luke 22:34)

Jesus knew that Peter needed to take a clearer look at himself. Peter had seen himself as fiercely loyal, incapable of faltering in defense of his friend. But in the crowing of the rooster Peter found the depths of his true character. He really *did* deny the Lord. Jesus' words undoubtedly replayed in Peter's mind, burning into his soul a lasting memory and sorrowful reminder of his lack of loyalty and giving him a keen awareness of the Lord's ability to know his true mettle. He was weak in the very area he so easily boasted he was strong. Although this was a painful discovery, it was a pivotal point in Peter's ministry. Out of Peter's humbling denial came the birth of much-needed character strength. He faced the real workings of his inner self and grew from the encounter.

A TRUTH REVEALED

"This came for you today," I said, handing a large yellow envelope to Charlie.

"It's from Aunt Phyllis," he said. "Why would she be sending me mail? It's not Christmas."

Aunt Phyllis is Charlie's mother's younger sister. We rarely got mail from her. This envelope was curious indeed. A bit like receiving Pandora's box.

As Charlie opened the envelope, a letter dropped out.

"I found these papers while cleaning the attic," the letter read. "I know your mother will be unhappy with me for sending them to you, but I feel I must. I've kept them all these years. Now they belong to you. Perhaps they will help you understand your life, and your mother's."

Birth certificates, marriage licenses, and photos fell from the envelope. What a fun package! In over fifty years my husband had never seen these documents. As we began to look them over, confusion set in. Something must be wrong. Things didn't.fall together in the right time sequence. His parents' marriage certificate was dated long after his birth. What had the family hidden from him all these years? What mystery was he uncovering?

"I was born out of wedlock!" said Charlie. "I'm illegitimate! This secret has been kept from me all these years."

Shock came over his face. "I've got to call my mother."

Suddenly I understood the annoyed avoidance she had displayed when, on our last trip to Boston, I'd so comfortably asked her about her own pregnancy and the birth of her only son. Unknowingly I had invaded a tightly locked room tucked carefully away in the archives of her heart. She had lived with this secret most of her life. It was her intention to die with it as well.

At first Charlie felt betrayal. Not just by his mother, but by his whole family. His father knew. His grandmother knew. His aunts knew—all six of them! No one had told him. For over fifty years his entire family had concealed the circumstances surrounding his birth.

After the hurt and the anger and a lengthy, emotional conversation with his mother, Charlie began to feel compassion for the woman who had given him birth. Out of love, she had sheltered him from a truth that was unacceptable in the era when he was born. A child born out of wedlock in the thirties brought reproach to the family. Charlie's mother bore the shame herself. This was her gift to her son. Unfortunately, the unspoken truth had also kept her from being close to her son for most of his life. For years Charlie wondered why his parents divorced when he was so young. He had the gnawing thought that the family was not telling him something important. Finally, by knowing the truth, the walls were coming down.

It is common to remember grief, sorrow, fear, or abuse in greater measure than times of enjoyment. Pain touches our lives in deeper ways. Because of this, many will dread looking back, choosing denial over discovery. Yet, the privilege of revisiting the past, if done for the right reasons, is greatly to our advantage. We are not going in search of blame, but in search of truth. The truth really does set us free. It frees us to know our own fears and to celebrate the life we have been given.

DOWN MEMORY LANE

Our mental filing cabinets hold journals that are ours alone. As unique as our fingerprints, so are our journeys on Earth. We are all designer originals. What are the real scenes on the canvases of our lives? Do we really have the courage to look? Will we dare to see the journey God has already brought us through?

In the early years of our marriage we didn't have full knowledge or psychological acceptance of our own histories. We were constantly looking at life through ill-matched lenses, each thinking the other's life-management skills were askew. The things we didn't understand about ourselves were blocking our unity as a couple. It became clear that the little boy and the little girl of our childhood held the key to our present personalities.

We felt the future of our marriage would be brighter if we embarked on a new journey—a trip down memory lane to obtain an accurate account of our earliest days and the events that brought us to the present. So Charlie and I set forth to discover the roots of our individuality. Who were we? Whom did we really marry? Beyond physical intimacy and food, we weren't sure what brought enjoyment to the other. We were too busy managing the craziness of life to pursue the enchanting intricacies of our mate. What were our real desires, hopes, and fears?

The foundational environments and belief systems of our developing years, whether negative or positive, created two people who acted out the by-products of those elements. These two diverse people were now trying to live under one roof as husband and wife.

We didn't spend hours on end in a counselor's office. I went on three different occasions just to clarify my thoughts and not get caught up in self-pity. For us this was a journey of faith, constant prayer, and dependence on Scripture to shed wisdom on every memory we were to uncover. Revelation didn't happen in a day. Over time, new memories and new truth emerged. Not all of it was pretty, but all of it was a part of who we are today.

Fortunately, our minds do not recall everything at one time. I'm thankful. That gives us time to process events without becoming overwhelmed. In this way we can systematically apply God's wisdom to each of the images that emerges.

Our differences were popping up all over the place. What eye-openers! The short phrases recapping our earlier years are listed in the chart on the facing page.

It was easy to see that nearly all of our root characteristics were drastically different. There was a big contrast between the harshness of Charlie's childhood and the not-perfect, but gentler, lifestyle I had experienced. Our realization of one another grew. In fact, we began to have compassion and newfound patience for the person we'd married.

Although different, our childhoods had equipped us with gifts to perfect our marriage union, not destroy it. When necessary, Charlie had the ability to boldly confront issues; and when there were hurts to heal, I was easily drawn to give comfort. Both of those qualities enhanced our family unit.

By looking back, we saw the formation of our personalities. We discovered the origin of many of our emotions. We had fears of rejection. We had learned to be defensive. We learned how unreasonable it is to expect a spouse to react to life in the same way we do. Our differing responses to events and emotions now made sense. Our hard drives weren't wired the same way. And if they had been, one of us would have been unnecessary! So being different was a good thing as long as "different" honored the Lord.

Using his ethnic background as an excuse, Charlie had become accustomed to loudly venting his opinions because, after all, "he was Italian." Everyone was expected to understand the personality of this ethnic group and overlook any offenses their habits might create. His Italian heritage somehow granted him special privileges.

Among those was the right to speak his mind—in whatever way he saw fit. Insults were to be understood as acceptable expressions, not rudeness, despite the tone of voice. His father banged on the table and yelled and got what he wanted. Charlie used the same approach. Angry dominance and intimidation were normal patterns for him to mimic.

Charlie's Story	Maxine's Story
Born out of wedlock; parents later married	Second of four children
Lived in Italian ghetto of Boston; city boy	Lived on small farm; country girl
An only child	Lived in the Pacific Northwest
Parents divorced when he was three	Sensitive to mistreatment
Lived with his father and grandmother	Lived with her father and mother
Ridiculed for not having a mother	Ridiculed for being small
Didn't speak English until the age of ten	Excelled in school
Son of a Mafia head	Father a millworker/farmer
Money equaled influence and power	Very little money; frugality
Altar boy in the Catholic church	Rarely attended church
Parochial schools, reform school	Public schools, Good News club
Wore hand-me-downs	Wore hand-me-downs
Received coal in his Christmas stocking	Received fruit and candy in her Christmas stocking
Cruel treatment by priests and nuns	Raised herself in many ways
Saw loan-sharking, prostitution, cruelty	Mother was busy with self-interests
Had many jobs (newspaper route, etc.)	Father's love not verbalized
Met his mother in teen years	Parents divorced when she was sixteen
Mother struggled with alcohol	Left home at age sixteen
Married for the first time at the age of nineteen	Married for the first time at the age of seventeen
Lost all close-knit relatives by the age of twenty-two	Dealt with death once: grandpa
Enlisted in the army	Was the mother of two children by the age of twenty
Is a sports fan	Enjoys cultural events and nature

Through the eyes of remembrance we were now able to explore this pattern. We discovered the angry outbursts were only cover-ups for genuine feelings. There was a fear of rejection if the real feelings were expressed because they were considered signs of weakness in his neighborhood. Anger, on the other hand, was thought to represent a strong emotional stance.

There was no marital relationship between a father and a mother in his boyhood home for Charlie to view as a model for his own adult life. His father only had bitter words to say about his mother. He grew up with a negative impression of the value of a wife. He had felt the rejection of his own mother, combined with the angry attitude of his father toward the woman who gave him birth. His father died when he was twenty-two, and his grandmother six months later. When that happened, Charlie broke all the furniture in his apartment and enlisted in the army. He was a lonely young man with a satchel in his hand. At the time we met, he was in the midst of his second divorce.

My childhood was drastically different. Along with my three siblings, I was the offspring of a generation that believed children should be seen and not heard. Love was assumed but never spoken. I don't recall my parents ever resolving an issue in front of us. I believe they let many things go to avoid conflict.

A loud outburst was uncommon at our house. *Damn* was the only curse word I remember either of my parents using, and that wasn't too often. As a sensitive child, I felt deeply hurt and abused by loud, abrasive behavior. Charlie and I were definitely not on the same page when it came to expressing our emotions. It was like mixing oil and water. One always floated to the top, while the other sank to the bottom.

Growing up on a small farm, I rose early in the morning to help feed the animals, had a pet chicken, rescued fish when the irrigation water overfilled the pond, and played with my favorite bride doll. Being small in stature, I experienced a lot of teasing—or it was thought I was incapable of doing certain tasks. That only made me more determined to accomplish them. I learned early on to stuff my feelings, as it was not acceptable or safe to vent emotions. Shedding tears meant being taunted by my siblings. So when I was really sad I sat with the dog—and cried alone.

My father was a man of few words. The word I remember best from childhood was *no*. He would usually say no to my desire to take clarinet or dance lessons or to join a Brownie troop. I learned there wasn't much point in asking. But that didn't take away my dreams. In the fourth grade I wanted to join the school band and play the clarinet, but I wasn't going to be allowed to rent an instrument. It cost money, and we didn't have enough for stuff like that.

Mother had often said, "Where there's a will, there's a way." So I became resourceful, found out what the school had to offer, got a pair of drumsticks . . . and joined the band. In revisiting this memory I found I had a great deal of perseverance. Today I still have the will to do something, and if it's at all possible, I will find a way to pull it off.

My life revolved around school, family, and the farm we lived on. Just before my sixteenth birthday my life changed dramatically. My parents separated and filed for divorce. My mother moved far away. We four children, aged twelve to sixteen, stayed with our dad. In the months prior to finalizing their divorce, my father spoke very harshly and unfairly to me. Without telling him, I left for Los Angeles to join my mother.

I didn't know it then, but this was a huge pivotal point in my life. Living in Los Angeles was difficult. Mother was into her own lifestyle and wasn't prepared for a teenager to join her. Within a couple of weeks I went to live with a family who needed help with child care. It was there that I met a man I married a year later, at the age of seventeen. After seven years and two children we were divorced.

Charlie and I were very different in our foundational selves when we met. More than a city-boy, country-girl merger took place. Our marriage represented two very different walks of life. We celebrate life differently, handle crises differently, express love differently, view money differently. We are *different!* Out of our two histories we needed to make a life that worked for both of us. A tall order representing a challenge neither of us had given much thought to.

I've come to realize that many, if not most, couples enter marriage just like we did, without a clear look at the basic differences that have collectively formed who they are as adults. The euphoria of infatuation swept them into marriage.

LEARNING TO LIKE OUR DIFFERENCES

When we retrieved the history of our individual roots, we looked at them abstractly without labeling them "right" or "wrong." On paper these histories were nonthreatening expressions of our lives, experiences recaptured to reveal the inner reasoning processes. We were "outsiders" doing a research project on ourselves. This was not a time to judge the environments we grew up in. It was a time for learning. Our education was off to a good start.

As we allowed ourselves to embrace our differences, it became OK to attach the beauty of our own distinct qualities, childhood formation, and traditions to our journey as husband and wife. Those things revealing dysfunctional behavior and excessive fears could now be brought under scrutiny. We were able to search for healthy alternatives.

Holidays are hard for blended families. There may be grief over family members who cannot be present or strain over the logistics necessary to work out a happy ending. I grew up celebrating Christmas on Christmas Eve. Charlie's family celebrated on Christmas morning. Nothing was wrong with either observance. But we both had different expectations. This made holiday time a hassle.

To enjoy Christmas we needed to blend our two lifestyles. We now open one special gift on Christmas Eve and do the rest of the gifts on Christmas morning. It's a great solution. The children love having one gift to enjoy the night before and also look forward with anticipation to Christmas morning.

As we got deeper into the discovery process we were surprised to learn that many of the qualities that drew us together in our courtship were building walls between us. Yet they were the very elements that made dating each other exciting! They made us feel special. One day I had to stop and ask myself: "When did we stop having fun? When did the differences become annoyances?" (The truth is, a few weeks after our marriage.)

In the early years of our marriage I was obviously the "people" person and Charlie the "time-alone-with-you" person. It wasn't long before the time-alone person was finding fault with the people person as I involved myself preparing social events for our church. We had numerous arguments and a lack of understanding for each other. I was feeling restricted. Charlie was feeling neglected. Why didn't we see this before the wedding? Why did it matter now?

Courtship is a time of discovery and of enjoying shared moments. In most cases couples can't get enough of each other. Yet their lives are still separate. So there is less expectation in courtship and a greater willingness to enjoy the world of new adventures.

Marriage is different. The personalities don't change, but expectation levels do. Neither of us wanted to lose the excitement we felt in our dating days or live without the qualities that drew us to one another. Now we had to schedule our time to meet the needs of both personalities. I began to include Charlie socially, giving him a portion of responsibility at social events. In pouring coffee he made lots of new friends and felt included. We listened to his needs as well. We planned times to steal away for weekends alone. Today the people person and the time-alone person are doing much better. The best part is that we reaffirmed both personalities.

UNCOVERING GENERATIONAL SINS

Revisiting the past disclosed a pivotal source of wisdom. It unexpectedly opened our eyes to generational sins. This concept, with its compelling evidence of family sin, became a breakthrough for our family. We found explanations for many unhealthy personality traits.

"For I, the Lord your God, am a jealous God, punishing the children for the sin of the fathers to the third and fourth generation of those who hate me, but showing love to a thousand [generations] of those who love me and keep my commandments." (Exodus 20:5b–6)

You can imagine our surprise when we found that the Bible speaks about generational sins. A parent's choice to sin affects generations to come. In our family there is convincing proof of this truth. But in our society of mediocrity and ease, we fail to see that parental unrighteousness becomes a punishment to children and even carries on to grandchildren—the very people we love the most!

It's hard to recognize generational sins because they are so much a part of our daily life. And we don't recognize them as punishments because, after all, these traits are common to our family. We brush them off as part of our ethnicity or we let our feelings justify sinful actions as an inherent part of our personality.

When we question whether these same behaviors are also common to the character of Christ we often come up with another answer. Yet if we choose to deal with the sins of our fathers and mothers, we will be in line for the blessing that awaits those who live God's way. Better yet, this blessing passes on to our descendants in greater measure than the transgression. We have a lot to gain by recognizing sin's trickle-down effect.

A generational sin is sin that leaves its mark on others. Don't confuse this with meaning that we will pay for the sins of others. We are each individually responsible for our own choice to sin. We cannot pay for someone else's sin. Yet our personal sin contributes to the detriment of others, in particular our family members, because we are the closest to them. God deals with each of us face-to-face for the deeds we have done while in the body.

"Fathers shall not be put to death for their children, nor children put to death for their fathers; each is to die for his own sin." (Deuteronomy 24:16)

I don't like to leave this verse standing alone, for as believers in Christ we have an even greater hope. We have a Savior who has taken upon Himself to remove the sting of death. He died in our place, paying sin's price, that we might be called *righteous*. As a believer, I need not fear sin's death.

> The words "it was credited to him" were written not for him alone, but also for us, to whom God will credit righteousness—for us who believe in him who raised Jesus our Lord from the dead. He was delivered over to death for our sins and was raised to life for our justification. (Romans 4:23–25)

As children, my husband and I had caught what we saw modeled. My mother had chosen flight to deal with interpersonal difficulties. Consequently, I had never seen my parents resolve hard issues, so I brought both of those patterns into my own adult life. I felt the need to escape when troubles came, and I was very uncomfortable with relational conflict. So I stuffed feelings until they got to the boiling point.

Charlie was uncomfortable with relational conflict too. He just handled it differently. He angrily banged his fist on the table, just as his father had done, to gain control of the situation. Discipline was always overdone or came with a verbal threat. Again, this was a generational pattern. His father kept him out of trouble by threatening to break his kneecaps. God's idea of conflict resolution is neither fight nor intimidation.

Both of us came from families who chose divorce over reconciliation and unconditional love. We both repeated the cycle. We wondered just how many families in our ancestries had been affected by the same sinful life-management skills. We knew at least two generations dealt with divorce, and we suspected anger and unresolved conflict had enjoyed much greater longevity.

Charlie and I want to leave something better behind for our family. We are determined to break generational strongholds. Through prayer—and new behaviors—inasmuch as it depends on us, we will halt the rebellion of our ancestry. Satan has set down deep roots in particular areas of our family histories. We are declaring war on his underhanded ways. They do not fit God's design for Christian living. They are only cancerous growths on the lives of future generations. Our children need a healthier model to follow.

This determined effort has drawn us closer as a family. We see these generational strongholds breaking. The walls are coming down. Rather than driving off to a weekend of casino action in Reno, we choose to attend family camps and entertainment with a wholesome outcome. Instead of angry responses, we are instilling a greater effort to listen and find resolve, not control. We are creating a new legacy—one that will bless many generations to come.

JUBILATION

Some years South Africa experiences locust swarms so large they block out the sun. The devastation to crops is catastrophic! The food supply is cut dangerously short. Everyone fears the years the locusts eat. Yet, to everyone's amazement, the following year produces a bumper crop. The dead bodies of the locusts actually serve as a rich fertilizer for the soil. So there is jubilation over the abundant crop gathered at the next harvest.

> "I will repay you for the years the locusts have eaten—the great locust and the young locust, the other locusts and the locust swarm—my great army that I sent among you. You will have plenty to eat, until you are full, and you will praise the name of the Lord your God, who has worked wonders for you; never again will my people be shamed." (Joel 2:25–26)

We are witnessing this in our lives. The dark years of divorce, the struggles to adapt in our own strength to blend our families, the years without prayer, and all the anger and selfishness were devouring days—days given over to the locusts. But when, by God's grace, we chose to recognize them as bearers of death, something wonderful began to happen. A heavy spirit gave way to the light of His presence. Out of the discoveries made by looking back at the years of childhood and desolation came fresh nourishment for our lives.

What we put to death we won't miss because we will have gained something much better. Now each day given to us by God is a fresh opportunity to plant seeds of righteousness and write a fresh legacy. We are far better educated in the good things of family life, much more concerned with the choices we make in our marriage, much more in "like" with each other. Most of all, our hearts are now grieved by the things that bring unhappiness to our Lord. If they displease Him they will bring misery to us. We no longer want to invite the locusts to dine on our family.

God blesses that which is brought under His authority. He is more interested in where we are going than in where we have been. He truly does replace the years the locusts have eaten!

Growth and Application

Commit to memory Joel 2:25–26.

1. Describe your childhood. Compare notes with your spouse. What similarities did you discover? What differences surfaced? (for example, ethnic backgrounds, discipline methods, holiday celebrations, etc.)

2. Do you have a deeper appreciation and understanding for one another as a result of looking back at your individual roots? What did you learn about yourself? What did you learn about your spouse?

3. How can these differences become tools of enhancement to your family unit?

4. Why is it important to understand generational sins? In looking back did you discover any generational sins? Describe these. How have they affected your family? How can you stop them from affecting the next generation?

Prayer of Application

Lord, thank You for the courage to look back at our individual histories. What an eye-opener! You have seen us through so much. With Your help, Lord, we can bring beauty out of our differences. We can see the corporate strength available to our marriage when we utilize our unique gifts. Thank You for revealing the effect of generational sins on our family. Walk beside us as we rid ourselves of these. Our desire is to leave a heritage of godliness for the generations to come. Amen.

NOTES

1. Ron Rathburn, *The Way Is Within* (New York: Berkley, 1994), 63.
2. Kevin Leman and Randy Carlson, *Unlocking the Secrets of Your Childhood Memories* (Nashville: Nelson, 1989), 40.
3. Fred Littauer and Florence Littauer, *Freeing Your Mind from Memories That Bind* (Nashville: Nelson, 1988), 141.

Chapter Five

WHEN ANGER RULES

I t's a beautiful day. The snow is probably perfect," I said, while making breakfast for the children. "Why don't you finish eating and I'll take you up the mountain? You can spend the day skiing."

"Great. Let's hurry," said Mike. "What should we do with Heidi?"

"She has so many accidents," I said, "we'd better tie her outside while we're gone."

Heidi, our cocker spaniel puppy, was famous for frequent unpleasant household problems. So we found just the right spot to tie her, and off we went to Mt. Ashland. As the day went by, she barked, annoying the neighbors. They called the authorities and filed a complaint.

My husband had been home from work only a few moments when the police arrived notifying him of the nuisance complaint, which led to his embarrassment and the angry attitude with which he greeted us when we arrived home.

"Do you realize the embarrassment you caused me?" he yelled. "I didn't want that animal in the first place. Now there is a complaint against me."

"I'm sorry," I said. "I had no idea she would bark so much."

As the verbal assault escalated, I felt attacked and let his words bring out my defensive attitudes. Soon I was yelling back. I'd engaged in his game, enabling it to continue. In a few moments whatever fun I'd had with the children in the snow was long gone. No more smiles; no more laughter. The children went off to their rooms to escape what was taking place, and the dog and I were both unjustly in the doghouse! Satan had definitely entered the room! His angry agenda sucked out the joy, like a leech, and left us emotionally anemic.

For several years our home was a minefield of surprise attacks followed by a cycle of apologies. We never knew when the next round would begin. The children and I were often surprised by a husband and father prone to bouts of rage. Most of the time we didn't understand why something as small as leaving a light on created such a stir. In turn, I felt the only way to be heard was to turn up my own volume. So I did. In a short time I would respond with the same angry fuel. Anger had become the preferred method of exerting control and spewing frustration.

Anger is a chosen family-management skill. We are such territorial beings, protecting our stuff and defending our rights. We get upset over the smallest things. If someone sits in our favorite chair, borrows our tools without asking, uses our private office, fails to do a job well, or takes a postage stamp, we feel violated. From these rude actions we find fuel to feed emotions of anger.

A great deal of anger takes place behind closed doors and is hidden beneath a veil of secrecy. We attempt to keep up a good public image. But what upsets us in our workplace and we feel we cannot release there, we often take home to our family and begin venting in our "safe" place. Outsiders may never detect our inner struggles with anger, while our family copes with our secret.

Or the opposite may be true. The world may become our stage and everyone our enemy. You may be a person known for angry outbursts and even visits by the police. People may keep their distance, not knowing how to intervene and not wanting to experience the fallout themselves.

If anger was handled as God intended it to be there would be no domestic violence. Our families would feel secure. Peace and fun would reign at the center of our homes. We owe it to our families to learn the truth about anger. If we fail to understand this potentially volatile passion residing within the soul of man, we will continue to be caught off guard by its attacks.

In the same way that camouflage is used to conceal battle strategies, our misuse of anger is used to conceal genuine heart issues. Digging beneath the angry surface will expose our real feelings. In our case, Charlie feared gaining a poor reputation in the community because of his dog. He was selfishly motivated— not concerned about upsetting his family but with what others would think about him.

We can only be in control of anger when we don't lose control. Satan uses our blindness to anger's truth to keep us from focusing on God's will for our lives. He cunningly arrives at a moment when all seems to be well and in an instant turns our world upside down. That is exactly what happened to me. That particular day I didn't even see warning signs of his arrival. I finished my day of fun with the children and expected to come home to a similar evening. Unaware of his cunning ways, I invited Satan in.

LEARNING ABOUT ANGER

If we operate from a mind-set lacking the knowledge of anger's physiology, we are vulnerable to Satan. Gary Jackson Oliver and H. Norman Wright, noted Christian counselors and authors, have helped me to understand a great deal about anger. They have allowed me to see a picture of anger that frees me to exercise self-control with this emotion.

Anger is a normal part of close relationships. Whenever two people begin a relationship, part of what attracts them are their similarities and another part of what attracts them are their differences. Opposites do attract, but not for long. It doesn't take very much time for differences to lead to disagreements. Disagreements may involve the emotions of fear, hurt, and frustration. Fear that our relationship is threatened and that we will never be understood. Hurt over what has been said to us and about us or over how it has been said. Frustration that we've had a similar disagreement before and this is the same song, twenty-second verse. Disagreements often involve anger and lead to conflict.

At that point we have a choice. We can choose to spend our anger-energy by dumping on our spouse or child, showing our victim where, once again, he is clearly wrong and we are right. Or we can throw up our hands in futility and stomp out of the room. By that act we communicate one of two things. Either the other person is not worth taking the time to work out the issue with, or communication between the two of us is impossible. Both choices lead to feelings of hopelessness and helplessness and set us up for more failure in the future.

However, there is another option. We can acknowledge our fear, hurt, or frustration and choose to invest our anger-energy by seizing this opportunity to better understand our loved one. One of the most practical ways to "bear all things, believe all things, hope all things and endure all things" (1 Corinthians 13:7) is to develop the habit of working through our differences. This takes time and involves listening, asking questions, listening, asking more questions, and finally reaching understanding.[1]

When anger is out of control, we are incapable of effectively communicating our real feelings. The further away Charlie and I got from communicating true emotions, the more we were blinded to the mask anger had become. We thought anger was the problem. What we didn't realize was that anger was only a cover-up for something deeper. For this reason anger is clinically spoken of as a "secondary" emotion. There is always a much greater primary emotion beneath it. Most often the real emotions are associated with fear or loss—fear of rejection if real feelings are expressed or grief over lost relationships.

IT'S AN OLD STORY

Provoking anger is not a new strategy for Satan. Let's go back to Genesis and see where it all began.

> So Cain was very angry, and his face was downcast. Then the Lord said to Cain, "Why are you angry? Why is your face downcast? If you do what is right, will you not be accepted? But if you do not do what is right, sin is crouching at your door; it desires to have you, but you must master it." (Genesis 4:5b–7)

From the time of the first family, unresolved anger and unnecessary conflict have existed. Here we are now, thousands of years later, displaying the very same behaviors, proving beyond a shadow of a doubt that Satan's influence continues in our modern day. His desire is still to destroy relationships, just like he did between Cain and his brother.

The moment self-serving, angry words leave our mouths we openly invite Satan to share in our life, our spouse's life, and our children's lives. At that point he has, by personal invitation, entered our room. By *room* I mean the temple of the Holy Spirit known to the believer as *self*. When Satan can tempt us to do his bidding in life's frustrating moments, we in turn allow him to affect relationships closest to us.

Anger was not Cain's real issue. He was jealous. He felt humiliated. God had accepted Abel's gift and not his. He knew what an acceptable offering should be but didn't bring it. God even brought it to his attention, giving him a chance to do what was right. Unhealthy anger was merely Cain's tool of choice to gain the upper hand. It did not prove to be an effective one. Cain had greater consequences to live with as a result of his anger than if he'd done the right thing. Even burying his brother in the dirt did not hide his sin from God.

Recognizing how Satan gains entrance to our room is crucial. Otherwise, we allow him to continue to nullify God's work in our lives. We can learn to lessen his visits and shorten his stay. As we experience victory over ill-spent anger, we can even arrive at a point where the door does not open to him. We will choose to deny him access.

Since we all experience anger, we know that some anger is good. It's a God-given emotion. What does God have to say about the subject?

> "In your anger do not sin": Do not let the sun go down while you are still angry, and do not give the devil a foothold. (Ephesians 4:26–27)

God is not saying we will never be angry. Anger is a neutral emotion given to us to benefit our lives. We have turned it into a negative emotion of possession. When it comes to anger, God sets some guidelines in place. He commands us not to bring sin into our anger and He puts a time limit on how long we are to remain angry. His reason for this is well taken. Anger that persists gives the devil a foothold in our lives. Anger is only expressed properly if God's commands are observed.

A FAMILY DESTROYED

While I was preparing this chapter, the Associated Press released a heartrending story depicting all too well the devil's use of anger in a blended family in Florida. The family's suicide was meticulously planned, down to the Post-it notes pasted on toys and furniture to indicate who should inherit them.

The husband (and father) had been married before and had grown children. Now he had an eight-year-old son with his present wife. The wife was distraught enough to succumb in submission to the murderous plan of her husband. Clutching rosary beads and leaving a written prayer on the table, she climbed into bed with their son and allowed death to come to her and her child. The husband then turned the gun on himself. His anger toward an older son had festered, allowing Satan to enter with devouring vengeance. Blaming this older son for his financial woes, the father left a note behind for him to read what was the ultimate display of sickening, long-seething anger.

Our intentions were to die on January 8, your birthday! We wanted you to remember the day that your cold and heartless actions, lack of love and compassion, caused the destruction of a perfectly good family.[2]

Could this kind of selfish hate-laden anger come from the heart of a father? Regardless of what our response to that question would be, that is exactly where it did come from. Love had been swallowed up in an all-consuming anger. It was obvious there had been much division between this man and his grown son—enough to bring about the ultimate payback! Not only did this loveless action harm his son but the entire breadth of the family structure shared in that destruction.

Our anger is not a license to sin, and sin is never justified just because we are angry. Our own personal actions still matter to the Lord. Take another look at Ephesians 4:26–27. We can see the result of unresolved anger. The devil got a foothold with this Florida family. It is just as easy for him to gain a foothold in my family. I have choices to make.

The father of this family could have made other choices—healthy choices to aid his wife and children. Choices expressing love in a manner favorable to the Lord would have brought reconciliation, not death.

POWER TO RESIST ANGER

It makes a big difference when we realize there is power within our reach to resist destructive anger. Satan's identity and schemes are not hidden from God's children. It is God's will that we be equipped to disarm him. He is a mighty foe, but we can refuse him entrance to our sanctuaries. It will require a battle plan. The strategy I try to put into practice involves four proactive steps.

Step 1. Recognition:
What are my anger trigger points?

Many things have the potential to bring about unhealthy

anger. Recognizing points of personal vulnerability is the first step. Do any of these sound familiar?

- Wounding words
- Physical discomfort (health issues, weather, abuse, etc.)
- Defending others
- Peer pressure
- Work-related unfairness
- Difficulty in family relationships
- Self-pity
- Inconsiderate drivers
- Unmet expectations
- Silent treatment or rejection from others
- Financial woes or greed
- A sudden change or a crisis

Step 2. Acknowledgment:
How does my anger cause a downward spiral?

Since unhealthy anger is sin, and sin separates us from God, we begin to walk out of His will. Our rebellion begins a spiral down into

⇓ Rebellion against God

⇓ Rebellion against one another

⇓ Self-defense mechanisms fly into action

⇓ Unity of home life is broken; relationships are strained

Each step takes us deeper. Ask yourself two questions: "What step am I at now?" "Am I willing to get off before spiraling further downward?" God's standards have not changed. Since He cannot bless us while we are living outside His design for Christian living, it is important for us to realize when we are beginning to spiral downward. We are always free to choose to get off this spiral at any one of the above four points.

Step 3. Self-examination:
Who am I?

We need to know ourselves. I spoke about this subject in chapter 4. Behind closed doors the private self behaves differently from the public self. We all let our hair down at home. Childish patterns of the past quickly pop up. As adults we are still responding to issues the way we did when we were children. Only now we are having sibling rivalries with our spouse!

> When I was a child, I used to speak like a child, think like a child, reason like a child; when I became a man, I did away with childish things. (1 Corinthians 13:11 NASB)

I grasped this concept clearly as I read David Seamands's book *Putting Away Childish Things.* Who we are at home is who we *really* are. The mask is off. Our behaviors, in their rawest sense, are paraded before those we claim to love the most.

> This little child of the past makes himself most clearly known in the place where a child is most comfortable—the home, and in those personal contacts and relationships which feel most like home. The hardest place to live maturely is with close friends, a roommate, a sweetheart, colleagues at work, and with family. For the little child tends to take over in close relationships.[3]

We can learn about ourselves. We can identify those childish behaviors that remain and "put them away." We can mature into reasoning as an adult. Examine the following list to see if you have allowed yourself to be a participant in Satan's ploys of family dissension. Many tools of his trade are reflected in our everyday, commonly used responses. Place a check mark beside the items you recognize as personal patterns.

- I am easily offended and easily angered.
- I withdraw and use the silent treatment.
- I use anger the same way my parent did.
- I use my ethnic background as an excuse for my temper (for example, "I'm Italian").
- I am a poor listener.
- I withhold love from others ("paybacks").
- I withhold forgiveness until I feel like forgiving.
- I don't accept forgiveness easily when asked to.
- I blame others before I examine my own actions or attitudes.
- I enjoy talking of my accomplishments.
- I don't get adequate rest.
- I consistently overwork.
- I have difficulty holding a job.
- I pout or cry often.
- I am a perfectionist; mistakes make me feel of less value.
- I often break promises.
- I abuse substances often (alcohol, drugs, etc.).
- I often use coarse language and curse words.
- I shout to make my point.
- I am physically abusive (shoving, slapping, etc.).
- I don't accept criticism well, even if it is helpful.
- I often criticize others and even poke fun at them.
- I believe God only cares about my salvation, not my daily life.
- I keep a list of wrongs others have done to me.
- I don't draw near to other Christians for fellowship.
- Prayer is not a regular activity for me.
- I have no daily plan for reading God's Word.
- God's Word is not relevant to my life choices.
- I seek God only when things are in crisis.
- I have no hesitation concerning debt or credit.
- I focus on me first.
- I have to be right.

Each of these statements could easily represent a childish pattern carried into adult life. Satan is delighted with all of these behaviors. They further family dissension. They keep us from growing into the maturity God has for us.

If we really want to put away improper anger and march to the beat of God's drum, we will have to be brutally honest with ourselves. This could be embarrassing. It will be humbling. But only if we admit we are hanging onto childish behaviors that result in childishly improper anger will we be able to begin walking and talking like mature men or women. Then we can express a more accurate witness of the God who lives within us. We will bring honor to our Lord when we display His character in its true form.

Step 4. Strategy:
What is going to be my plan?

I need to establish a strategy for escape before I come under attack again. How can I follow through differently next time? I am certain anger will have a "next time" in my life, so I must be ready. The best offense is a good defense. No professional team plays ball without first working out a strategy to help them win. They even watch films to become familiar with the opponent's game plan.

For me, implementing the winning plan God laid out in James makes sense.

> Submit yourselves, then, to God. Resist the devil, and he will flee from you. (James 4:7)

I will never have a winning strategy apart from God's wisdom. I can't do it in my own strength. I also know that without a plan I will lose the next bout with anger as surely as the football team that never practices.

It is helpful to view anger as an addictive agent, like alcohol or drugs. If you contend with anger often, you have become a "rageaholic." At our house it became a habitual pattern for life management. We had to break the addiction to anger. What about a twelve-step program? I think this one is worth trying.

1. Memorize James 4:7; it will prove invaluable.

2. Believe God has the workable solution.

3. Come apart for a designated cooling-off time (one to six hours).

4. Use the time apart wisely; begin by seeking the Lord in prayer.

5. Write down what you understand the issue to be, not your mate's view.

6. Come back together with an attitude of reconciliation.

7. Determine to be a good listener—respect and affirm what you hear.

8. Offer forgiveness, remembering that the Lord has forgiven you.

9. Put pride aside—being right is not the loving answer to any argument.

10. Be willing to agree to disagree if necessary; it's OK to think differently.

11. Once compromise is accomplished, follow through willingly.

12. End with a meaningful form of touch with one another.

With these twelve steps we see a progression into proper problem resolution and reconciliation. Anger does not have to be unhealthy. In its proper context anger alerts us to issues needing to be dealt with. It can be a good thing when used wisely. Conflicts will arise within every family. Some behaviors may need to change for the family to go forward. Important decisions will have to be made. Anger is the emotion lifting us to a passion for change. Jesus cleared the temple in Matthew 21:12–13 not to destroy the people, but to bring about a needed change in the use of the temple.

The best part of learning about anger is that I now see times of disagreement with others as being completely in God's permissive will and capable of bringing about a positive result. The right kind of anger gives me the opportunity to confront issues and extend grace. There is no devaluing of the people involved.

Misusing anger brought me to see the dark side of who I was capable of being. Once, finding no other immediate coping mechanism, frustration heightened. I picked up my beautiful crystal bowl, a precious wedding gift, and smashed it on the kitchen floor. This really startled me. I never thought I could do such a thing. But now I could see the world of evil lying within every human spirit. When a person is pushed into a corner and feels no way of escape, domestic violence is easily birthed. The 911 tapes replaying Nicole Simpson's fearful voice as O. J.'s threats are heard in the background and the photos of her face should heighten our concern for the family. Anger should never go to this level.

We are not always able to know how we will react until circumstances become overwhelming. That is why it is so important to understand anger before we are in an emotionally heated moment so that its use is under the directive of the Lord. With a proper understanding we can look at life through different lenses. We can see multiple choices. We are able to release the offender and allow God to do a work in his life too.

Educator and minister Tim LaHaye has said, "You need to realize also that you are responsible to choose how you will respond in anger-producing situations. No one 'makes you angry.' Anger is your response to others' actions. You make you angry."[4]

I now look at times of Satan's tempting as opportunities to test the godly character traits growing in my life. I know God has allowed these tests to take place. I would never know my strengths if there were no times of testing. These tests of my maturity in

Christ are not comfortable, but they help me focus on God's plan while removing the irritation of the event. I am able to evaluate the circumstance in light of God's sovereignty. I even add a little lighthearted flair by mentally preparing a scorecard naming my test and the date I came to grips with my carnal nature once more. For example:

Exam # 63: self-pity: _____Date _____Passed _____Failed
Exam # 64: listening skills: _____Date _____Passed _____Failed

This helps me remain accountable to walking the talk of my Christian faith. It's fun to imagine God giving heavenly diplomas when we graduate from this earthly place. I'll be happy to move my tassel to the other side. How about you?

Growth and Application

Commit to memory Ephesians 4:26–27.

1. When are you most likely to lose your temper and become angry?

   What effect does your anger have on family members?

2. From James 1:19–20, what is the relationship between listening, speaking, and the use of anger? Explain the relationship between anger and righteous living.

3. Describe a time when you let the sun go down on your anger. How did you feel? Did you realize you were giving the devil a foothold?

4. From step three of the chapter text, what behaviors best define you? In what way can you actively put away childish behaviors? How would your family benefit?

Prayer of Application

Lord, forgive me for the times I have fallen to Satan's schemes with unhealthy anger. Please examine my heart and reveal my unhealthy habits with anger. I want to learn to respond appropriately and not give the devil a foothold. Help my spouse and I develop a strategy for using anger in mature and healthy ways, not letting the sun go down on our anger. Lead us to a greater depth of intimacy in our relationship by helping us to "put away childish things." Amen.

NOTES

1. Gary Jackson Oliver and H. Norman Wright, *When Anger Hits Home* (Chicago: Moody, 1992), 87.

2. The Associated Press as reported by the *Mail Tribune* (Medford, Ore., March 1997).

3. David Seamands, *Putting Away Childish Things* (Wheaton, Ill.: Victor, 1982), 11.

4. Tim LaHaye and Bob Phillips, *Anger Is a Choice* (Grand Rapids: Zondervan, 1982), 144.

Chapter Six

WHO'S
IN CHARGE?

I was eight when my stepfather moved in," fifteen-year-old Brent said. "Suddenly I felt like an outsider. I had to adapt to new and different rules and ways. My mom always had to check with my stepdad about everything. She thought differently from him on a lot of subjects, but what he said went. He disciplined me for stuff my mom never did. He made me start doing things I had never had to do before, like rinse out empty pop cans . . . and never drink from someone else's drink."

"How did that make you feel?" I asked.

"I felt like I was a parasite. Like I was leaving germs everywhere."

"Did other things change as well?"

"He wouldn't let me do stuff without a reason," Brent continued, pushing his auburn hair back from his face. "I couldn't even talk on the phone after eight o'clock at night. I suddenly had to watch everything I did and said in order to stay out of trouble."

"I guess a lot of these changes must have made you angry," I said.

"Yeah," Brent admitted. "He wouldn't even let me use the bathroom by my room. I had to go to the other end of the house and ask if someone was in the bathroom I was told to use before I was allowed in the one across from my room. And . . . he felt he could walk in on me anytime he wanted."

"What else did you find difficult at your house?" I asked.

"Well . . . I used to play on the lawn," the young man said sadly. "Since my stepdad came, I can't even play on the lawn anymore because he thinks I will ruin it."

"How have you managed to adapt to so many new things?"

"Well, sometimes my mom prays with me, and she lets me spend a lot of time with my friends," Brent said. "That way I'm not around the house so much."

Brent is like a lot of children in blended families. A stepparent moves in and a coup takes place. So who's in charge? The old family government, with its familiar rules, is given over to a new ruler. The subjects (the children—and the spouse) of the newly formed kingdom are expected to comply willingly. But had they been given a vote, they would have voted against many of the new statutes. There is much about the new regime they don't like. It was better the old way. But—in many families—they do not have a say. They are the silent majority.

BALANCED DISCIPLINE

"What if you fear the children will grow up to be bad people?" Nick, a relatively new stepfather of preschoolers, asked. "That's why I make sure they are strictly disciplined at home."

"Do you have reason to believe your children will be bad people?" I asked.

"Well, no," he said, "but I want to insure they won't."

"Disciplining to ward off what might happen won't be effective," I said. "A dad who applies loving correction will raise good children, children who learn to trust. One who instills unwarranted fear will raise insecure children."

"Charlie," Nick said, addressing his next question to my husband, "how did *you* figure out what is really balanced discipline versus too much control from a father?"

"I finally realized I was just not trusting God," Charlie said. "I wanted to be in control. Because of that, I was exasperating my children. I asked God to forgive me, and I began to enjoy who my children were, focusing more attention on what they did right. I didn't have to make them good people. They already were. I just needed to see them through God's eyes. When I was able to do that, I learned a father's discipline, as God defines it, is only necessary once in a while. It should be reserved for outright disobedience, and then administered in love so the child's spirit is not crushed."

A summary of studies of family relationships observed that "much of the clinical and theoretical literature on stepfamilies has suggested that how well stepfamily members adjust to their circumstances depends on how issues pertaining to the role of the stepparent are managed."[1] Effectively integrating the stepparent into the family's life structure is a must. Going about this tall order is where we run into snags. Instilling fear will be an ineffective approach.

In most blended families, the household of primary influence on the children is made up of a birth mother and a stepfather. That is how our blended home began.

I believe most stepfathers want to do a good job of parenting but they may lack the skills to do it well. Their own home of origin may not have exhibited good parenting skills. Like it or not, vow that we won't, we often perpetuate a parenting style similar to what we grew up with. So it is easy to begin with poor methods and think they are OK.

There is the "Captain" father. He wants to groom a shipshape family. So from day one he corrects every behavior he is not pleased with in the children, from how they chew their food to whether they put on a belt with their jeans. If he can just fix the kids, his home will be happy. And his new wife will be so pleased, even proud of him. This doesn't work—probably because he wants respect for rules, not relationships.

A family with a Captain father will be frustrated. Family

members will begin choosing sides. Moms like me feel the discipline is too harsh and doled out too often. Our hearts are torn between our children and our husband. We try to intervene with the stepfather on behalf of the children.

But Captain husbands interpret a wife's concern as a lack of respect for their authority in the home. So the couple is now at odds. The children still see their mother as their primary source of discipline, love, and protection. Her heart is soft toward them, just like before. They are accustomed to her boundaries and her methods of correcting inappropriate behaviors. Because the parents are divided, the children are confused as to who is really in charge. The parental authority of the home has been weakened and discipline is now a major obstacle.

Then there is the "Mr. Rogers" father. His temperament is the opposite of the Captain's. His goal is not to fix the children, but to develop relationships with them. They will draw near to him because he puts relationships ahead of rules. He is supportive of the personhood of his children.

In this home, respect for the stepfather begins to grow soon after the marriage. His goal is not to replace the children's father. He takes time to talk with the mother about parenting and discipline issues. He realizes change will be difficult for the children. So he moves slowly into their world. This couple works together to forge new boundaries for their family because the father figure would rather have fun, offer encouragement, and help when he can. Even though his role is not dominant in the beginning, he is confident in the significant role he plays. This family will do well as it moves ahead. The family is not divided and the parents are not divided as they raise the children.

When Blake was a teenager he was caught in a tough situation but was fortunate to find a supportive attitude in his stepfather. He writes a bittersweet letter:

My dad was pretty upset when he found out my girlfriend was pregnant with my child. Unfortunately, to this day, he has been unable to make the transition from being angry to being supportive. He has always seen adversity as an opportunity to teach me a

110

lesson, rather than an opportunity to show his love. My dad was the second person I called after my daughter was born on Sunday night. When I told him the news, the first words he said were, "Well, I guess you're gonna learn what it's like to be a father." During that phone call, he never told me congratulations. He still never has. Now she is three.

His letter continued:

I didn't talk to Carl (my stepdad) until the next day when I returned home. I went in the kitchen, where he was reading the paper. This might sound overly dramatic, but I swear it's exactly what happened: He looked up and saw me, smiled, and said, "Congratulations." There have been many times when my stepdad has been much more of a father than my dad.

PLANNING FOR DISCIPLINE

These stories show that effective parenting skills are possible for both the natural parent and the stepparent. We can implement appropriate structure in a blended family. Discipline and love work together. They make delightful companions. Both are time consuming but share the same goal—the good of the children.

Prior to our marriage we didn't discuss parenting details at any length. We made a lot of assumptions. We were already parents, so we thought we knew the job description. In my mind a mom would know how to be a mom, and a dad would know how to be a dad. Love them, feed them, correct them, and watch them grow. But what worked in our past nuclear families wasn't working in our blended family. This was a different man with a family standard unlike mine and unlike the family structure the children were accustomed to.

Almost immediately discipline was a problem. This quickly became one of the "biggies" in our house. It affected all of us, not just the children. We could not parent effectively unless we could bring a halt to the division surrounding this subject. Only in unity would we be able to develop and administer a discipline strategy capable of guiding our children into lifelong, socially acceptable behaviors. Somehow we had to go beyond the familiar do-what-I-say patterns of the past. The only way to make this happen was to renew our minds about discipline.

In *The Jack and Jill Syndrome* counselor Patricia Rushford brings understanding and fresh insight to the word *discipline.*

> Every child needs a parent who loves him enough to discipline him wisely. How do we do that? Perhaps one of the first keys to effective discipline is understanding what it actually means. Many tend to use the words *discipline* and *punishment* synonymously. Although discipline may include chastisement, correction, punishment, and penalty, it has far deeper implications. To discipline also means to guide, instruct, train, prepare, indoctrinate, develop, moderate, and restrain. It implies a state of orderliness, habit, regimen, and adherence to certain rules, as opposed to the chaos, confusion, and disorderliness of the undisciplined.
>
> Effective discipline then must incorporate not only forms of punishment, but also methods for teaching and guiding a child into an orderly and self-disciplined way of life. Discipline is something we do *for* our children, not something we do *to* them.[2]

Discipline is an act of love, not an opportunity to vent frustration and impose suffering. It is a loving means to train, prepare, and mold a child. Parents are the most instrumental teachers in the child's world. They set the boundaries that hem a child into a safe place of nurturing. Discipline should bring order to the child's life, not confusion. Until discipline is meted out in love it will have limited effectiveness and the potential to produce rebellion rather than positive change.

Parents whose goal is to administer effective discipline will take time to form a plan. They will clarify behavioral boundaries and just consequences. After they have discussed these disciplinary guidelines, they are ready to convey their values to the children. The children will see Mom and Dad standing together in the government of the home.

The plan should subject all children to the same standards. Then a younger child will feel as secure as an older sibling. For example, if it is wrong to lie, then it is wrong for everyone. The children should all understand that they will be busted if they lie. But parents will need to administer consequences differently. These will have to be individually tailored and age appropriate. A four year old will not receive the same punishment as his fourteen-year-old brother. His understanding is not the same, nor his attention span as long.

GOD'S OPINION ON DISCIPLINE

What do we need to know about discipline? To start with, I believe we need to know God has an opinion on the subject.

> And you have forgotten that word of encouragement that addresses you as sons: "My son, do not make light of the Lord's discipline, and do not lose heart when he rebukes you, because the Lord disciplines those he loves, and he punishes everyone he accepts as a son." (Hebrews 12:5–6)

We are to follow God's pattern of discipline. It is to encourage a better behavior, it is done in love and because of love, and it should not cause a child to lose heart.

> All a man's ways seem innocent to him, but motives are weighed by the Lord. Commit to the Lord whatever you do, and your plans will succeed. (Proverbs 16:2–3)

Because we vary in personality, we will vary in methods and attitudes toward discipline. Our ways may seem innocent to us, but would the Lord consider them innocent? If we are doling out punishment to satisfy our own frustrations, our motives are suspect. If our goal is to love the child and guide him to an appropriate behavior, we will have the proper motive and our children will grow in understanding. We parents need to discern whether we are using selfish or God-centered motives in correcting the behaviors of our children.

Chuck Swindoll has offered sound advice for discerning right motives from wrong ones:

Only God's two-edged sword is able to pierce behind the action to the motive, deep into the thought life, to expose the whole truth. We need to listen to His counsel as we open our eyes and ears to His truth. When we do this, we tap into the most phenomenal source of information available to mankind.[3]

The Word of God is the sword that is able to cut to the quick of our motives. When Charlie and I married and our two households came together, the different discipline styles in the blended families our children were a part of threw our family government into a state of confusion. The children wondered what had happened to yesterday's rules! Their world was turned upside down.

As their mother I felt Charlie made too many new demands but didn't want my husband to feel he wasn't the head of the house. So I tried to enforce as much of the new as I could. Perhaps I could help the children understand his expectations. I began policing my children's behaviors to lessen the chance of offending my husband. I can see now that my motives were wrong. My goal was to find a peaceful space, not just to train the children. But I was in a real dilemma and unable to successfully bridge this gap for a long time.

Some families come to ruin over this issue. For us, there was a missing element in the core structure of our family unit. It was called relationship. The emotional foundation between Charlie and his stepchildren was missing. He could not appreciate the adorable, rosy-cheeked baby boy who scooted across the floor as he mastered the art of crawling. He wasn't around at that time. When I remarried, Mike was already an active six-year-old. Somehow the gap between the stepparent and the children that should have been filled by a loving, trusting, and respect-filled relationship had not yet been closed. Yet without this bridge we couldn't expect the children to respect the new parent figure in the home.

Stepparents are generally advised by clinicians to focus on developing warm, positive relationships with stepchildren before assuming an active disciplinary role.[4]

We now know that our first mistake was in allowing the stepfather to take an equal role in the discipline of my children too soon after our marriage. There had been no adjustment period. Charlie was a stranger to them. Family feelings between my children and Charlie were not yet established. Since loving relationships take time to develop, the children didn't readily accept the fact that his authority was really substantial in the home. They saw a lot of rules. They didn't feel a lot of acceptance.

Charlie's immediate outpouring of discipline made Andrea and Mike feel they could never please their stepfather. It made me feel caught in the middle, loving and protecting my children while loving and attempting to honor the new head of our household. At times I just could not allow the discipline imposed by my husband to be carried out against my children. It wasn't reasonable. This placed me in an awkward position, as it taught the children to question Charlie's authority and gave them hope that Mom would change the consequences imposed for unacceptable behavior. It allowed them to play us against each other.

We would all have fared better if the children continued to look to me, their biological parent, for discipline during the first few months we were a blended family. Then, little by little, their stepfather could come alongside me in a slower manner, demonstrating warmth, discussion, interaction, and even prayer with the children. With this delay, the children would have had the chance to become familiar with Charlie and adjust to receiving parental discipline from this new man in their lives.

THE IMPACT OF A PARENT

Lynn, a thirty-eight-year-old mother of two, lay in a hospital bed recovering from surgery. As we began talking, the conversation turned to her concern for her family.

"Being married to Jake for the past ten years has been very difficult," she said, tears softly dropping to her cheeks. "He can't bring himself to love my son. Jim was only nine when I married Jake. Now he's nineteen, and Jake still refuses to resolve the relationship. He knows how much this hurts me."

"I can see it really tears at your heart," I said.

"I'm scared something will happen at home while I'm here in the hospital," Lynn said, "and that I won't be there for Jim."

"Has your husband gotten physical with him in the past?" I asked.

"There have been several times when I've stopped Jake from punching him. Jake tells me he just doesn't like my son.

"Our little girl sees how her daddy treats her brother," Lynn continued, frustration rising in her voice. "She isn't learning to love like I want her to, because her father is so ugly to my son."

"It's difficult to understand how an adult can make a conscious decision not to love a child," I said, reaching to hold Lynn's hand. "Moms just aren't wired to watch their children live with daily rejection. That can only bring a deep wound into the marriage relationship."

"I'm losing my feelings for my husband. I feel I can no longer trust him. If I could do it over again, I wouldn't marry him," Lynn admitted through her tears. "We're Christians! Why doesn't this man, who says he loves Jesus, love my child?"

Lynn raises a very valid question. Many times I've sat with a parent who has retold this same, heartrending story. I wish it didn't happen so often. If parents could only understand how significant they are in the lives of their children. They are the ones who will make the deepest impact on a child. Parental acceptance is so necessary. An effective stepparent must open a space in his heart and tuck each child in. We simply cannot say we love Jesus and choose to reject a child.

In his book *Daddy Loves His Girls* T. D. Jakes gives a great description of the impact a parent has on the development of a child:

> It is obvious that a father is significant to the wellbeing of a young man. It is from our fathers that we receive the first pattern we can expect to resemble in some way. It helps to be able to contour our rough edges in alignment with someone we admire. . . . I figured he represented what I would be someday.[5]

Whoa! What we model as parents represents what our children will emulate as they grow into adulthood. This sheds new light on the responsibilities of our parenting roles. Contouring a child's rough edges should be a gentle process, such as that of a potter working at his wheel to form a beautiful vase that will one day hold a rose. Gently and with much patience his hands mold the soft clay. Too much pressure will push the clay off center, make the vessel unsymmetrical, and may even break it. But by molding the wet clay gently with water-dipped hands, we remove friction and the vase grows into an object of balance, service, and loveliness.

For a child to be appropriately molded, parents need to look at the model they are displaying before their children. Children mimic well. They catch what they see better than they follow what they hear. That is why it is important to align our lives to God's design. As moms and dads we need also to remember who is in charge—Almighty God. We will answer to Him, and He has given us a high calling to personal accountability. So disciplining our children really begins when we dare to discipline ourselves.

The mouth is a good place to start. If we want them to use good words, we must use good words first. How can we expect positive behaviors from our children if we exhibit bad behaviors ourselves? The old cliché "Do as I say, not as I do" is really a cop-out, setting up a double standard in our homes. This statement says, "My behavior and your behavior are not the same; adults act differently." It also says, "I have higher standards for you than I do for myself." A child will see you as a hypocrite and disregard your authority. Parents, guard how you lead your family. God has set a standard for you to follow. Children are a gift from God, whether your children were acquired naturally or are stepchildren as a result of a blended family. God cares how we treat our little ones.

> "And whoever welcomes a little child like this in my name welcomes me. But if anyone causes one of these little ones who believe in me to sin, it would be better for him to have a large millstone hung around his neck and to be drowned in the depths of the sea." (Matthew 18:5–6)

This is a strong warning from God for those who mistreat the precious little ones entrusted to their care. Abuse comes in many forms. Often emotional abuse is more devastating than physical abuse. Neither form of abuse is condoned by the Lord.

While preparing this chapter I came across a startling statistic in the 1997 *Journal of the American Academy of Forensic Sciences*. This statistic alerts us to what is taking place within our society:

> In a Federal report from 1992–95, the government summarized by stating that since 1992 there have been 5,000 deaths of children by parents and other caretakers. More children die at the hands of their parents than in car accidents, house fires, falls or drownings.[6]

I shudder to think how many of these precious children were part of a blended home where one of the parent figures failed to discover God's design for love or discipline. Recently I was horrified as the news reported the finding of the body of a three-year-old child whose small frame showed a history of repeated physical abuse by her mother and a male parent figure. This time the abuse went too far and the child didn't survive. For the sake of our children we must learn a better way and cherish the little ones God has given to us.

If you have been a parent who has withheld love and caused a child to feel unaccepted in your home, seek God's forgiveness. God is able to restore you to your children. Genuine repentance paves the way. Be mature enough to ask your stepson or stepdaughter to forgive you; ask your natural children to forgive you; ask your spouse to forgive you. Embrace the value of each child God has allowed you to care for. It is a high privilege to nurture those little ones created in God's very image.

> Sons are a heritage from the Lord, children a reward from him.
> (Psalm 127:3)

Charlie and I each married a ready-made family, and we knew it from the start. It wasn't a surprise when we took on stepparenting roles. We didn't stop parenting because the words "I do" were uttered. Each spouse's children were an important part of both of our parental responsibilities, whether the child lived with us primarily or just came for visitation. This is the family God has placed under our leadership—lock, stock, and barrel! There are joys to be revealed and blessings to receive from each child as we open our hearts to cherish the reward God has given us. There is pain to reap when we don't.

DESTRUCTIVE CONSEQUENCES MAY COME

Stepchildren exposed to high levels of parental conflict are doubly disadvantaged compared with children from other types of families . . . not because they experience more intrahousehold conflict than children in original, two-parent households and not because they experience more interhousehold conflict than children in single-mother households, but because they are exposed to *both* sources of conflict, which, taken together, means that they are less likely to live in low-conflict families and more likely to live in high-conflict families.[7]

These are significant findings. We must realize children in blended families potentially have much more exposure to conflict than children in original, two-parent families, even if conflict is present. This continual conflict, if not put to rest, sometimes results in serious consequences.

Brad was remarried to a woman with two boys. His only child from his first marriage lived with Brad's ex-wife in another city. Brad was a miserable stepfather. He failed to exhibit acceptance and love to his stepsons. He often spoke of an inner desire to flush them down the toilet.

His second wife endured his temperament and occasional physical abuse as they raised their own two children alongside her sons. For this family time didn't seem to make things better. Eighteen years later heated family conflicts were still a constant occurrence. Relationships were full of extreme emotional highs and lows—a time bomb waiting to explode. One day it did.

The two boys were now grown men in their twenties. One

summer day Brad became abusive toward their mother. They'd had enough of his ill temper and drove to the house to confront him. It wasn't long before a fight broke out. The boys, being younger and stronger, began to give Brad back a portion of what he had dished out all those years. The tables had turned. He was now on the receiving end. Not able to deal with this humiliation, Brad chose to commit suicide. A very sad ending leaving scars on the whole family.

Pain cannot be held down forever. One day its voice will rise, screaming to be heard. It will be given expression. This time it took a parent's life. Often it is the child who chooses suicide.

CELEBRATE EACH CHILD

Praise the Lord. Blessed is the man who fears the Lord, who finds great delight in his commands. His children will be mighty in the land; the generation of the upright will be blessed. (Psalm 112:1–2)

An effective parent fears the Lord and finds delight in the instruction of the Word. He learns how to celebrate each child and give him a sense of value, so that one day he will be an influential person in his own world. He will be equipped to spread godliness into another generation, and the blessing baton will pass on into the future.

Hug your children often, and they will learn they are loved. Speak kind words, and they will learn to communicate effectively. Listen to their hearts, and they will know they have a voice. Allow them to fail, and they will learn to have mercy on others.

Training children is a hands-on project. We have to make opportunities for them to be included in the family business. It makes them feel important, even though they are young. Center some fun around the things each boy or girl enjoys doing. In this way you will actively enter into the world of your children. You will probably be amazed at the interests your children have. Each one has been gifted so differently. One of our sons was very interested in model rockets when he was younger. He would build a rocket and then want us to watch it blast off. I have to admit that if it weren't for Mike, I would not have understood model rockets. They were fun!

A great way to include children in family decisions is to have a family calendar. Hang it in an obvious place. Allow each child to choose a family activity once a month. When the activities are written down, everyone can do his best to be available for the family fun and each child can see that he is getting a turn. If your children are too small to choose for themselves, pick age-appropriate activities, like a trip to the zoo, and put their names on the calendar. You act as their proxy. Fun doesn't have to be expensive. Make a "family fun" budget if necessary. Some ideas to get you started:

- Do an art project, e.g., finger painting, coloring, models
- Go fishing
- Decorate a "funny" cake
- Collect fall leaves, seashells, rocks
- Make homemade ice cream
- Have frisbee fun or toss a ball
- Take a bag of bread to feed the ducks at the pond
- Design a child's menu night . . . let them cook
- Have a backyard camp-out

My husband has never been an avid fisherman, but my son loves to do such things. So to make a special, fit-to-order vacation memory for Mike, Dad got fishing licenses for the two of them at Yellowstone Lake. It was fun for me too, as I watched them bait hooks together and then reel in beautiful trout. We still talk about how good those fish tasted.

Remember, our goal is to build value into our children, to celebrate the joy of childhood, and to ease the discomfort of change within the blended home.

Focus on the Family's Dr. James Dobson has sound advice when he says, "Pick your battles carefully. Make sure they are over issues that are important." Cut some slack—don't sweat the small stuff. Life is too short for so much rejection and sorrow. Life is too short *not* to consider the value God places on our child rearing. As this chapter ends, ask yourself: "If my children were to emulate me, who would they grow up to be?"

Growth and Application

Commit to memory Psalm 127:3.

1. As you read Psalm 127:3, how are we to appreciate the children in our family?

   Do you think this statement is limited only to our natural children?

   Do you consider children a blessing or a burden? Why?

2. On a scale of one to ten, ten being the greatest, how would you rate the conflict level in your home? _____ How has change played a role in the conflict?

3. After reading Matthew 18:5–6, do you think God places a high level of accountability on us for our parenting skills? _____ How does this relate to our discipline techniques?

What kind of parenting changes do you think God would want you to make?

4. How do you celebrate the children in your family? Name them individually and give a brief description of how you have done this.

What could you do to show greater appreciation for each child?

Prayer of Application

Lord, how beautifully You express Your love of children. We want our lives as parents to be a reflection of that image to our children. Forgive us for the times we have failed as parents to show appreciation for our children and for times we have disciplined in ways we now see were inappropriate. Create in us a real love not only for our natural children, but also for our stepchildren. Each one is a gift from You. A gift You have placed in our care. Give us creative ideas to help each child feel loved and accepted. We ask that our ears be open to listen to our spouse where family change is needed and not become defensive. Our desire is to train our children in a way that will leave a godly heritage for the next generation. Amen.

NOTES

1. Mark A. Fine, Lawrence H. Ganong, and Marilyn Coleman, "The Relationship Between Role Constructions and Adjustment Among Stepfathers," *Journal of Family Issues* 18, no. 5 (September 1997): 503, summarizing Crosbie-Burnett, 1989, and Visher & Visher, 1988, 1996.

2. Patricia H. Rushford, *The Jack and Jill Syndrome: Healing for Broken Children* (Grand Rapids: Revell, 1996), 124.

3. Charles R. Swindoll, *Living on the Ragged Edge* (Waco, Tex.: Word, 1985), 147.

4. Fine, Ganong, and Coleman, "The Relationship Between Role Constructions and Adjustment Among Stepfathers," 520.

5. T. D. Jakes, *Daddy Loves His Girls* (Lake Mary, Fla.: Creation House, 1996), 47.

6. Lawrence A. Dobrin, "Parental Homicide: Child Abuse at Its Worst," *Proceedings* (American Academy of Forensic Sciences) 3 (February 1997): F31.

7. Thomas L. Hanson, Sara S. McLanahan, and Elizabeth Thomson, "Double Jeopardy: Parental Conflict and Stepfamily Outcomes for Children," *Journal of Marriage and Family* 58, no. 1 (February 1996): 153.

Chapter Seven

CHILDREN
IN THE MIDST
OF CHANGE

Early one afternoon, I received a phone call from my son's second-grade teacher.

"Mrs. Marsolini, I need to talk to you about Mike," she said. "He threw his food in the cafeteria today. This is odd behavior for him. Did something new or unusual take place in your family? Change often triggers conduct normally uncommon to a child."

"I'm as surprised as you are," I replied, puzzled. "Mike doesn't throw food at home. Were any of the other children throwing food as well? He sometimes joins in with others."

"A couple boys were doing the same thing, but they both say he threw the first spoonful."

"I'll talk with him when he gets home from school," I said. "Thank you for bringing this to my attention."

I listened to Mike's story about the incident when he came home from school. I chalked it up to misbehavior and gave him an appropriate consequence. But his teacher's comments about change stuck in my mind. Truthfully, there were a lot of changes happening in his life. The more I thought about it, the more I realized that throwing food was his way of focusing some attention on himself. After all, even negative attention is attention. And everyone was so wrapped up in the new baby. Mike was the youngest until two months ago.

Change alters the familiar. Sometimes it exchanges a known quantity for an unknown one. Other times it only modifies, giving a fresh look, as a coat of paint does to the exterior of my home. Change can be a scary thing, a fun thing, a sad thing, or a welcome breeze on a hot afternoon. It enters our lives accompanied by an array of emotions.

Yet change is to life as oxygen is to air. To live is to experience its presence. A baby in his first year of life changes rapidly in appearance, alertness, and dexterity. If photos are not taken every couple of weeks the stages of development are lost to our memory. By age one the child goes from total dependency to multiple skills. He now holds objects (cleverly gets most of them in his mouth), speaks a few words, and is often walking. Remarkable change is taking place. It doesn't stop.

In blended families there are added dimensions to the speed of change within the child's world—actually within the entire breadth of the family structure. Instead of feeling secure, children can become fearful or angry. How can we make these transitions easier for our children? I believe there are many ways.

First, we can take time to identify the changes and acknowledge their existence. Second, we can care about their outcome and converse about them with the children on their level of understanding.

Mike was still dealing with the loss of his relationship with his birth father, a new home in a new neighborhood, a new school, new friends, a stepfather, and a baby sister. His role as the youngest had been displaced. His father and his former friends were not as accessible as before.

These were big changes for a little boy! He expressed his dismay the way many children do—through behavior. Youngsters are not adept in speaking what they are feeling. They are at the mercy of adults, trusting their needs will continue to be met. We

parents can easily overlook the deeper issues and overcorrect behavioral manifestations.

DEALING WITH LOSS

Understanding loss takes time. It is difficult enough to deal
with our own sense of loss but even more difficult to embrace the
sense of loss our children experience. Laura Sherman Walters
covers this topic well in her book *There's a New Family in My
House.* We parents owe it to our children to help them through
the grieving process.

> All of the literature indicates that children need to mourn longer
> than we realize, and we must give them that time. Get books to
> read on the stages of grieving and storybooks for your children,
> who are not as experienced as you at handling life's hard lessons;
> neither are they equipped emotionally to deal with pain or make
> sense of their circumstances.[1]

Divorce brings death to a family structure. My children didn't
want their relationship with their birth father to stop—but it did.
After their stepfather adopted them, several years went by without any contact from their birth father. I didn't realize it at the
time, but they were grieving, as if there were a death in the family.
They mourned the loss of relationship with their father but dealt
with it silently. An important part of their lives had passed away. I
viewed their lack of conversation regarding him as a statement of
"we're adjusting just fine." I didn't shut the door, but we didn't go
into that room either.

My husband's children were dealing with the same silent
grief. The secret phone calls we received once in a while let us
know Dad was in the back of their minds, but nothing could be
done. As long as their mother insisted on keeping them from
him, we had no way of bridging the loss of relationship they felt.

Childhood sorrow is more serious than we realize. Divorce
does not guarantee a continuing relationship between the absentee parent and their children, even if the decree stated it to be so.

Broken relationships for adults can mean the loss of a loved parent for a child. Even for children who continue with a visitation schedule, the home they were initially secure in has passed away. The daily interplay with their loved parent is gone. A grieving process is taking place within the child. Somehow we need to put ourselves in his shoes and set aside our own negative emotions toward our ex. We need to ask our children questions about what they are feeling when they think about their absent parent. "What do you miss most when you think of Daddy?" "Does that make you sad?" "Would you like to pray about that?" Let them see our concern. Let them know Jesus cares.

Jesus understands grief better than any of us. Sorrow touched Him as He heard of John the Baptist's death and again when Mary and Martha cried out for help while trying to cope with the death of their brother, Lazarus. Jesus identified so much with their sorrow that He wept too. But He also brought them comfort. He has the same compassion for us when life brings sorrow our way.

> He heals the brokenhearted and binds up their wounds. (Psalm 147:3)

When a divorce and remarriage occurs, familiar family roles change. A time of reconstructing relationships is needed. This does not mean the loss is not felt, but that we say good-bye to the way life was with that person. Daddy won't be home each night, but he will be here to get you on Saturday. By bringing closure to what was, we are able to open new doors to enjoy the relationship as it exists today. As we help our children understand what it means to form new family connections they will be able to heal the wounds of lost relationships and grow into acceptance of new family roles.

DEALING WITH BIRTH ORDER

Dr. Kevin Leman gives us great insight into the mysteries of birth order:

In any family, a person's order of birth has a lifelong effect on who and what that person turns out to be. Are you an only or first born? You are a different person than you would have been had you been born later. Are you the baby in the family? Things would be different, and so would you, had you been born first. Are you the "squeezed" middle child? You can look up or possibly down and think about how it might have been had you been born earlier or later.[2]

I am trying to comprehend the effects of birth order on human development. According to the definition above, I am a squeezed middle child: child number two of four children. I was not as watched or fussed over as a number one child or a number four child. My younger sister, child number three, and I probably made more independent choices than our older sister or younger brother simply because of our birth order. We were ignored on a more consistent basis. My older sister was the pride and joy of our parents, Dad in particular, as would be any firstborn child. My brother being the youngest, and the only boy, also received an abundance of attention. Mother doted on everything he did or said. He was the cute one.

Birth Order in the Traditional Family

In a traditional family setting there is an acceptable adjustment when each child is born. If there are more than two children, the birth order for all siblings between the first child and the last child changes. The firstborn always keeps her special position in the birth order. She is Mommy and Daddy's first attempt at parenting and everything she does is so exciting, so perfect. And with only one child they have plenty of attention and training time to give her. This child soon learns that a great deal is expected from her. After all, her parents brag about her accomplishments to all who will listen. Many number one children become overachievers and, because of this, are likely to exhibit more fears than children born later.

The last one born to the family also retains his family birth position. He continues to be the baby. By virtue of being the youngest, there are a great number of family members catering to his needs. It is common to expect less from this child and be more lenient with him. He can grow up with mixed signals. One attitude is that everything he does is wonderful. The other is that everyone makes fun of him for being the youngest. He may not put out enough effort to accomplish his goals or be good at taking personal responsibility, but he will know how to get the attention of the whole family by being more animated and more of a character. Dr. Kevin Leman, author of *The Birth Order Book,* is a last born. He has some interesting observations to make.

> Youngest children in the family are typically the outgoing charmers, the personable manipulators. They are also affectionate, uncomplicated, and sometimes a little absentminded. Their "space cadet" approach to life gets laughs, smiles, and shakes of the head. Last borns are the most likely to show up at the elementary school's "sing" or the Sunday-school picnic unzipped or unbuttoned in some delicately obvious area. . . . It stands to reason then that the family clown or entertainer is likely to be the last born. . . . What I wanted was attention. That was my thing in life—getting people to laugh or point or comment.[3]

Middle children are the ones having to deal with change in birth order. The baby-of-the-family status is theirs for only a short time. Often they are too young to fully remember the experience before the next child has arrived to take the title. But, like Mike, not always. In the blended family they move over, but it takes an adjustment. When my niece had her third child in her nuclear family, her second child, nearly three at the time, became moodier and more mischievous. For a while she would try to push the baby away to get back in Mommy's lap herself. She needed to regain assurance of her position in the family. We often overlook this basic childhood need after remarriage.

Middle children, by virtue of being caught in the middle, usually mediate better and exhibit fewer fears. They find it easier to mature with balance because they have had to give more frequently. They get more hand-me-down clothing and make more compromises within the family. This child may start out looking to the personality of the older sibling but will usually decide not to compete, but instead to go in the opposite direction. He finds it necessary to carve out a personal position of importance. (Sometimes they throw food.) However, we must remember that these are the children most likely *not* to feel special in the family lineup.

Birth Order in the Blended Family

What about birth order in the blended family? A blended family brings a much greater adjustment, even trauma, to birth order. Our blended family began with a nine-year-old girl, a seven-year-old boy, and a five-year-old girl from my husband's prior marriage. I brought an eight-year-old girl and a six-year-old boy to the marriage. Fortunately, for us, none of the children were in their teen years! Those years would have brought even greater competitive challenges. When both spouses have children, like us, the family unit now has two firstborns, two babies, and perhaps many middle children. This is a recipe for ready-made competition! Understanding birth order will be a major step in grasping the warring tactics within the family.

If we are aware of the issues surrounding birth order we can help our children diffuse competition in the home. We can help them understand that it is normal to experience feelings of competition with their new siblings. We can help them be less anxious if we let them know that we comprehend the changes they are undergoing.

However, an effective parent will do his best not to take sides in an issue between stepsiblings. It is better to become a mediator. For example, do your best as parents to treat both firstborn children as if they still retain the title, though they now share it with another child. Neither should have to lose, but both can learn to compromise, even take turns at winning.

Middle children may make the adjustment the easiest, even if they feel more squeezed, because they already see being squeezed as normal to their role. Once again, the danger with middle children is that they may feel invisible in the family. Find creative ways to make their "centered" position feel significant to the family unit.

Jealousy is prevalent between stepbrothers and stepsisters. It's often the easiest to see in the youngest of each family—maybe because they are the most juvenile in intellectual maturity. Both still feel like the baby and are each expecting to be fussed over as the "cute" center of attention within the family. They can display many amusing antics, or even outright naughtiness, as they vie for center stage.

FAMILY MEETINGS

Parents play the most significant role in stepsibling adjustments. Children will try to drag parents into the competition. In fact, they may be looking to see this "Brady Bunch" fail in hopes of returning to the family they had before. By allowing them to pit us against one another, our weak spot is discovered and the children see the hope of pulling their birth parents back together. So be on guard. Minimize divisive attempts and competition by attempting to maintain neutrality while expressing loving concern.

A parent's continual defense of a birth child at the expense of a stepchild weakens family adjustments, heightens frustration, and hinders the children from developing problem-solving skills. Both step- and birth children have valid points to consider. Both have intrinsic worth within the family. Yet feelings of parental protection can easily cause us to excessively side with our birth child.

We know this in the family as favoritism. Parents who guide their home by establishing favorites will find it difficult to win the hearts of their stepchildren. These children want to feel just as special, just as heard. A better approach would be to begin having family meetings. The blended home is a great place to begin negotiation training for life management. What we consider a hassle to deal with can be turned into an opportunity for family growth.

A simple approach for family meetings is to make the meeting resemble a game. Each child writes two things on a piece of paper. First he writes down what he sees as working well within the family. Next he writes down the issue he's concerned about. Place the papers in a bowl in the center of the table. (You may have to help younger children with writing.) Dad and Mom take turns from week to week moderating the meetings. As the papers are drawn out one by one the discussion begins with what is working . . . a positive note.

Let each person have a couple of minutes to speak. After establishing an encouraging tone for the meeting, move to the troubling issues with the same attention. Remember, it is against the rules to make fun of the concerns of other family members. The goal is to show sensitivity and seek a remedy. Some issues may have to be tabled, allowing Mom and Dad to come to a decision later. If that happens, schedule a time when the issue will be resolved. A good thought to remember when dealing with children is to say yes if possible to their concerns. This will increase individual confidence for sharing problems at future family meetings.

In families the need for outside counsel may arise. When family meetings work well, we are made aware of problems too difficult for us to overcome without expert guidance. It is always wise for parents to recognize when intervention is necessary and get the help their family needs. Dr. Earl Henslin applies the same sense of urgency to emotional healing as he does to attending physical needs.

> If their teen needed blood donated because of an auto accident, the members of the family would line up at the blood center immediately! But when it comes to injured relationships, that is a different story.
>
> It needn't be. Family members can contribute to and stimulate recovery in many ways: attending family seminars together, reading and discussing books that deal with an issue the family struggles with, even holding a weekly family council. That family council can be a place where members pray for one another and share feelings and problems. Each member of the family needs to have a time to share openly without judgment or recrimination— a time to talk about happy and joyful stuff, and yet to share what hurts, too.[4]

MOVING DAY

When two families come together one family usually moves into the home already occupied by the other family. Half of the new family unit has been displaced by the move, leaving behind a house they called home, has perhaps changed schools, and has said good-bye to close friends. The other half of the family has had their turf invaded. Suddenly there is not as much closet space, and time for use of the bathroom has significantly dwindled. This is tough! It is easy to see how the children on both sides could be disgruntled.

It's hard for children to leave friends and familiar neighborhoods behind. Parents often overlook their feelings. We expect a lot from our children where lifestyle adjustments are concerned. We assume their flexibility is limitless. Once again, understanding the changes in our children's worlds will help us bond as a family.

I was concerned about Andrea. She had two very special childhood friends in the old neighborhood. Tommy and Tammy were her best buddies. She liked her backyard, her pink bedroom, and her social climate. But after the divorce, when she was only six, many changes affecting her took place. We moved away from the familiar neighborhood. Like it or not, a new world was being formed around her. Fortunately, the new neighborhood had a delightful little girl just her age living down the street, and a new friendship formed within a few weeks.

Life is much more complex for teenagers. With body changes comes a more self-conscious view of who they are as persons. Changing familiar environments can become a critical issue.

Tonya, a slightly overweight teen, turned fifteen a few days before her home sold and her mother informed her she would be moving to another city. She was so uncomfortable with this change she rebelled by refusing to attend school in the new location. In her mind there was no reason to make new friends. She liked the ones she had. The thought of a new neighborhood was totally distasteful. She especially didn't want to try to fit in at a new school. What if they didn't like her? What if she didn't like them? Despite the pressure put upon her by her mother and the authorities, she eventually dropped out of school.

I can understand her feelings. While my parents were divorcing, I began my junior year of high school in Los Angeles, far from the little community I'd grown up in. I had no friends. In fact, I knew *nobody*. I was very uncomfortable with the classroom expectations in my new environment. Even though I managed to persevere through these changes, this was a most difficult year for me.

Parents can do several things to become sensitive to the changes their children are experiencing. Healthy parental attitudes make a big difference.

- Open up communication lines; talk with your children about their feelings as they relate to change.
- Begin to pray together for new friends and a sense of belonging.
- Encourage your children to invite other children to come to your home.
- Allow your children to bring a friend along on a family outing.
- Don't forget the old friends; go out of your way to continue those friendships.
- Share with your children the changes you are experiencing yourself.
- Set an example by feeling positive about your new environment.

PREPARING SPACE

Connie is in her first marriage. Her husband, J. R., has been married before and has two children, a boy and a girl. The couple is celebrating six years of marriage. The children live with their mother most of the time but visit often with Connie and their father. In the beginning of their marriage, the children, then aged eleven and seven, spent every other weekend with her and J. R., plus one evening each week. Connie was wisely concerned about the lifestyle she was entering into, and she wanted to get off to a good start. Their first home was a small, seven-hundred-square-foot cottage with barely room for the two of them. Financial pressures prevented them from moving into a bigger home.

"From the beginning I wanted the children to feel they had some personal space," Connie said. "Figuring out how to do this was a challenge. I knew there would never be bedroom space for them. Our spare room was very little, and it doubled as an office. We managed to squeeze in a bed for Janee, but Isaac had to sleep on the Hide-A-Bed in the living room. The most important thing we did was to purchase a dresser—just for them. They each had two drawers for their own things. This small amount of privacy allowed the children to feel that part of them stayed at our house all the time."

Her smile widened as she continued to talk. "After two years we were able to move into a three-bedroom town house. Now there would be more space, or so we thought."

"What do you mean?" I asked.

"I discovered I was pregnant. This was such exciting news— my first baby! But, now what? Again, we were facing more space constraints. Having a bedroom for each of the children was once more an impossible dream."

"So, what did you do?" I asked, placing my cup of tea down on the glass-topped table in front of me.

"This time it was harder," Connie said, taking another sip from her cup. "I grieved because I knew my baby would not have a special nursery just for her. But even though my husband's children were not with us all of the time, they were still very important. I wanted them to feel as loved as the new baby."

"You are a very wise stepmother."

"J. R. and I began brainstorming," Connie said. "Isaac was now fourteen, and our only boy. He needed a greater measure of private space. Janee was still young enough to share a room with the baby, but we wanted her to feel part of the room preparations. We didn't want her to feel like she was living in a baby's world, so we let her contribute ideas to the room decor. She loved being included in the choices."

"It's easy to see your blended family is working well together," I said. "You kept the baby from taking center stage in a threatening way to the other children. By doing this you have remained sensitive to the needs of all three children."

"As the children get older, they spend even more time with us," Connie said. "We have learned to leave visitation flexible and the door open to accommodate changes in their mother's schedule. Recently we bought our own home, but we still could not afford one with four bedrooms. Isaac is now seventeen, Janee, thirteen, and Elizabeth (our baby), three. So much diversity in the children's ages continues to impose new privacy issues. With the help of relatives we're making a private room off the garage for Isaac. He's being consulted on colors, decor, and furnishings as much as possible. With this addition, each of the girls will now have her own room as well."

Because this family kept personal space a priority and worked well together to solve privacy issues, they continued to instill a sense of value in each of their children. J. R. and Connie have shown us how it is possible, even in the smallest of homes, to create personal space for each child.

SIBLINGS AS "NEIGHBORS"

Privacy is important to all of us. Blending families often means bedrooms have to be shared because of space. The child who used to call a room his own is now being told to share his quarters with a stepsibling. He may not like this idea. There could even be resentments. To ease this transition it is important to make individual space boundaries for each child. Would two dressers fit? What about individual closet space, room dividers, separate clothes hampers, and wall areas for personal decor expression? Most important, emphasize respect for one another's things.

Do not plot harm against your neighbor, who lives trustfully near you. (Proverbs 3:29)

137

I marvel at the teaching opportunities in the blended home. One of those wonderful lessons to be learned is who our neighbor really is. Does it include a sibling we didn't even want in the first place? Our parents and our siblings are all our neighbors. They live trustfully under the same roof with us; even those who come for visitation. It is up to each of us to do his best to respect what belongs to other family members. We must learn to ask before borrowing their stuff. And it helps to say "Thank you."

There are many storybooks available to reinforce the principles we are trying to teach our children. Try to make some of these available to read to the children, particularly at bedtime. Most children's books are written so creatively they bring the lesson home to the child's mind in a delightful way. A way that says, "Life should look like this."

"So in everything, do to others what you would have them do to you, for this sums up the Law and the Prophets." (Matthew 7:12)

If blending turns out well, the children will learn conflict resolution skills at an early age. In homes like ours, selfish attitudes cannot survive too easily. We *all* have to learn to give to make life a little easier for the whole family. We all have to do chores! We all share in the fun too.

I JUST GOTTA BE ME!

While children may be compliant on the outside, they may feel differently inside. As a teen, Mike had a terrific poster hung over his bed that he used to say what he felt unable to verbalize. It was a poster full of penguins, but in the center was one solid white penguin. The caption read "I just gotta be me!" This was his way of sending us a message. "Look at me. I'm OK doing things differently from you. Value me, just because I'm me." He felt we were trying to make him fit a mold of who we thought he should be. He wanted to have fun, not always be doing something "important." It was time we heard him. Time we relaxed and enjoyed his fun-loving nature.

A teenager from a blended family told me, "I feel like a rag doll. Neither of my parents knows what to do with me; they just pass me back and forth like a toy. They don't hear me. I know they're just waiting until I'm old enough to be on my own."

Do our children really know we like them just because God made them the way they are? Do they have to be just like us, or do we take an interest in their interests? Do they understand our desire to be a part of their world? Or do we live with them as if they are a burden rather than a blessing? If we take the time, I believe we will discover delightful personalities inside our sons and daughters. They have lots to share with us, if we let them. It would be very sad to miss the joy hidden in a child's heart. Let's make the decision to know our children. Then when they leave our homes one day, they will be confident they are persons of value.

SAFETY ISSUES

I wish I didn't have to write on this subject, but it would do a great injustice to the family if I did not. The safety of our children has to be a big concern. Fearful children and angry children do not feel safe. At some point in their short lives adult trust has been betrayed. Their hearts begin to pull away . . . inward . . . fearful of confiding in a parent. Sometimes anger in a child or rebellious conduct is the result of his being fearful of being hurt again. Today we often hear of young people, even as early as age nine, viciously hurting—even killing—their parents or their peers. Counselor and author Patricia Rushford writes:

> If they are not [nurtured] enough, if their needs are not sufficiently met, if they are too often treated cruelly or with contempt, they will put up defenses that will eventually cause them to harden. As children become increasingly damaged, they become more rigid, afraid to take chances, afraid to bend.
>
> Unfortunately, once a child hardens, it's extremely difficult to bring him back. He may become inflexible and unwilling to trust, and our attempts to influence him can be like trying to carve our initials into stone.

Sometimes it's possible, sometimes not. Hardness of heart and loss of trust, hope, and resilience present one of our greatest challenges in caring for wounded children. Yet love, the presence of God in our lives, and belief in a child's ability to overcome the past can soften even the hardest of hearts.[5]

Privacy and Incest Issues

Blended families need to be doubly aware of safety issues. Privacy should be guarded among stepfamily members. Whereas a nuclear family unit bonds from birth and perhaps is quite comfortable walking through the house in underwear or a nightgown without a robe, this can cause problems in a blended family. Children come along after the honeymoon stages in a traditional marriage, but children of blended families observe the honeymoon stages of a parent at the same time they are forming their own ideas regarding sexuality and intimacy. There are also issues not just between parent and child but between sibling and stepsibling.

Incest is increasing its horrendous impact on our families. Every day a multitude of children is scarred by this dreadful sin. These scars last a lifetime and send a message to our children that we parents are not able to protect them.

A grandfather angrily told me of the sexual abuse of his eight-year-old granddaughter. Her stepfather, acting out his sexual depravity, took advantage of the mother's absence. The girl became the helpless prey of his incestuous act. The stepfather underestimated the child's courage, however. She was brave enough to tell her mother. Fortunately this mother listened, and in this case the man was prosecuted and went to jail. But he left many scars behind. The girl is now in counseling. Her innocence has been taken from her.

We cannot continue to allow children to be robbed of the beauty of childhood. Somehow we have to do our best to build hedges of protection around them. If grandparents are near, perhaps you could ask them to participate in caring for your children if you work outside the home, or perhaps you could pay a day care facility (one you have researched thoroughly). Safety issues need to be a top priority.

The lack of blood relations makes it easier for some young people to cross the line with stepsisters. Erin, a young teen, told me of her ordeal with the teenaged sons of her father's wife. She was forced to have oral sex with them or face physical harm. And, to make matters worse, they threatened bodily harm, not only to her but to other family members, if she told.

These same boys did other cruel things, like burning her with hot cigarettes and taunting her with bouts of vicious verbal abuse. Where were the parents? Why didn't anyone notice what was going on? Why was she so afraid to tattle that she was unable to reveal the truth until she was in her midtwenties? I wish there were adequate answers to these questions.

Kelly's story is similar to Erin's. She was younger, only ten, when her stepbrother held her down while his friend raped her. These are young people who are now siblings living under the same roof.

Our children's actions toward each other need to demonstrate that family is a safe place to live, not a place to fear interrelating with one another. We parents must be closely involved with the lives of our children so that we will be trusted confidants in times of improper behavioral issues between siblings. We must make sure our children understand that lines are drawn in some very specific areas of family living.

It is our parental responsibility to create a safe haven where our children will be nurtured properly. They need to know the dangers in their world so they will be prepared to say "no" and bring their problems to us. Safe family boundaries mean no promiscuous sexual circumstances will be tolerated.

Alcohol or Drug Abuse

Squarely face the habits of family members. Does anyone misuse alcohol or illegal drugs? Is anger out of control? Alcohol, substance abuse, and rage often go hand in hand. Both parents and children answer their alluring calls. As addictive behaviors continue to influence our culture we see an increase in domestic violence. For families to be healthy these habits cannot be left unchecked. We must find methods of intervention.

Physical and Emotional Abuse

Children sometimes live in fear of physical abuse against themselves or a parent. Safe boundaries within the home have to be established. No one has the right to abuse another family member, either physically or emotionally. Abuse is not discipline. It is malicious, self-serving, out-of-control behavior. Let's call it what it is. Don't allow denial or fear to keep you living under this type of family oppression. This allows the abuse to continue and weakens your ability to get help. Face the truth about what is really going on "behind closed doors" and let the children see that help is available. Silence never opens the door to freedom from abuse. God does not intend His children to live as victims and, indeed, has made a way out. If any form of abuse is taking place, begin to pray for a healthy solution to be found.

> Therefore let everyone who is godly pray to you while you may be found; surely when the mighty waters rise, they will not reach him. You are my hiding place; you will protect me from trouble and surround me with songs of deliverance. (Psalm 32:6–7)

Angry, Abusive Children

Sometimes the safety issue is a child's abuse of a parent. Drugs, alcohol, or just anger at parental control are contributors. A child can cause a lot of damage if he cannot find proper restraints for behavior and nonphysical ways to address his problems. Our juvenile justice system is bulging with troubled young people. Much of our television programming and movies lend themselves to violent solutions. Young people often confuse what is perhaps fictitious in the motion picture industry as being a possible real-life answer. We all know from news broadcasts that today there is an increasing number of young people in our schools with guns and knives. We parents must make it our business to look for signs of substance abuse or aggressive behaviors in our children and intervene. Don't blow these conducts off as a stage the child will grow out of. It is far more serious.

WHEN CHANGE OCCURS—AGAIN

What happens to the children who are caught in multiple marriage families? The second marriage ends in divorce, and their world shatters once again. How do they know whom to trust?

Liz was only two and a half when Jan, age twenty, married her father, Bert. Liz's father was away on a military tour of duty when her mother abandoned her to the care of a baby-sitter. This was Jan's first marriage, the second for Bert. Jan wasn't ready for motherhood, but Liz needed full-time care. She was a difficult child from the beginning, already able to lie and misbehave without a second thought. By age six she stole frequently.

"Because of the way she acted, I didn't even think she liked me much of the time," Jan said. "After five years I walked out of her father's life, unable to cope with his substance abuse.

"One day I went back to get some things and tell Liz goodbye," Jan said. "She was sleeping, and I woke her. She sat straight up. Tears began to roll down her cheeks.

"'Mommy, Mommy, I thought I was dreaming,'" Liz cried as she reached for me. 'Are you really here?'

"Until then, I never really knew I was the one Liz thought of as 'Mommy,'" Jan said. "What could I do? Her father and I were divorced now. My heart was broken. I had no legal right to remain in this child's life, but morally I couldn't abandon her. Her father and I talked and agreed I would begin taking her for visitation."

Two years passed. One day Liz's birth mother came back into her life. Eventually Jan lost track of her stepdaughter, married Eddie, and had two children with him.

As the years went by, Liz occasionally contacted Jan. They spoke on the phone and from time to time saw one another. But Jan's new husband and Liz did not get along well. Liz's relationship with her birth mother was not a healthy one. In fact, substance abuse continued with both of her birth parents. She was a very troubled teen. By age twelve she was hitchhiking between Arizona and California. One day Jan received a phone call from a woman in California.

"I have a teenager here. Her name is Liz," the female voice on the telephone said. "She's a runaway claiming to be your daughter."

It became clear that their mother-daughter bond would not be broken. Liz had so many problems that Jan was unsure what could be done. She tracked down her ex-husband Bert. He agreed to have Liz come live with him again. This effort failed as well. Liz bolted and ran once more. Jan started making phone calls to see what could be done if and when Liz was found again.

"I began to pray," Jan said. "I didn't know what else to do. But I remembered hearing of the work Youth for Christ was accomplishing with group homes for troubled teens. I felt in my heart if Liz could only go there she could get the help she needed."

The Lord is a refuge for the oppressed, a stronghold in times of trouble. (Psalm 9:9)

"God is so good!" Jan said with a deep sigh of appreciation. "When Liz was found I discovered God had gone before me. My prayers were answered. She was already in a Youth for Christ group home in Portland! In this environment she began to do well, and she graduated with honors from high school three years later. She became the longest live-in teen the shelter had kept. They became family to her. Today she is married with a child of her own, and I'm the grandma.

"'I don't know why you thought you wanted to marry my dad,' Liz told me one day, 'but I know God had it happen so you could be my mom.'"

Jan and Eddie also divorced, and Jan married for the third time. Liz is more a part of her life today than ever. In fact, Jan is filing adoption papers to make their mother-daughter relationship feel more concrete.

"If you love your stepchild it will be a rewarding experience," Jan says today. "In fact, Liz is one of the best gifts God has given me. I can't imagine my life without her. Often I didn't have any solid answers, but I was always there to listen and love her. I never felt free to turn my back on her."

TELLTALE SIGNS

Parenting is a position of privilege. We know our children better than anyone else does. We have been with them all their lives. Because of that we can sense when things aren't going along as they should be. A sudden change in school grades, a new group of friends, not wanting to get out of bed, changes in eating habits, defying authority, and lack of zeal for life are a few indicators that children may be struggling to cope with life's changes and are crying out for help. Our children could even be suffering from depression brought on by grief.

Being available to our children will let them know their voice is important. A distraught and fearful child may have something very serious to tell us. Are we approachable? Do the children know we will listen and not brush them off? Let's do our best to be attentive parents and to notice when things are not "business as usual" for our youngsters. Then we will be able to help them through the tough stuff life sends their way.

Growth and Application

Commit to memory Psalm 147:3.

1. Change is common to blended families. List the changes your family has faced.

How have you been sensitive to these changes?

2. Describe the birth order of your children. Why is this issue significant to the family? Have you been able to establish personal space for each child? In what way?

3. Have the children been given time to grieve? In what way?

How does understanding death, as it relates to a prior family structure, make you more sensitive to their needs?

4. Read 1 Corinthians 6:18–20. Why does God give us such an important warning about sexual sins?

What does the physical body represent? At what price were you bought?

What do you think it means to "honor God with your body"?

Prayer of Application

Lord, our children are so important to us. We ask for Your guidance as we help them to assimilate all the changes in their lives. Thank You for revealing the grieving they are experiencing. Give us the wisdom necessary to lead them into healthy adjustments with family members. Please give us ears to hear and hearts of compassion for our children. Allow us, as parents, to be aware of safety issues within our home and to instill safe boundaries. As we begin to implement family meetings, we pray that our home will reflect our trust in You and our desire to understand our children. Amen.

NOTES

1. Laura Sherman Walters, *There's a New Family in My House!* (Wheaton, Ill.: Shaw, 1993), 103.
2. Kevin Leman, *The Birth Order Book* (New York: Dell, 1985), 55.
3. Ibid., 132.
4. Earl Henslin, "David and His Family Tree," in Dave Carder, Earl Henslin, John Townsend, Henry Cloud, and Alice Brawand, *Secrets of Your Family Tree: Healing for Adult Children of Dysfunctional Families* (Chicago: Moody, 1991), 35, 37.
5. Patricia H. Rushford, *The Jack and Jill Syndrome: Healing for Broken Children* (Grand Rapids: Revell, 1996), 76.

Chapter Eight

THE IMPACT
OF MONEY

Let's sit here," I said, nodding in the direction of a table nestled in the corner of the quaint coffeehouse. Soon Jim and Linda had ordered their coffee and joined me.

"Thanks for meeting me today and agreeing to talk with me about finances and remarriage.

"At this time the two of you have been married for eight years," I said. "That's a wonderful testimony for a second marriage. But you told me earlier that money was a difficult issue to resolve right from the start of your marriage. Could you tell me about the initial financial problems you each encountered after saying, 'I do'?"

"Things were really different for me," Linda began. "At that point my expectations of married life were still stuck at the level of my prior marriage experience. I wanted Jim to take care of me monetarily just like my first husband had. My ex-husband's income was very impressive. We were able to buy spontaneously, go anywhere, and do just about anything we wanted. There was always plenty of money to purchase more property, dine in fine restaurants, and vacation in any part of the world. This was how I lived for over twenty-five years. I was a housewife, a mother, and a community volunteer. It was only after the divorce that I went looking for a job. Boy, was that scary! I was nearly fifty years old."

"So, you really saw an immediate difference in your financial picture after your divorce," I said, taking another swallow from my iced peppermint mocha. "What kind of job did you get, and how long was it before you married Jim?"

"The first job I got was working at the jewelry counter in a local department store," Linda said, reminiscing with a laugh, "for six dollars an hour! A few months later, I met Jim at church. I was immediately attracted to his sensitive nature. Within a year we were married."

Jim grinned. "When I met Linda I took her at face value. She was a working girl behind the counter at Penneys," he said. "I assumed we were on the same page financially. She was a clerk, and I was a hard working guy. It never even crossed my mind she had been accustomed to such a privileged lifestyle."

"Now I expected Jim to care for me financially," Linda added, "maybe not at the same income level as my first husband, but with the same feeling of financial security. But, Jim's income was nowhere near what my ex had been able to provide. In fact, his salary was then, and still is, probably less than average. Jim brings home only two thousand dollars a month! I still wanted to eat out, take vacations, and buy nice clothes. It just wasn't possible on my husband's wages."

"Jim, how did you feel knowing Linda struggled with your limited income?" I asked, gazing expectantly at the ruddy-cheeked outdoorsman sitting across the table. The softness of his dark eyes reflected the gentle spirit his wife had spoken of earlier. He set his coffee cup down and began to share his feelings.

"At first I didn't know why Linda was so unhappy. She hid her feelings, not thinking it was OK to share them with me. Finally, I took her by the hand, and we started having lengthy talks on the couch. And we prayed. Little by little I learned she was struggling with the money stuff. I wasn't used to eating at Jacksonville Inn or Mon Desir weekly, so I was totally insensitive to her wish to do these extra nice dinners so often. I got resourceful when I recognized her needs weren't being met. I took some odd jobs, cut back on my own hobbies, and worked overtime when possible. But both of us had to give a little to make the finances work. We found restaurants that weren't so expensive. We agreed to save the nicer restaurants for special occasions.

"It's quite obvious the two of you held totally different financial expectations. How long did it take to begin pulling together to effectively meet the needs of your new household?"

"It took us four or five years to work through all the money stuff," Jim said, his eyes looking down at the table.

"I received a combination of assets in cash, stocks, and properties as a result of my divorce settlement," Linda explained. "I put that money in my own personal account and I resented having to share it. It didn't take long for me to figure out that Jim's smaller earnings meant that I had to put some of *my* money into *our* household expenses. In the beginning of our marriage my attitude wasn't very good about this. It really annoyed me that I had to help provide for *us*. I was never expected to contribute money in my first marriage. In my mind, providing the household money was a husband's job.

"And I discovered that Jim had not been real good about paying his bills on time. It just didn't seem important to him to keep his payments current. This bothered me! So I began to pay the bills, but I was irritated that I had to assume this responsibility."

"After Linda wrote out the checks," Jim explained, "she brought them to me to sign. This really helped me to take an active part in the finances of our home, to pay things on time, and it gave my wife the support she needed."

"We found some solid help when we finally took a class on finances," Linda said. "The study helped us through a really stressful period. We were exposed to Christian concepts on finance, and even though Jim was unemployed at the time, we made it through. We were able to recognize our unhealthy attitudes. We were finally able to form a workable budget and to recognize our spouse as a God-given counselor."

"Together we started forming a plan to increase our income," Jim commented with added fervor. "I desperately wanted Linda to know my intentions to care for her needs were genuine. I also came into the marriage with some assets. The property I owned and lived on before I married Linda included some timberlands and a fixer-upper house. We decided to sell off a portion of the timber to bring in some extra money. With the timber proceeds, I fixed up the house as a rental. I did much of the work myself, so that saved a great deal of money. This rental has increased our monthly household income, after expenses, by about five hundred dollars a month."

"One day," Linda said, "I realized that I was the one who was not being realistic. Jim is the man I chose to marry. Money was not the reason I wanted to spend my life with him. I wanted him because he loves the Lord, he's sensitive to others, and he's a thoughtful husband to me. His resourcefulness showed me he was more than willing to work with me to accomplish new financial goals.

"My thinking had been selfish and unfair. I was placing expectations on my husband that he could never fulfill. I had to take my bitterness up with the Lord. I had to repent. The Lord helped me to become content, rather than resentful, in sharing my interest income to support our lifestyle. It was my turn to make some choices. If I wanted to keep some of the comforts I'd grown accustomed to I would have to pull together with Jim as a financial team. This simple partnership attitude greatly enhanced our marriage.

"My expectations of my husband are now reasonable. He already earns, by honest means, a salary in keeping with his vocation. I was the one wanting to keep a higher standard of living than he could provide. Now we work together. Both of us contribute money. This has resulted in more than enough to meet our monthly needs and have fun too."

"How do the two of you handle the household expenses today?" I asked.

"I put my salary and my rental income into our joint checking account each month," Jim answered. "This covers much of the household expenses, plus my child-support payment. My children are still in their teen years."

"I put a portion of my monthly investment proceeds into the joint account," Linda added. "The remainder of my investment income gets deposited into a personal savings account to cover extra tax payments, our vacations, and my personal car expenses. This seems to work well for us."

"Let's touch on a related subject for a few moments," I said. "Linda, you have grown children. How did they accept your marriage to Jim?"

"It was difficult for them," Linda responded, her face expressing sorrow for the lack of understanding she found with her adult children. "It still is. My sons confronted me on the money issue more than once. Because of my assets, they were sure Jim married me just to get *their* inheritance. But that wasn't the case. To reassure them, I put into a living trust the assets I had received as a result of my years of marriage to their father. My children will still be the beneficiaries of that portion of my estate."

"Jim, is this how your property assets will be dispersed too, one day?" I asked. "Will your children inherit the property holdings you had prior to marrying Linda?"

"Linda and I agreed on the inheritance issue from the start of our marriage," Jim said. "We felt the children from our prior marriages were entitled to the inheritance they would have naturally received had there been no divorce."

"I admire you both for coming to such workable solutions," I said. "As a couple you have not only found ways to successfully manage the personal assets you each brought into the marriage, but you are also pulling together to have a healthy financial footing for your home."

Jim and Linda's solutions may not fit every blended family, but couples like Jim and Linda have a lot of wisdom to share. Together they have overcome some of the major financial struggles of remarriage, combining their blended incomes and settling some critical inheritance issues. Their story shows us that financial solutions can be found for the blended family, if we will commit to self-examination and the overall good of the family unit.

INHERITANCE ISSUES

When Charlie and I married we had very few assets. His ex received half of the assets they had held prior to the divorce. He had just enough savings to put a down payment on a house. We were starting over financially.

Because all of our children were quite young, our inheritance issues were very different from Jim and Linda's. For a long time we couldn't bring ourselves to deal with the issue of a will. The proportions of who should be entitled to what, how much should be left, and in what form the assets should be left brought up too much disagreement. So, rather than fight over the issue of a will, we indefinitely tabled the whole subject. This was not the wise thing to do since none of us are guaranteed our next heartbeat.

Many years into our marriage, when we were finally able to discuss our estate matters and beneficiaries with a measure of sound reasoning, we prepared a will that made sensible provision for all of the children. We were even able to address the form in which our assets will be left. Ron Blue, financial planner and speaker, gives godly insight to the issue of inheritance in his book *Generous Living: Finding Contentment Through Giving.*

> Once you decide how much to leave your children and when to give it to them, you need to consider the form in which your assets will be left. Should you leave the farm? What about the family business? Is it better to leave cash, stocks, or real estate?
>
> In general, the answer to the "form" question is simple: Assets should be left in a form that will allow your children to accomplish their God-given goals and build their skills and strengths. Typically, this means that gifts should be left in cash or other liquid assets, such as stocks and bonds, which can be sold easily and quickly.[1]

As important as form is, this is only one portion of preparing a will. I find a lot of other very sensitive questions come up for the blended family. Who are the children I am responsible for? Am I willing to share my lifelong assets with my stepchildren? How do we guarantee that assets from a natural parent will be received by a birth child after remarriage? Since relationships require love to grow, I think these questions are best answered out of love in blended families that function well. As a mother and a stepmother, my heart is to see all of *our* children sense inclusion, not exclusion, when it comes to family matters.

Not all parents put relationships first. Often the divorce has left them too bitter to feel like being fair about inheritance issues. It isn't uncommon to see individuals fail to honor the intended inheritance wishes of a relative. These men and women become more possessive, rather than equitable, over the items being left for future generations.

"Julia, how old were you when your parents divorced?" I asked.

"I was nearly twenty and already in college," Julia said. "My mom and dad had been married over twenty years."

"You told me that a particular set of china dishes has caused a lot of family bitterness. Why is this such an issue?"

"These were special dishes passed down from my great-grandmother to my grandmother and then to our family," Julia explained with obvious annoyance over the subject. "Grandma wanted us to have them—my sisters and I—when we were grown. But my dad has remarried and taken the china to his home with his new wife and her girls."

"How do you feel when you think about these heirloom dishes being at his house?"

"I feel like we could be cheated out of what belongs to us," Julia admitted. "We are the natural grandchildren. His wife and girls aren't even related to us."

"Does your dad understand your feelings?" I asked.

"Oh, he says we'll get them someday. But we have no guarantee that that will happen if he dies before his wife does. Or his wife may decide to dispose of them at any time. They just aren't special to her like they are to us."

It's easy to see how bitter feelings can pop up over inheritance issues. When the nuclear family is no longer in existence, the security forming the fiber of family is disrupted. The children, like Julia and her sisters, sense the threat of a possible future loss of what rightfully would be theirs had the divorce not occurred. It's only natural for these grandchildren to feel entitled to the family china. Grandmother had said she wanted it that way. She didn't envision divorce or thoughts of another wife for her grandson. In Julia's family the china became such a serious inheritance issue their mother had its eventual distribution written into their divorce decree. But we all know that this is no guarantee that the china will eventually end up with the intended beneficiaries. That will be determined by the integrity of the individuals involved.

One of the biggest reasons to prepare a will is to provide guardianship for young children. If we were to die unexpectedly, who would care for them? How would their needs be met? Because of their tender ages, they have much greater needs than adult children. By writing out our wishes in a legal document we can be assured that others will know what our intentions are. We can provide educational funds for later. We can have the estate disbursed at appropriate intervals over the child's lifetime.

I think it is also important to consider our stepchildren in estate planning. Are we willing to prepare for a secure future for that child also? It helped me to cross bloodlines by remembering that as believers in Christ we are all coheirs with Him of a heavenly inheritance.

> The Spirit himself testifies with our spirit that we are God's children. Now if we are children, then we are heirs—heirs of God and co-heirs with Christ, . . . that we may also share in his glory. (Romans 8:16–17)

This brings me to the reality of who really owns it all anyway—God. I also see our heavenly Father's heart to share, just because we're His kids. Looking at my stuff this way gives me the perspective of passing along to the next generation—both my natural children and my stepchildren—the monetary assets and keepsakes God has so generously blessed me with while here in the body.

When the children are older, probably adults, it would be

good to hold a family meeting to discuss and come to an understanding about the written intentions we have for the disposal of our estate after our death. If we wait until death occurs, our heirs will be searching desperately for direction in the midst of a deeply emotional experience. It is kinder to begin these family discussions when there is no known emergency. This will give the children time to ask questions. It will give us the opportunity to bring clarity to our disbursement decisions.

It's possible that we may want to make some changes after meeting with our children. Family needs may surface that we have overlooked in our initial preparations.

Another suggestion is to bring an independent party into the meeting, possibly an attorney or financial planner, to help answer questions as they arise. By doing this we bring a more serious tone to the purpose of the family meeting.

The objective of a will is to bring closure to our estate, not to set up a wedge between family members. These few steps will (hopefully) prevent money from becoming a divisive issue after our death. The last thing my husband and I want to leave behind is an inheritance of bitter feelings that could cause our children's faith to flounder.

WHAT DOES IT MEAN TO LOVE MONEY?

Money—the very word wells up emotions in us. I marvel at how easy it is to become defensive over money issues. There is nothing we possess (outside of love) that is not impacted by money. Next to health, most of us recognize the almighty dollar as life's biggest necessity. Money has a dramatic influence on our physical existence. Without it we would not have a home to live in, food to eat, water to drink, clothes to wear, automobiles to drive, businesses to provide employment, schools for education, churches to worship in, medical clinics, or even a means by which to dispose of our garbage. City budgets could not be funded, so there would be no community services like police and fire protection. Maybe (worst of all) the entertainment we enjoy so leisurely (casually) would be curtailed.

The list could go on and on. Perhaps money issues were at the root of your divorce, and now in remarriage the pressures of money still pose an ominous threat to unity. For remarrieds it is likely the financial demands are even greater now. Most remarrieds bring along two incomes, but also two debt structures to resolve.

Along with greater financial issues comes the greater potential for sin to get the best of us. The monetary arena is no respecter of income levels or persons. Our dollars are neutral. We choose to give these currency creatures their high position of status, almost as if they each had a name and personality. It's time to mentally redefine money.

By defining money in its truer sense, as a tangible resource and practical tool given by God to be used as a medium of exchange through which our family's daily needs and even occasional desires are met, we give our currency a nonemotional identity. Yes, it is still an asset, but one that is to be directed by sound principles and godly judgment. By removing our emotional attachment to money we can scrutinize our actions, set goals, and see where we lack sound structure with personal finances.

The attitudes we hold regarding money cannot be isolated from God's standard. Some of these attitudes may be good. Perhaps we are giving to others, are budgeting our money carefully, and have kept debt to a minimum. But upon careful examination, do we discover we are guilty of excessive hoarding, greed, selfishness, or even theft? Do we withhold from family members what is within our means to supply? How do our stepchildren fit into our financial picture?

The Bible gives us a clear set of principles, laid out in some 2,300 verses, from which to form a godly financial footing. God knew we would have need of money. He also knew He would be competing with money for the lordship of our lives. Why? Because God says as humans we have a tendency to love money.

For the love of money is a root of all kinds of evil. Some people, eager for money, have wandered from the faith and pierced themselves with many griefs. (1 Timothy 6:10)

Keep your lives free from the love of money and be content with what you have, because God has said, "Never will I leave you; never will I forsake you." (Hebrews 13:5)

God knew, and warned us, that we would see our needs met through monetary means and praise the dollar. By trusting in money we develop a love of money. When this happens our love for God takes a backseat to our increasing appetite for money. We no longer see God as our provider. So we trade the truth for a lie when we believe that money, whether cash or easy credit, is supplying our needs rather than God.

YOURS, MINE, AND NOW OURS?

Talking about money is one of the quickest ways to mess up a relationship. In a second marriage it can become a divisive problem even faster. With *ours* comes many questions of *yours* and *mine*. The human psyche seems to be driven to look after its own. But when selfishness enters, trouble is close at hand. To keep money struggles at a minimum, blended families will have to build a workable plan for the *total* household income and expenses. Reasonable goals can't be developed until we address several pertinent questions.

- Will both spouses continue to work?
- Who will manage the checkbook?
- Should separate checkbooks be kept for "his" money and "her" money?
- How do we reduce debt?
- Is there a plan for savings?
- How will we determine who pays what bills?
- Should there be rigidity or flexibility in money matters?
- What is a reasonable household budget?
- How will we combine assets or preserve those from a prior relationship?
- What about allowance money for the children?

• How will education costs be met in the years ahead for all of our children?

These questions are probably only the tip of the financial iceberg facing many remarrieds. Yet if we don't resolve these identifiable money issues, frustration, bitterness, and competition will set in. Some of the simpler financial questions, such as who will write out the monthly bills, are best answered by giving those tasks to the spouse who has the greater talent for tending to clerical-numerical tasks.

Unfortunately, most financial questions are often difficult to resolve in the blended family. Many husbands or wives are exerting excessive control over family members via the family purse strings. Rather than confronting the underlying conflicts of fear, sinful habits, selfishness, or anger that reside within themselves, these individuals shout and blame and refuse funds for necessary items. In these homes, resolving financial questions is nearly impossible. Certified financial planner Russ Crosson writes:

> It is important that we understand the source of marital conflict. The real source of this conflict is our desire to each have his or her own way (Isa. 53:6). Money may appear to be the source of this conflict, but all too often it is simply a vehicle through which the real problem manifests itself. The ultimate solution, of course, is for each spouse to walk in the Spirit and maintain a close relationship with the Lord.
>
> In the marriage relation[ship] (1 Pet. 3:7) it is important to understand that men and women perceive money differently. These differences underlie why money is generally the avenue through which conflict arises.[2]

OUR EXPERIENCE WITH FINANCES

For the first ten years of my second marriage the whole money arena made me very nervous. After Charlie and I married we decided I would quit my job. As a stay-at-home wife I would write out the bills each month. Charlie would earn, and give to me, the necessary money to cover the monthly expenses. Since he was his own boss, we drew out a salary in keeping with the amount of income that had been generated each month. Self-employment is different from being handed a check from an employer on payday. The amount of take-home pay can vary from month to month.

After I wrote out the checks to pay the monthly bills my accountant husband would look them over. I felt like I was being graded on my ability to pay the bills. He looked carefully at each expense as if he had not contributed to its accumulation. His questions always led to my having a knot in my stomach and feeling accused of unnecessary spending. From there the conversation would turn to comparing the monthly amount of child support going out with the much smaller amount coming in from my ex. I often got defensive over the unfair fuss that arose when we paid our bills. This was never a good day at our house.

Several years later (perhaps now I was considered a trusted partner) my husband was able to care about the obvious stress brought about by this money process, and we began to talk about resolving the issue. I was relieved to know we could finally view the household money as *our* money and not just *his* because he went to work and earned it. A specific amount was then determined for the month's bills and given to me without question. Any additional expenses were discussed as they came up. I was so relieved to know my husband finally cared about the negative emotional impact money was having on me—and on us!

THE "BIG" ISSUE OF CHILD SUPPORT

Child support can become a very intense issue. This is one of those subjects capable of blatantly exposing our love of money. Maybe because too many who are ordered by the court to pay don't follow through with their responsibility. Or maybe because they look at it as a trade-off for visitation with the children, and that privilege is being withheld from them. Whatever the reason, we all understand child support is a normal consequence of divorce. As long as we live in blended families, with children to raise, child support will be a part of our routine lifestyle. We don't have to have a bad attitude about it, whether we are paying it out or anticipating its arrival.

When pain follows or anger sets in before the ink is even dry on the support check, it's time to question why. When we begin to burn with rage because the support check hasn't arrived on time, we need to question why. These are the keys to whether we love money more than we value a peaceful relationship with our family members. Pain and anger are symptoms that we aren't looking to God as our provider but are trusting in money.

As couples cope with tension brought about from child support checks, blame becomes the focal point. I think part of the reason so much tension arises is that too often the family budget is so close to the bone that the support check either makes it or breaks it in regard to paying the monthly bills. So it's easy to get mad when the check doesn't come before you get a late-payment notice from a creditor.

In some families the needs surrounding the stepchildren constantly pivot around whether or not the support check comes in. Our children, meaning *all* the children in our household, should not be made to feel like financial burdens. When the importance of money gets to this level it damages our family relationships. The children come to see their security as something provided by a means outside their home. And our anger over the money tells them they are right. Because of our outbursts they can even come to believe that money is a measure of personal worth. By not paying on time or not paying at all, the absentee parent is telling the children they are less than acceptable, perhaps even unworthy of being cared for.

Christian parents have a responsibility to honor Christ by placing more value on the well-being of parent-to-child relationships than on the arrival of the check. We need to send forth a good testimony of our Christian faith to the world around us. Believe me, others are watching. Accepting the inconvenience of child support with integrity not only makes life easier for us and for our children but also gives worth to our Christian testimony. It is a demonstration of our inner faith.

Faith in action brings peace, not hostility. It shows others, especially our spouse and children, that God is our true source of provision, not salaries or child-support checks. Sure, we need things money can buy, but God knows that too. I've learned that exercising prayer in place of anger does more good toward having our family's needs met than complaining or worrying.

I often hear about individuals who are dragged into court by an ex-spouse for an increase in child-support payments. This is tough. If you are an ex attempting to do this I would caution against it in most cases. Actions like this can backfire on our children's world. These court appearances also have the potential to increase bitter feelings between satellite families. It's not that the parent doesn't want the child to have additional needs met, but they have a life to live too. The added financial pressure can mean their own household will suffer greatly, and they may even have to declare bankruptcy.

That is what happened to the Kelly family. Brian had finally gotten a promotion with a nice increase in salary. For the first time in his marriage to Kay the couple was able to purchase a home for their blended family. The papers were signed. They happily moved in.

But within weeks their joy was turned to overwhelming financial difficulty. Brian's ex decided to take him back to court for additional child support. Despite Brian's displaying their monthly income and expenditures, the judge ruled in favor of his ex, and Brian's monthly support payments were dramatically increased.

The consequence of this judgment devastated their family. He and Kay were unable to keep their home and the furniture they had just purchased (on credit). Angry feelings set in, along with sleepless nights. Brian and Kay are trying to hang on, but it's a struggle for them to form a home for their children from what is left of their fragile financial picture. They feel like bankruptcy may be their only option. They also realize their future is held hostage by the whims of his ex-wife until his children are considered emancipated. It seems their life has been put on hold.

Just because we know our ex has been given a raise or has experienced a change in financial ability does not mean we are entitled to more money. We should be sensitive enough to consider the needs of their family as well as our own. Every family lives within a unique set of financial boundaries. That includes the family of our ex. Those boundaries are tied to the income and expenses the family members alone are privy to. Why create an extra financial burden for the family in which our children are growing or with which they spend visitation?

FIND HELPFUL TOOLS

There are ways in which the blended family can begin to rise above the weight of financial worries. Combining two debt portfolios under one roof is not for the faint of heart. Added expenses can quickly bring fresh ammunition into a marital relationship, fueling explosive arguments. If we don't want money problems to get the best of us, we need to add some financial tools to our lives. One of the smartest and easiest tools to implement is a budget.

Believe it or not, most families don't budget their money. Budgets seem to be scary things. A lot of people view them as a negative concept. There are usually three reasons why people choose to avoid budgets:

1. We don't want to know how bad things really are.
2. We feel a budget will bring restrictions to our lives.
3. We have more than enough money and can't see why a budget is necessary.

For those who find budgeting a new concept there are many helpful books and computer programs available to help us today. The important thing is simply putting our apprehension behind us and getting started.

A budget represents a navigational tool for tracking our income and expenses. Like a compass, it gives direction so we don't get off course as we chart our financial journey. Because a budget is practical we are able to set reasonable boundaries for our financial needs and obligations. This simple tool gives us the ability to exercise control over our hard-earned dollars instead of trying to catch up with where our money went.

Healthy budgets allow for flexibility if monthly needs change. Because of this, it is necessary to reevaluate expenditures from time to time. There may be a month when the hot water tank unexpectedly goes out (like it did for us in July) and a replacement is needed immediately. If our savings are not enough to cover the cost of this item then this is one of those times to take a fresh look at the budget. Let's get creative. Let's learn to quiz ourselves. Could we get by with a smaller food budget this month? Could we take fewer trips to town to save gas money? Is there a way to add extra income this month? By preplanning flexibility we preempt bad attitudes. We program our minds to deal with emergency expenses before they happen. This flexibility allows creativity rather than frustration to surface in crisis times.

Are you beginning to see how much order a budget can bring to our lives? By structuring our money, with the use of a budget, we are in a better position to keep our joy, hold anger at bay, and diminish the tears brought about by financial woes.

Another tool for increasing financial savvy is to take courses that teach biblical financial principles. In 1990 my husband and I became involved with a nationwide financial study called Crown Ministries. These materials offered us biblical financial counsel. It was different from the worldly financial counsel we had embraced. This study included twelve, practical, easy-to-follow weekly application lessons. Through this class our lives were transformed. Christ was brought into our finances. We were able to build a foundation of financial unity based on biblical principles. Even though my husband worked in the financial arena every day of his life, we needed God's perspective—not the world's. When we understood that God does not view money the way the world does, that paved the way for better goals and better attitudes.

Because God spoke to us through Scripture, we were given an unthreatening environment in which we could set financial goals without fighting. At last we drew up a will. And within three years we were debt free, mortgage and all!

Statistics continually support the view that money is an underlying factor in over half of all divorces. What should our real focus be? I believe it should be the same as God's—to love people, even if it costs us something, and to use money as the tool it is intended to be. Money does not have feelings, but people do. It was never meant to come before the love we give the Lord or our family members.

Howard Dayton, founder of Crown Ministries, researched the biblical teaching on money and discovered the incredible amount of Scripture devoted to the subject.

> That's why Jesus talked so much about money. Sixteen of the 38 parables were concerned with how to handle money and possessions. Indeed, Jesus Christ said more about money than about almost any other subject. The Bible offers 500 verses on prayer, fewer than 500 verses on faith, but more than 2,350 verses on money and possessions.
>
> The Lord said a lot about it because He wants us to know His perspective on this critical area of life. He dealt with money matters because *money does matter.*[3]

If Jesus took time to place a warning label on money, that is reason enough for us to look at it as a serious issue.

WHAT ABOUT ALLOWANCES?

In a blended family a plan must be drawn up that demonstrates fairness and consistency with allowance money. Some parents give allowances. Others do not. Some parents choose to give children money with no strings attached. Other moms and dads tie allowance money to chores done around the house. Whatever the method we use to dole out allowances, it is important to understand the reasoning behind and the benefits of getting money into the hands of our children.

The word *allow* means to permit, consent to, or let one have. Thus allowance money is a predetermined amount of money we willingly give to another, in this case to our minor children. Since the nature of children is to learn by experience, parents must create learning opportunities.

The first step in teaching financial faithfulness to our children is getting money into their hands. An allowance is the easiest way to accomplish this step. With parental guidance this *allowed* money creates numerous ways for parents to teach sharing, impart trust, and develop marketing skills in our children. Through these lessons their self-esteem is elevated. Being trusted with money gives children feelings of accomplishing big-people stuff, just like Mom and Dad.

A child is ready to use money by age three. She is quick to comprehend that it costs money to buy candy and toys. She even likes putting pennies in a piggy bank to save for a later use. By grasping the moldable moments present in the child's early years, healthy habits with money can begin to form.

A great way to start teaching money lessons to a young child is with three jars or three boxes. Make it fun. Take an afternoon with your child as she decorates and labels these money containers. Label one for *Giving,* one for *Saving,* and one for *Spending.* With these three jars we can teach a child three money concepts:

1. How to share with God and others
2. Delayed gratification by saving for more expensive items
3. Seeing immediate desires come to pass from the spending jar

As the child grows older, or as her money increases, take her to another money step. Allow her to become familiar with the banking system. Open a savings account in her name. Let her take her own money to the bank and deposit it, just like you do. Then, when the statements come in, show her how she gains interest from leaving her money in the bank.

Part of learning is making room for failure. At some point our child will probably make a decision that won't end happily. Maybe the toy she saved for and finally bought broke soon after she brought it home and the store will not take it back. Rather than berating her for a bad purchase, remember that adults sometimes make bad spending choices too. This is a wonderful time to gently teach a hard lesson, but one necessary to life. Not all toys that look like fun are made well. Her next purchase can be looked at with more attention to quality and not to the television advertisement.

Bailing our kids out of tough brokenhearted times isn't necessarily the best thing to do. It actually hinders their growth. They need to learn that life sometimes disappoints us. It will be better to buy our child an ice-cream cone, talk about better choices for the next purchase, and express sadness over the broken toy. Because of these valuable life lessons, I am convinced that the benefits of an allowance far outweigh the financial burden on the family budget.

SAFEGUARDING THROUGH UNITY

A house divided cannot stand. A house united is a fortress of strength. Privatizing money—viewing the dollars we earn as *his* or *hers* and not as *ours*—poses a threat to our marriage. The best scenario for money and marriage is to look at money as community property. Personal spousal allowances then emerge from a two-become-one perspective.

Holding on too tightly to personal earnings gives negative feedback to a spouse. I never felt secure while my husband held such high esteem for the things that represented his hard-earned dollars. Or when he would spend money without considering my thoughts on the item to be bought. The statement I heard, loud and clear, from his actions was "It's my money; I'll spend it my way." I finally decided it was easier not to oppose the next jukebox he wanted to buy. God impressed upon me that as a wife it wasn't my job description to change my husband. My job was to love him. God's job was to change him. It was better for me not to fight his spending decisions but instead to allow the Lord to work in his life. It was better for me to learn unconditional love.

WHAT ABOUT BETRAYAL?

Healthy marriages share an honest vision of all monies brought into the home. These couples plan financial goals together. They also hold a true picture of all indebtedness. Clarifying finances should begin long before the wedding day. By discussing the money stuff, hiding nothing, trust begins to build from the start. The inability to discuss money before the wedding is a good indicator it will be even more difficult to talk about after the wedding.

"Boy, was I surprised after I married John. He was my second husband," Ellen said. "I was so mad I could have spit."

"What happened to bring about such anger?" I asked.

"John hadn't told me the truth about his finances. I had no reason to question his honesty or to think we wouldn't have enough money to meet our monthly bills. He worked as a long-haul trucker and proudly boasted that his yearly wages were in excess of thirty-five thousand dollars," Ellen said with disgust. "Money was something I didn't think I would be worrying about. But it wasn't a week after we were married that the notices started coming in the mail. He was behind in his PUC road fees by thousands of dollars! The penalties were mounting, and now his wages were being garnished. Soon he talked me into selling the house, the one my children and I had been living in, to pay the back debts. Wanting to be the helpful spouse, I foolishly went along with this bright idea."

"It doesn't sound like it worked out well for you," I said. "Did you find more troubles because of that decision?"

"Oh, yes!" Ellen answered, rolling her eyes in exasperation. "I couldn't find a house to rent that we could afford in the same community, or even in the school district where my children were attending school. Everything became a bigger mess. I was upset. My children were upset. The only one who found any real satisfaction was my husband. His bills got paid. He didn't have any ties to the old neighborhood, so that wasn't an issue to him. Then I discovered he'd taken money to be in partnership with his daughter—they were buying a truck together—with *our* money, only I wasn't in on the deal. Our fights became more frequent. Eight months later we filed for divorce."

"For there is nothing hidden that will not be disclosed, and nothing concealed that will not be known or brought out into the open." (Luke 8:17)

Secrets don't keep forever. Honesty up front is always the best way to begin a relationship. Ellen felt betrayed by John's secret financial troubles and behind-her-back schemes. Money secrets like this eventually rise to the surface. It's only a matter of time.

Couples who want to safeguard their marital future will look at the financial aspects of their relationship during the courting stages. I think that's why we call the premarriage stage "engagement." It allows us time to engage in conversation with the one we love on issues that will be important to our future together. Money is definitely one of the big issues.

Knowing the individual financial condition of the one we intend to marry allows us to enter marriage with our eyes wide open. It's the loving thing to do. We have a right to know the extent of the debts and the assets that are being brought into the relationship. This shared knowledge creates a fair playing field for the marriage to be built upon.

Surprises with a negative monetary impact are really untold truths. When they are discovered they speak volumes about our inner self. Secrets say our self-image is too fragile to entrust to our mate. Our fear of rejection supersedes our ability to be truthful.

Blind trust can prove very foolish. Husband's like John don't want to muddy the waters until after the wedding. At that time they feel the commitment has been sealed. Their sweetie will be mad but their charm will get them through. By concealing the true picture they assure themselves of a bride delighted to say, "I do." The romance of the moment is not disturbed.

This is shortsighted living. While the moment was enjoyed their future intimacy was jeopardized. Honesty would have prevented Ellen's trust in her new husband from being shaken. And the secret he kept only worsened his money problems. The debt he owed continued to grow with penalties and interest. In the end it weakened his relationship with the bride he had promised to love and to cherish. Falsehood is not an expression of love. I can think of nothing more shocking than to find hidden truths that not only cost us money but have the potential to bring feelings of regret to a marriage partner.

A wife or husband who discovers hidden financial issues should begin to pray for wisdom. Most relationships are still salvageable. As ugly as the circumstances are, praise God that He has allowed this secret to surface so you can deal with it. Susan was furious when she discovered Carl had concealed the fact that he hadn't paid his federal taxes for six years. But she was also wise enough to seek counsel. Together they made a plan. They followed the advice of a tax professional. They filed the overdue returns and pulled together to solve this difficult financial issue. Yes, there was a big price to pay. But Carl was repentant. And they were determined to resolve this exposed secret *together.*

Forgiveness will be a major issue for the one who feels betrayed by a spouse. But without forgiveness the betrayal cannot be overcome. Forgiving seventy times seven is the biblical understanding of forgiveness. In other words, God is telling us not to limit how often we extend this marvelous gift of grace.

We must remember that forgiveness and trust are two different things. To forgive is to act without any strings attached. It is our gift of releasing the one who has offended us. In doing this we are also blessed, because we are no longer in bondage to the bitterness of the offense done to us.

Genuine forgiveness is always a win-win solution to relational difficulties. It opens the door for new trust to build. Trust is something we earn through actions consistent with a life of integrity. Trust is shown by performance. Susan and Carl's consequences were not erased. But they were able to work together to get their financial house in order—after forgiveness had taken place—and after efforts of integrity were seen from Carl. It is exciting to see God bless what is brought under His authority.

UNDERSTANDING DEBT

Debt is consuming our culture today. Most Americans have no savings. They live with debt that consumes 80, 95, or even more than 100 percent of their accessible income. Families live from paycheck to paycheck, month to month. There is no provision for an emergency. There is no money, apart from credit, left to enjoy in their leisure. Most adults have bought into the Madison Avenue plan for living in today's world and use credit—often. The underlying statement is, "You deserve to enjoy what life has to offer. Deprive yourself of no good thing." But debt is *not* God's will for His children. The only debt God intends for us to keep is our debt of love toward one another.

> Let no debt remain outstanding, except the continuing debt to love one another, for he who loves his fellowman has fulfilled the law. (Romans 13:8)

All debt—outside of love—presumes upon tomorrow and adds stress to today. God is not being cruel by giving solid counsel on accumulating debt. He knows we will best serve Him, and be pleasing to our fellowman, if we are not loaded down with financial pressure. When we owe money to others our focus is on repaying the debt. We are in effect their slave until the debt is paid in full.

John M. Montgomery, author and management consultant, expresses well the attitude of today's generations in his book *Money, Power, Greed.*

> We live in a buy-now, pay-later generation. Well-meaning, normally sane people from all walks of life follow a pied piper named Madison Avenue into a river of debt; sometimes they get in so deep it takes years to climb out on dry land. This buy-now, pay-later syndrome is another snare from the devil himself. It seems that life will not be worth living unless we can get ahead of, or at least keep up with, the Joneses. We no longer are satisfied with just our "needs," we want all the trimmings and gingerbread surrounding the needs—bigger, faster, more luxuriant autos; more versatile, "energy and water saving" appliances; exotic vacations to faraway places; all on the "easy monthly payment plan." We can even take a trip to the Holy Land and "walk where Jesus walked" on credit, so say many Christian magazines.
>
> Bookstores are filled with books telling us how to "borrow and grow rich"; how to find "ready sources" of money; how to become a "millionaire."

What we seldom read about, however, is the pain and heartache of debt. Madison Avenue does not tell about the day when all the debts must be paid and there is no money to pay them. All they tell you is how to consolidate your debts so that you no longer have a dozen "small" payments, each one with a different rate of interest, but only one monthly payment that is stretched out to last until your children graduate from college. That way, they say, you can have money left over each month for other things you "need." Neither do the ads tell about broken marriages, suicides, alcohol and drug addiction caused by debt.[4]

The best way to avoid debt is to embrace God's Word as truth on the subject. Heed His wisdom. Next, create a simplified lifestyle so that it is possible to live on less money than you make. In America today most debt is incurred for things we don't need. We go into debt for things we desire and then tire of before they are even paid off. To come out from under this burden our want list will need to be replaced with a thankfulness list. We all have so many things to be thankful for. And with prayer God is able to provide the things we really need. In His way and in His timing our needs will be met. The secret to financial freedom is found in putting God first, in realizing He thinks differently than the world does. When I do this I am amazed at how much peace follows.

"For my thoughts are not your thoughts, neither are your ways my ways," declares the Lord. "As the heavens are higher than the earth, so are my ways higher than your ways and my thoughts than your thoughts." (Isaiah 55:8–9)

Growth and Application

Commit to memory Hebrews 13:5.

1. Has the subject of money been an area of difficulty in your marriage? How?

Have inheritance issues been part of your unresolved financial problems? Why or why not?

2. Have you and your spouse set financial goals?

What would you like to see accomplished with the use of money in the next five years? (for example, pay off credit cards, pay off a car, begin college fund, vacation plans, etc.).

After writing these goals down discuss them with your spouse.

3. Have there been secret financial issues in your marriage? Describe them.

If you are the one guilty of "hiding," have you asked for forgiveness?

If you are the one who was kept from "seeing" the truth, have you forgiven?

How have you worked together to alleviate the stress these issues have caused?

4. Read 1 Timothy 6:10. What warning is God giving us regarding money?

Why is it so important that we understand our own attitude about money?

Prayer of Application

Lord, Your Word is such a faithful counselor. Forgive us for not including You in our money matters and for loving money above our devotion to You and our family. Our desire is to use money as the tool You intend it to be and to trust that You will provide for our needs. As we set financial goals, give us the wisdom to free ourselves from selfishness and the servitude debt has placed us in. The only debt we desire to keep is the debt of love to one another. Amen.

NOTES

1. Ron Blue, *Generous Living: Finding Contentment Through Giving* (Grand Rapids: Zondervan, 1997), 132.

2. Russ Crosson, *Money and Your Marriage* (Dallas: Word, 1989), 30.

3. Howard Dayton, *Your Money Counts: The Biblical Guide to Earning, Spending, Saving, Investing, Giving, and Getting Out of Debt* (Longwood, Fla.: Crown Ministries, 1996), 8.

4. John M. Montgomery, *Money, Power, Greed: Has the Church Been Sold Out?* (Ventura, Calif.: Regal, 1987), 125–26.

Chapter Nine

THE INFLUENCE
OF GUILT
AND SHAME

Stepfamilies were recently the focus of the popular television documentary *20/20*. As commentator Deborah Roberts interviewed actress Suzanne Somers, her husband, Alan Hamel, and her son, Bruce, I began to hear about the role guilt played in their family. Although uninvited and left unspoken for years, guilt was a primary influence stopping the effective blending of both families into one. Guilt's powerful presence, hidden beneath the layers of Alan's moods, had undermined their happiness, stolen their joy, and thrown their lives into angry, inexplicable confusion. I found this interview impacting because the story line was nearly identical to our own family's blending history. By merely changing the names, this could easily have been an interview with our family. I'd like to share a portion of the program with you.

> *Alan Hamel:* Well, when I first met Bruce, I really liked him. And when he moved in with me, it all changed.

Deborah Roberts: What changed?

Alan Hamel: Well, you know, I was fresh out of a marriage. And I had two children, one of whom was a son who is the same age as Bruce. And I felt very guilty. And every time I looked at Bruce, I thought, you know, "Why am I living with somebody else's child? I should be living with my own child."

Deborah Roberts: To Suzanne's horror, Alan simply ignored Bruce.

Alan Hamel: If Bruce was in this room and I walked in, I'd probably turn around and walk out. . . . I really made him invisible. He was living in the next bedroom, but I ignored him and I didn't want him around.[1]

Later in that same interview I learned how Bruce felt as the recipient of Alan's moody behaviors.

Bruce Somers: . . . I probably felt scared, because I was always judging Alan's moods. Because I just wanted him to like me. I just wanted to have peace in the household, and it wasn't . . . There was always thick air in our house. . . . [Alan would focus on his children, joking with his daughter, Leslie, rough housing with his son, Steven] I wanted to be a part of that, and there was an invisible shield. . . . It could be happening right here, and I wasn't invited into that, and I'd have a silly smile [on my face] like "They're so cute." But, in retrospect, those are some of the more painful memories. Just you, feeling kind of alone in my own house.[2]

Lingering, deep-seated, seemingly immovable guilt felt by a parent figure like Alan adversely affects the entire family unit. His inability to turn back the hands of time deepened his sense of having blown it as a husband and father. At the same time, the reality of living with a new wife and child deepened his need to rise above the guilt, but it wasn't happening.

The ghosts of relationships lost with his first family became stumbling blocks to Alan's developing relationships with the new family. His inability to divulge his feelings weakened him as an effective spouse and parent. Those feelings made him so uncomfortable he was stuck between the proverbial rock and a hard place —the old family and the new family. The guilt dug in deeper. It was left unspoken for a great length of time. When his family confronted him about his behavior, he hid the bad feelings behind words of denial and a game of smoke and mirrors (shifting blame). He left his wife and stepson to draw their own conclusions as to why he wouldn't participate like a regular dad with the family.

When Suzanne questioned her husband's actions, he answered with a classic case of denial and even accusation.

Suzanne Somers: It was so clear that he preferred his children over Bruce. And that would be fodder for the fight later that night. "Can't you be nice to Bruce when the kids are over?" He didn't—"Don't you see you just ignore Bruce all the time? Why do you do that?" And he'd say, "I don't ignore. I don't know what you're talking about. You know, you're the one with the problems."[3]

Suzanne and Bruce both knew something wasn't right about the way Alan interacted with the family, but they couldn't get beneath his moods. Year after year he stuffed the guilt into deeper recesses of his mind rather than expose his true feelings to those he lived with. His family was left to cope with his denial of responsibility and unspoken sense of guilt until one day they were forced into family counseling. Alan's daughter went into drug rehab, and Bruce exploded with an angry punch at his stepfather. Those two shattering events were the catalyst to healing their family. They finally had to talk about *all* of it.

IS GUILT NECESSARY?

Let's consider a world where there was no guilt. Would we really want that? Our immediate response might be yes, but after giving it some thought I think most of us would say a resounding no.

A world without guilt would be horrible. People would have no sense of right and wrong. Life as we know it today would cease to exist. From our government systems to our personal lives, all boundaries of moral behavior would be meaningless.

There would be no policemen, no arrests, no trial by jury, no prisons, no remorse. The word *criminal* wouldn't appear in the dictionary. We would have no laws to govern us as a people. Today we think of government as being too big. But in a guiltless society, government would be far too small. We would all live in fear.

Without guilt, our eating habits would be out of control. It wouldn't matter how many hot fudge sundaes we ate at a single sitting. From a chocolate lover's point of view, that sounds like a wonderful freedom, but on the other hand, sin and foolish behavior would run rampant among us. Everyone would truly do what felt right in his own eyes. With no sense of wrongdoing, each one of us would simply be "expressing" ourselves. Punching someone in the mouth would be as OK as giving someone a hug. Robbery and rape would be as acceptable as singing praise songs to the Lord. The most assertive person would win out. A survival of the fittest. What a mess!

It is easy to see why we need checks and balances to set healthy boundaries. God really did know what He was doing when He created guilt as a necessary component of a healthy, fully operational conscience. The conscience separates us from all other created beings. It gives us the ability to respect one another by operating within appropriate limits.

BOUNDARIES

Train a child in the way he should go, and when he is old he will not turn from it. (Proverbs 22:6)

Watch a small child. See how quickly he goes from tears, to time-out, to joyfully returning to play. My young nephew David is a delightful example. When in trouble he will go—crying loudly as if he were dying—to his time-out space. He continues wailing for a few minutes. Then, suddenly, as though turning off one switch and turning on another, his voice returns to normal. He actually says, "All done now." His mom releases him from his confinement, lesson learned, and a smile quickly returns to his face.

Like David, we are all developing character traits important to life. Because we are God's children, we will receive His methods of training. When we were toddlers our parents enforced boundaries in our lives. Obedience to those limits brought approval from our parents. Disobedience brought displeasure. We caught on quickly that stepping out of the boundaries resulted in less-than-pleasant consequences. Discipline was simply a form of love given by parents who really cared. Those boundaries keep us safe.

But as adults we no longer have Mom and Dad standing beside us telling us what to do. Now we have to rely on our past training—and the Word of God.

The mature Christian recognizes God as *Father*. He knows that God's Word places reasonable, loving boundaries upon his life to keep him safe. When those boundaries are not heeded, we feel guilt and suffer consequences.

How do we know when guilt and shame are present in a healthy degree? Only by taking what we feel and examining it against what we know to be true from the Word of God.

A PROPER BLEND OF GUILT AND SHAME

"This is the covenant I will make with them after that time, says the Lord. I will put my laws in their hearts, and I will write them on their minds." (Hebrews 10:16)

God's law placed in our hearts and written on our minds makes up the moral code we are to live by. With our hearts we care; with our minds we reason. Something has to govern the choices we make. That something is known as the conscience.

Because God is holy, His laws represent true righteousness.

A holy God cannot act apart from holy absolutes. These laws written on our hearts and minds represent His holy thinking and define what we know to be a healthy conscience. These moral absolutes are meant to make the conscience a blessing, not a curse. But being the crafty humans we are, we add our own dimmer switch to suppress the intended function of a healthy conscience. Guilt is not something we like to feel. It makes most of us very uncomfortable. We come to believe that if we don't think about our inner feelings of guilt, we can escape them. That's not possible. We can't run away from our God-given inner voice of right and wrong. Our conscience, since it is created before birth, is a constant part of who we are.

Guilt will always grow larger when we believe it is necessary to keep it a secret. We may try to hide our guilt by living a lie. When we are asked, "What's wrong?" we say, "Nothing," or divert the conversation: "I've just had a hard day at the office." By denying our feelings, we have to place blame somewhere else. In a normal course of events those little lies, one after the other, eat away at our personal relationships. As the days go by, those closest to us recognize that our words and our actions—just like Alan's—don't match up at home.

Because the conscience plays such an active role in our lives, it is natural that guilt and shame will play significant roles as well. If we feel guilty or shameful after divorce and remarriage, the conscience is just doing the job God intended it to do. It is pointing out our failure to conform to God's values. That's a good thing to become aware of. By interpreting our failures correctly we can discover that failures are also opportunities for growth.

How many of us really see the beautiful side of guilt? Dr. Frank Minirth of the Minirth-Meier Clinics has gone so far as to associate guilt with the work of an artist. If handled properly, the influence of this powerful emotion is capable of putting the finishing touches of the artist's brush on our lives.

An engraver uses tiny amounts of acid, applied in carefully measured doses, to clean and make perfect the designs. Rough edges are smoothed, and the fine lines are more clearly defined. The work of art becomes even more beautiful because of the acid.

In a similar way, God uses small amounts of guilt in our lives to cleanse us of our flaws and help us rid ourselves of our imperfections. The guilt serves as a warning signal, which alerts us that we are doing things we shouldn't be doing and that our lives are moving in directions that aren't good for us. . . .

Guilt, like acid, when used in small doses is a powerful but positive force that can make a godly work of art—a human being—even more beautiful than it was. Guilt can shape and even strengthen us. We suffer from it, but we're better off because of it. If we use guilt as we should, it will prevent us from making the same mistakes the next time.[4]

I once visited the Sistine Chapel and witnessed an amazing work in progress. Many artists were gently refurbishing the paintings of Michelangelo. The walls were a mixture of contrasts. On some walls were the dulled images of work done centuries before. But on the walls where the restorers were at work, a beauty shone forth so complex my attention was drawn to every detail of the old masterpiece. It was a thrilling experience.

This is what God wants to do for us. Like the old masterpiece, we, too, can come forth in beauty. The canvas of our life is not yet finished. If we are attentive to those feelings of guilt and wisely let them touch up our character, we will bring forth the beauty God has placed within. But if we become consumed with our feelings of guilt and shame and fear the Master's touch, we will keep the canvas from being completed. The beauty gets buried.

WHICH PATH WILL I CHOOSE?

When the conscience is disturbed by guilt, an automatic, preprogrammed reaction kicks a progression of events into action. There are two possible paths to take: guilt that moves to conviction and concludes in restoration or guilt that moves to shame and concludes in destruction (chart).

PATHWAY ONE
*Guilt⇒Conviction⇒Acknowledge Responsibility⇒
Repent⇒Pardon⇒Restore*

PATHWAY TWO
*Guilt⇒Shame⇒Fear Exposure⇒Cover up Behaviors⇒
Depression⇒Destruction*

The choice we make with our first feelings of guilt determines which path we will travel. In many ways, the path we then choose is based on preprogrammed factors at the core of our being. Are we fearful? Are we secretive? Are we able to admit our shortcomings and accept consequences? Are we looking to God for help, or are we hiding from Him? Our degree of sensitivity to our inner motivations will determine whether guilt will lead us to choose the path of eventual restoration or the path full of potholes leading pell-mell toward destruction.

PATHWAY ONE
*Guilt⇒Conviction⇒Acknowledge Responsibility⇒
Repent⇒Pardon⇒Restore*

On Pathway One, guilt is immediately brought under the convicting work of the Holy Spirit. We don't blame others. We don't fear exposure. We don't get hung up on shame. The individual choosing this path readily acknowledges guilt, seeks forgiveness, feels pardoned, and does his best to bring restoration to those who have been wronged. This path allows for pleasant sleep; peace replaces anxiety. On this path our character becomes more beautiful. Changed behaviors demonstrate positive steps toward maturity. Applied to divorce and remarriage, this means truly facing up to the consequences of divorce and its effects on you, your spouse (present and ex), and your children.

THE POWER OF CONVICTION

From the moment we embark on Pathway One, we find a powerful resource at work. It is called conviction.

> "When he comes, he will convict the world of guilt in regard to sin and righteousness and judgment. . . . But when he, the Spirit of truth, comes, he will guide you into all truth. He will not speak on his own; he will speak only what he hears, and he will tell you what is yet to come." (John 16:8, 13)

The real solution to guilt over any issue is that it be resolved through the God-given process of conviction. To be under conviction is to see the opportunity for positive change to occur after we've messed things up. Sometimes the Holy Spirit says things we don't want to hear, but if we heed them they are always for our own good. There will be a growing desire to make things right again. To seek forgiveness, to take responsibility, to replace something I've broken, to tell the truth.

Conviction, then, is a reasoned, thought-out process, not an emotional state. The work of conviction moves guilty feelings to the place where they can become building blocks to godly character. Conviction—not lingering guilt or ill-kept shame—allows God to work on us from the inside out through loving means, exposure of truth, and sound reasoning. By understanding conviction, we see consequences in a different light. We see them as instruments needed to move us toward healthy change in our lives. When we can embrace conviction as a friend, the fear of condemnation has been replaced with a fresh appreciation for the work of the Spirit within us.

Search for Significance is a book that clarifies our need for conviction.

> Christians are freed from guilt, but we are still subject to conviction. The Bible frequently speaks of the Holy Spirit's work to convict believers of sin. He directs and encourages our spiritual progress by revealing our sins in contrast to the holiness and purity of Christ.

. . . His conviction of believers is not intended to produce pangs of guilt. Our status and self-worth are secure by the grace of God, and we are no longer guilty. Conviction deals with our behavior, not our status before God. Conviction is the Holy Spirit's way of showing the error of our performance in light of God's standard and truth. His motivation is love, correction, and protection.

. . . Conviction is the privilege of those who believe, and is given by the Holy spirit. Guilt brings depression and despair, but conviction enables us to realize the beauty of God's forgiveness and to experience His love and power.

Guilt focuses on the state of being condemned: I am unworthy.

Conviction focuses on behavior: This act is unworthy of Christ and is destructive.[5]

Mature believers are sensitive to the prompting of the Holy Spirit. When our hearts are troubled, we understand that God is not punishing us, but placing us under the work of conviction. We are being nudged by the Spirit toward a needed change. Because the Holy Spirit is at work, we have the power to halt behaviors that are out of God's will. God's purpose for a troubled conscience is beautiful. It's not about punishment. It's not about shame. It's about maturing in godly character traits.

I sought the Lord, and he answered me; he delivered me from all my fears. Those who look to him are radiant; their faces are never covered with shame. (Psalm 34:4–5)

PATHWAY TWO
Guilt⇒Shame⇒Fear Exposure⇒Cover up Behaviors⇒
Depression⇒Destruction

On Pathway Two, the same initial guilt is felt. But this person copes in an entirely different way. Instead of acknowledging the guilt and seeking spiritual restoration, he quickly changes guilt feelings into self-disgust and shame. He feels like a loser. The action isn't the problem; *he* is. The shame becomes who he is.

186

And because he fears exposure, he rushes to cover up his bad person. Denial is a common first line of defense. Then he adopts any number of addictive behaviors to maintain an acceptable mental machismo. These behaviors can include outward addictions and emotional addictions. A few addictive behaviors:

- withdrawal of intimacy from those closest to us
- anger to somehow intimidate the opposition
- illicit pleasures, i.e., alcohol or drug abuse, sexual liaisons
- shifting the focus by blaming others
- overwork to excel in another arena of life
- excessive spending

If the behaviors on this list describe someone you know, or even yourself, you need to realize these behaviors are characteristics of a life already addicted to shame. Yes, shame is an addiction that goes unidentified in many individuals. We tend to think of shame as just a feeling, but if it lasts more than a few hours or a couple of days, it is more than that. It has become a controlling and lingering personal identity. Because shameful behavior has the capacity to consume our identity, it is similar in operation to addictive substances. Shame that lingers is an addiction.

Most addictions start out subtly but steadily grow into life-threatening problems. The person on Pathway Two is a good candidate for depression. Fear of exposure and fear of rejection result in a hopeless quality of life. This path can lead to destruction. Sadly, some have chosen suicide in a last-ditch attempt to put their troubled consciences to rest.

Vicki Underland-Rosow, the author of the book *Shame: Spiritual Suicide*, discusses shame as it relates to addiction.

> The more I learned about shame the more I saw it as very different from feelings such as hate, love, anger, fear, happiness, or joy. It has a bigger presence in one's life than these feelings. It takes over. It operates like an addiction. Addiction is any process over which we are powerless. Then I began to see that shame supports addiction and addiction supports the experience of shame.[6]

An addiction to shame actually feeds an addiction to abusive behaviors. And the addiction to the wrongful behaviors becomes food for our shame. A vicious cycle is in motion.

Shame is an "underground current, a major force in the lives of most Americans, resulting in spiritual suicide," asserts Underland-Rosow. "The spiritually dead often live on the edge, pushing the limits of danger, abusing themselves and others, vainly searching for self-worth. They become the 'walking dead.'"[7]

As long as we are guzzling the booze and can keep on feeling high, as long as we don't have to talk about it, life looks manageable. Some people even label this out-of-control lifestyle of escape as *happy*. But those near us don't see it that way. It is evidence that we are walking a tightrope between Dr. Jekyll and Mr. Hyde. When the hangover wears off and we are once again face-to-face with ourselves, the shame has only heightened because we are now also ashamed of being drunk the night before. In these real moments we will feel more ashamed and more convinced that we are truly a bad person than we did before our ill-chosen behavior.

LIVING THE SHAME CYCLE

I am all too familiar with this cycle of addictive shame. It was playing itself out at our house in the same way it had for Suzanne and Alan. Charlie felt guilty—just like Alan did. He lived with my children while he wished to live with his own children. Like Alan, he didn't address the feelings of guilt for several years.

And me? I was walking in the same shoes of confused disillusionment as had Suzanne. When I approached Charlie about his attitude toward the children, I heard the same story Suzanne heard. He quickly asserted that I was the one with the problem, not he. I simply was not understanding him. If I *did* understand, I wouldn't make him feel bad by trying to force a closer relationship between him and the children.

Often my heart was torn between my children's hurts and my husband's needs. I felt guilty for the less-than-fulfilling father-child relationship Andrea and Mike were experiencing. Try as I would to fix things between the children and their stepfather, it didn't happen. Try as I would to be sensitive as a wife, I was unable to accept many of my husband's actions. Because I didn't understand the battle that was raging in Charlie's conscience, I was now battling my own feelings of guilt and shame.

Because our family wasn't able to talk about our troubled consciences with honest communication, for years our family problems didn't improve. Although our defense mechanisms were different, my husband and I were playing the same game. We were addicted to shame—but we didn't know it. Neither of us understood enough about guilt—or shame—to put the proper label on the problem we had brought into this marriage.

SHAME'S EFFECT ON SELF-ESTEEM

Family therapist Laura Sherman Walters believes blended families have understandable reasons for the shame they carry. She also believes self-respect must be restored to safeguard future generations.

> In the case of blended families, there is the added shame and self-doubt due to the breakup of the original families. Consequently, there is not an abundance of self-respect. Parents cannot teach their children self-respect unless they practice it themselves. So steps must be taken that will heal the feelings of shame and inadequacy left by previous family problems.[8]

It sounds like shame may be a natural consequence of divorce. Divorce opens the door for shame to enter our lives because dissolving a marriage is a public expression of a broken promise. Breaking promises rightly makes us feel ashamed.

Shame that is based on genuine guilt before God mingles with social and psychological shame. Even if we are the spouse who didn't want the divorce, we can still feel guilty, or even ashamed, for a couple of reasons. First, because we assume we weren't a good enough husband or wife to keep our mate from leaving. We dupe ourselves into believing if only we had been a better marriage partner we would not be divorced. By feeling defective we begin to live under a blanket of shame. We feel personal embarrassment. What will our friends and business acquaintances think? We can begin to imagine that divorce has lessened our value within our peer group.

Second, it is common for the spouse who did not want the divorce to feel shame because she feels she has let God down by signing the divorce papers. This spouse really intended to have a marriage "for better or for worse." Now that opportunity is gone. All the tears, all the pleading, and even attempts at counseling have not stopped the divorce from taking place.

Because of the personal influence of shame, both partners can easily be living with deep-seated shame after divorce. If this shameful self-image, which results in low self-worth, is not dealt with, it will be taken into the next marriage. Consider the following equation:

> One husband with hidden shame
> + One wife with hidden shame
> = a shame-centered marriage

It will be difficult for shame-centered marriages to survive, yet lots of second marriages begin this way, made up of two very needy people licking their wounds of betrayal and rejection. Both are searching for someone to make them feel like a person of value. Neither one realizes that their internal need for love cannot be fully met until the shame is uncovered and properly dealt with. Because of this, these marriage partners may feel like even greater failures when their needs are not met in the new marriage. Only when they are able to recognize the paralyzing effects of shame on their lives will they be able to develop a healthy self-esteem and new marriage relationship which will, in turn, result in a healthy family environment.

MORE ABOUT SOCIAL
AND PSYCHOLOGICAL SHAME

Some shame originates in genuine guilt. We feel it because our actions have brought it about. But there is also a powerful

form of shame that results from Satan's efforts to undermine us—
to tell us we are unworthy as a person and cause us to believe
God made a mistake when He created us. If shame's very nature is
to kick our self-image into the gutter, it's not surprising that the
Enemy would use social and psychological shame as a weapon
against us—because it goes into the mind and is acted upon.
What is surprising is that Christians continue to choose a lie over
God's truth. God never intends for His people to live at gutter
level. We are to stand victorious. Even over shame. That would
be the result if we followed Pathway One and dealt with genuine
guilt directly. It would even be the result if we sought God's help
to overcome psychological and social shame.

> But those who hope in the Lord will renew their strength. They
> will soar on wings like eagles. (Isaiah 40:31)

The psychological aspects of this form of shame cause people to be hypersensitive to what others think and say about them.
They have a great need to be socially acceptable, yet feel there are
things about them that will never be good enough to gain the approval they think they need. Things they have no control over.

Pastor, professor, and counselor Dr. David Seamands speaks
insightfully about Christians who are overwhelmed by feelings of
low self-worth. He sees this mental image as an area where Satan
is able to capitalize on our weaknesses.

> Satan's greatest psychological weapon is a gut-level feeling of infe-
> riority, inadequacy, and low self-worth. This feeling shackles
> many Christians, in spite of wonderful spiritual experiences, in
> spite of their faith and knowledge of God's Word. Although they
> understand their position as sons and daughters of God, they are
> tied up in knots, bound by a terrible feeling of inferiority, and
> chained to a deep sense of worthlessness.[9]

I was told I was small from the earliest time I can remember. I
heard I couldn't do certain tasks because I was littler than other
children my age. And I was often the last one picked from a group

of classmates for recess games. I thought I could do just as much as the other kids, but they didn't. So I acted like it didn't matter.

But it did. I took in a personal message that said, "Maxine, you are not like the rest of us. You're just not big enough to qualify." I felt inadequate, like I had a flaw I couldn't fix. Being petite in stature seemed to be a bad thing. In my teen years, I tried to remedy the problem by buying fat pills to put weight on so I could be larger. It didn't work! I still weighed only eighty-four pounds when I was seventeen.

Today I know it doesn't matter what size or shape we come in. But growing up, I was left with a powerful message about myself as a person. At the time I had no idea I was actually ashamed of being *me*, based on what others said about me. I don't even think they intended their words to be hurtful. But they were.

Fortunately the Lord gave me a very determined nature. What they said made me angry. After the tears, I fought back by excelling in other areas. They might have stymied some of my physical activity, but they couldn't take away my inner drive to succeed. I remember when I was ten, my mother said, "Maxine, you can do anything you put your mind to. Where there's a will, there's a way." That message must have stuck as well.

A low self-image is really a bad case of tunnel vision. None of us is born with a bad sense of who he is. We take on this bad image of ourselves as we grow. A great deal of our self-value takes root in childhood and is reinforced throughout our lives by the people we interact with most closely. Sadly, divorce most often heightens issues of low self-image, and our self-respect is in even greater jeopardy.

I am convinced we are a combination of the positive and negative messages we continue to receive throughout life. Positive messages spur us on with joy. Negative messages become instant-replay tracks within our minds until we take the time to reprogram them.

We must be on guard against Satan when it comes to feelings of inferiority. He wants us to feel trashed and unable to live life with the abundance of joy God says is ours. The devil doesn't want us soaring like the eagles.

A simple way to start diffusing psychological shame is to identify the messages as well as their source. Most likely they hold the keys to unlocking our addiction to this type of shame. There are reasons why we hold a shameful image of ourselves. We need to know what they are.

Get a pencil and paper and write down what you have heard said about yourself in days gone by. Make two columns. Mark one "Positive Messages" and the other "Negative Messages." Maybe you'll remember a name you were called. Perhaps you were teased when you cried. Or maybe you were applauded for setting a record at a track meet. Whatever comes to mind, write it down.

After making the list, pray for the Lord to bring truth to you about whatever you wrote. Like me, you will find many of these replayed messages are not accurate statements of the person you really are.

SOMEONE ELSE'S SHAME

Sometimes you will find you have actually taken on a shame that was not even yours to own. It might have been an inappropriate act by a close family member that had nothing to do with your behavior. Yet because you bear the same name, embarrassment has spilled onto you. This is a false personal message. You have taken on the shame of another person.

This was Cindy's experience. Cindy's marriage to her first husband ended in divorce after twelve years. A few months later, she met and married Al. For the first three years things were tough financially, but they seemed to be a happy couple. But there was a secret side to Al. He was involved with pornography and excessive drinking. One day he crossed the line, sexually assaulted a young woman, and was arrested. The papers and the television stations buzzed with the news. Cindy felt so ashamed, so dirty, so noticed.

"How can I leave my house?" Cindy cried. "Everyone will know who I am. How could he do this to us? Doesn't he care about the humiliation the children and I have to live with? I just want to change my name, or better yet not even wake up tomorrow."

Cindy's story is one many individuals live with. Owning the shame of another is devastating. And it is false shame. We cannot dismiss the shame that binds us until we come to terms with what is real and what is not. Cindy would have done better emotionally if she could have separated her personal identity from her husband's actions. It took time to do this. But she did get there. Today, when Cindy is asked about her husband's behaviors she is able to say, "I was devastated, but my husband was the one who made some very bad choices. His choices brought horrible consequences on all of us."

NO MORE CONDEMNATION

In the book *Shame and Grace,* Lewis B. Smedes of Fuller Theological Seminary helps us to recognize how to move away from the negative messages that surround shame by applying the spiritual experience of grace.

> Grace overcomes shame, not by uncovering an overlooked cache of excellence in ourselves but simply by accepting us, the whole of us, with no regard to our beauty or our ugliness, our virtue or our vices. We are accepted wholesale. Accepted with no possibility of being rejected. Accepted once and accepted forever. Accepted at the ultimate depth of our being. We are given what we have longed for in every nook and nuance of every relationship.
>
> We are ready for grace when we are bone tired of our struggle to be worthy and acceptable. After we have tried too long to earn the approval of everyone important to us, we are ready for grace. When we are tired of trying to be the person somebody sometime convinced us we had to be, we are ready for grace.[10]

We only receive grace as we come to Christ. He is the grace giver. After taking this step it will still take courage to open the lid on Pandora's box and let out the secrets that have victimized us for so long. They have become familiar companions. Exposing the truth about the shame we hold is risky, but it is the only way to move forward in the healing process. So I applaud all who bravely take this step.

> There is now no condemnation for those who are in Christ Jesus, because through Christ Jesus the law of the Spirit of life set me free from the law of sin and death. (Romans 8:1–2)

What an amazing concept to be free from condemnation. We can begin to see the end of shame's lingering influence in our own lives. It is not God's plan for us to walk through life burdened by guilt or shame, so we'll need to apply some biblical wisdom. That is when we will feel the peace that accompanies the assurance of a full pardon.

It was such a relief to know that God wasn't going to condemn me because of divorce. Instead, He forgave me. If God wasn't going to condemn me, I didn't need to be concerned that people would. I was finally able to grasp a proper self-image. The pain of yesterday no longer hung its dark cloud over today's lifestyle. Because of Christ, I was free of Satan's hold.

WHAT ABOUT CONSEQUENCES?

Does forgiveness remove consequences? Not necessarily. We need to see consequences apart from issues of redemption. God is not loving us less when we experience the consequences of life's choices.

We have three beautiful grandchildren living three hundred miles from us. It would be wonderful to spend birthdays and holiday celebrations with them. But because of my husband's divorce, it isn't possible. Our children, the parents of these precious granddaughters, feel unable to have their mother and their father together at family events. So we lose.

Still today his divorce over twenty-five years ago leaves us with the consequences of fragmented relationships. We are on the outside looking in, longing to be included, yet not invited. When we see the children, it is on separate days for celebrations of our own making. His ex gets all the real holiday dates. What hurts the most is that year after year we get a fresh look at just how far-reaching the aftermath of divorce really is. Each trip to Portland reminds us there is no end to the consequences.

There is a cause and effect to all things in life. We choose whether to be bitter or to make the best of the less-than-normal relationships.

If we hit our thumb with a hammer we expect to experience natural consequences as a result of the action between the thumb and the hammer. But after the pain, discoloration, and loss of the nail, we see the consequences end. That's where divorce is different. We don't see the end. That's discouraging. Divorce brings a lifetime of consequences that would not have otherwise occurred. We will forever experience extra family issues. Some will be very difficult. But battling the consequences won't help. The best thing to do is spend more time in prayer. God promises to walk with us through every new trial.

> The Lord is my strength and my shield; my heart trusts in him, and I am helped. My heart leaps for joy and I will give thanks to him in song. The Lord is the strength of his people, a fortress of salvation for his anointed one. (Psalm 28:7–8)

Rampant guilt and shame ruling the life of a Christian makes a silent statement heard all too loudly by others. It says that what Christ did really wasn't enough. As Christians we have the life of Christ in us. Our friends are watching to see if it really does make a difference. Why would anyone looking at a Christian consumed by guilt and shame desire to know God? It appears He is ineffective.

If guilt or shame continue to hold us captive, we have not truly believed Jesus to be our source of victory. We are still trying to cover our guilt and shame by our own methods. Freedom will elude us forever until we give our guilt to Jesus. There is no guilt or shame He is not willing to cover. There is no life that cannot be given new joy!

Remember the two pathways. You will always have the freedom to choose the one leading to restoration.

Growth and Application

Commit to memory Romans 8:1–2.

1. In what way do you sense guilt and shame have influenced your family?

2. Take a few moments to write down the self-messages you heard from others.

Positive Messages   *Negative Messages*

How did you live as a result of these messages? Did you discover a hidden addiction to shame?

3. Why is it important to understand the work of conviction in the life of a believer?

How does conviction differ from guilt?

4. What are some of the consequences you have dealt with in your family?

What has your attitude been toward these consequences?

Prayer of Application

Lord, You alone are worthy of our highest praise. Thank You for bringing understanding to our struggles with guilt and shame. Please forgive us for holding onto the guilt You wanted to take from us. How foolish we have been. And as we look upon the messages we have taken into our lives from others, give us truth to dispel a false sense of personal value. Help us to live like the eagle.

And, Lord, we are now able to appreciate the use of conviction in our lives. Thank You for this great work of the Holy Spirit, given as a gift from You. Allow this gift to lead us to choices that please You and grow maturity in us. And, Lord, when the hurts from our consequences get heavy, please bring fresh thoughts of Your purpose into our lives. Amen.

NOTES

1. *20/20* (American Broadcasting Company, ABC News), 19 June 1998, ABC Transcript #1819, 12.
2. Ibid.,13.
3. Ibid.
4. Paul Hemfelt, Frank Minirth, and Paul Meier, *We Are Driven: The Compulsive Behaviors America Applauds* (Nashville: Nelson, 1991), 268–69.
5. Robert S. McGee, *The Search for Significance,* 2d ed. (Houston: Rapha, 1990), 168.
6. Vicki Underland-Rosow, *Shame: Spiritual Suicide* (Shorewood, Minn.: Waterford, 1996). Internet: http://www.ic.mankato.mn.us/web/shame/chapter1.html.
7. Vicki Underland-Rosow, *Shame: Spiritual Suicide.* Internet: http://www.ic.mankato.mn.us/web/shame/shame.html
8. Laura Sherman Walters, *There's a New Family in My House!* (Wheaton, Ill.: Shaw, 1993), 142.
9. David A. Seamands, *Healing for Damaged Emotions* (Wheaton, Ill.: Scripture Press, Victor, 1981), 49.
10. Lewis B. Smedes, *Shame and Grace* (New York: Harper Collins; Grand Rapids: Zondervan, 1993), 109.

Chapter Ten

ARMED
WITH
ATTITUDE

My eighteen-year-old daughter Andrea looked on eagerly as I opened the gift she had given me. Carefully I removed the colorful paper. Inside was a pillow cross-stitched on the front with a bear holding a bouquet of balloons. Next to him were the words "Pulling together against all odds."

"Yeah. That says it all," I reached over to give her a hug. "I love it."

"I thought it described our family well," Andrea said. "Somehow you always make me feel like we can keep pulling together."

"I guess I just believe God isn't finished with us yet," I said with a smile.

Andrea was right. At our house we were either happy or miserable. There weren't many in-between moods. Because our family struggled to feel like family, I often thought I was letting her down. Holidays were frequently the worst times. In spite of that, Andrea's positive attitude popped up in fresh ways to encourage me. She could easily have chosen to be rebellious, but she didn't. Instead, the pillow told the story. She understood. She saw my perseverance as a strength to value. Her attitude made me glad I had chosen to press on through the difficulties. Years later, the pillow is tattered but the message remains. It is a memorial to our family's growth.

On the other hand, my stepdaughter's attitudes were completely different. Things were tough for Sabrina during her teen years. Out of desperation her mother asked if she could come to live with us. We said yes. It seemed like a wonderful opportunity to get to know our daughter. But even though she was with us in body, she was far from connecting with us relationally. There seemed to be a chip on her shoulder we couldn't move.

Now that she is grown, I asked Sabrina to tell me why things were so difficult for her back then. She wrote these words.

> At first I was overwhelmed. I felt like I was invading Dad's new family, and I didn't feel like I fit in well there. I had a lot of feelings at that time, wondering who my father really was. I felt jealous of the fact that he had a new life with 3 other wonderful children.
>
> When I was 15 I had a lot of feelings, like should I live with my father? Would I be better off with him, or should I stay with my mother? At that time I didn't feel like that was working well. But, in short, I didn't feel like I could be accepted into Dad's life either. So the easiest way was to escape and go back to the life I was used to.
>
> Back then I couldn't understand it all. I just knew I wanted a better life, and I thought Dad could give me that. I had been getting into trouble at school. My mom was working full time, and I had no one to really talk to. I just felt so out of place with you guys, and jealous knowing if things could have been different I would have had my father while I was growing up.
>
> Now I know that things are the way they are for a reason, and no one is to blame. You and your children weren't at fault at all. Things just happened, and you and Dad found each other and raised a wonderful family together. Even though I wish I could have lived with Dad and received his love, it just wasn't possible.

Two daughters. Two different attitudes. One saw a family trying to survive despite its imperfections. The other believed we were the perfect family she could not fit comfortably into. In reality, both daughters were cheated by life. The only difference was their attitudes. To Andrea, we were her family, flaws and all. She was willing to work with that. To Sabrina, we were strangers whose lives she did not share. She envied the advantages her stepsiblings had. She wanted what they had, but her attitude kept her from seeing it was also available to her—all the time. It was as if she felt that holding onto a bitter spirit would somehow avenge what she had lost. Sabrina was unable to accept our love. The wall of hurt would not come down. Three weeks later she went back home to her mother.

ATTITUDE MAKES
THE INNER MAN (OR WOMAN)

Just as clothes make a statement about the outer man, attitude is a powerful proclamation of the inner man. Through words and body language we deliver an important first impression of who we are through our attitude. When we meet someone for the first time we quickly size them up. Are they warm and welcoming? Are they reserved and standoffish? They size us up, and we size them up. We set the tone for our time together. But that's not always good, since our attitudes run a wide gamut.

Like clothing, attitudes are highly visible to others. They need to be selected carefully. If we were to go into the closet and choose a black-and-green-checked shirt to wear with a pair of red slacks, what would people think? Unless we were "clown for a day," we'd get some pretty strange looks. People would conclude we had poor taste. Our attitudes can sabotage us just as quickly.

We all take care of our clothing, but we overlook the condition of our attitude. Sometimes it needs laundering. Looking into God's Word and soaking in its application is like a trip to the laundromat. With a little extra primping and a couple of wrinkles ironed out, our attitude will make a much better statement. It won't betray our Christian witness.

God clearly states that all attitudes should be modeled after the attitude of Jesus. He walked among us with appropriate attitudes. He was mistreated, just like we are. He was put down, spit upon, and punished for the sins of others. Yet despite the circumstances, He continued to live with a good attitude. He even prayed for His enemies and chose to forgive His offenders. How many of us would react the same way?

God isn't unreasonable. So there must be a way for us to make the same choices Jesus made. First we must see that attaining an attitude like Christ's is possible. It will never happen until we are convinced this passage of Scripture is a command from God and not a passive suggestion. If we can say in our minds, "God says it, I believe it, just do it," we will be able to put God's Word into action. At that point, we see a wrong attitude as disobedience to God. Only then will we desire to change.

SPONTANEOUS ATTITUDES

Our attitudes tend to change with the ups and downs of life. When we feel up, we greet the world with a cheery attitude. When we feel down, it is easy to let our disposition get out of sorts. Sometimes it's just the mundane exhaustion of a busy life that robs us of a high-quality attitude. When I'm too tired, working too many hours, or suffering with an illness, maintaining a positive attitude is hard. That's when it's easy to get into a grumpy mood and let that mood spill onto other people.

We are all spontaneous people. How many times have we been cut off by an inconsiderate motorist? We waste no time in expressing ourselves in words and even body language. With fist shaking and horn blaring, we let unpleasant words blurt forth. "Where did you learn to drive?" "Why don't you get off the road?" We are quick to vent our annoyance, and we even feel justified in doing so. But what would Christ have done? Would He show such a lack of respect for the careless driver? I don't think so. He probably would have shown him mercy.

We are told to do the same. Sure, we are cut off in traffic, but that doesn't give us license to act so rudely. What it does give us is the opportunity to display the attitude of Christ. Someday we may use poor judgment too. Would we like to see a fist shaking in our rearview mirror, or would we rather see a considerate motorist who despite our boo-boo gently moves over and makes room for us?

How would the people closest to us describe our overall attitude? Would they say, "Wow! He is so thoughtful. He is eager to help others in need. He always makes me feel so comfortable." Or would we hear something like, "She is always so angry and defensive. So many little things seem to upset her. I really have to watch what I say."

It's important to know our own predominant attitude. Other people already have us labeled. We can't begin to reprogram what we are not aware of.

In attempting to understand why we are who we are, we need to look at the things that have affected the formation of our personality. Some of these are

- our parents
- our relatives and friends
- our church
- neighborhoods
- our teachers
- compliments
- our fears
- physical or mental abuse
- criticism
- tragedies
- our health
- our financial status
- celebrations

When these outside influences combine with our God-given nature, they form the character traits that identify us as individuals. Since none of us have identical natures or the same outside influences we are unique in who we are. But among the strongest things affecting attitude are parental role models and peer pressure.

For my husband, growing up in the Italian ghetto of Boston meant strength was respected and weakness not tolerated. To protect himself from embarrassment and harm, he learned to be tough as a way to survive. But even if we think a particular temperament is necessary for self-preservation, we need to question whether that attitude is consistent with the attitude of Christ.

LEARNING JESUS' ATTITUDES

Jesus left us with some incredible instructions related to attitude. We commonly call this part of Scripture the Beatitudes—or, as I like to refer to them, the *attitudes to be*.

> "Blessed are the poor in spirit, for theirs is the kingdom of heaven. Blessed are those who mourn, for they will be comforted. Blessed are the meek, for they will inherit the earth. Blessed are those who hunger and thirst for righteousness, for they will be filled. Blessed are the merciful, for they will be shown mercy. Blessed are the pure in heart, for they will see God. Blessed are the peacemakers, for they will be called sons of God. Blessed are those who are persecuted because of righteousness, for theirs is the kingdom of heaven.
>
> "Blessed are you when people insult you, persecute you and falsely say all kinds of evil against you because of me. Rejoice and be glad, because great is your reward in heaven, for in the same way they persecuted the prophets who were before you." (Matthew 5:3–12)

Over and over Jesus says, "Blessed are you." That is very significant. It leaves us with a feeling of great anticipation. Then take time to notice how each attitude we are told *to be* comes with a promise. By living out the actions defining the attitude, we receive the reward. Then we feel *blessed.* To be blessed means to feel happy, joyous, and content. Rather than saying, "Blessed are those who mourn," we could substitute "Happy are those who mourn," or "Joyous are those who mourn," or even, "Content are those who mourn."

It sounds strange that those who mourn are actually those

who know true happiness, but that's exactly what God wants us to learn. The world views happiness in a much different way from the way God does. Most people think happiness can be found in outside activities, possessions, relationships, achievements, and lots of money. It's great to have happy things occur. We all like to enjoy life. But if happiness is based on external circumstances it won't last. Life is full of ups and downs. So there's nothing real to hold onto.

True happiness is determined by our internal attitude. Happiness that lasts only comes when we are content with who we are as individuals. And that feeling is only possible when we are in right standing with God. For this reason, Jesus found it necessary to address the crowd. In this setting He defined *new covenant* thinking.

This covenant built on grace fulfilled the requirements of the Mosaic Law. With it came mercy, promise, and a lasting sacrifice for sin. No longer would man's salvation be bound to a law he was incapable of keeping.

In the chart "Attitudes in the Beatitudes," it is easy to see each of the eight attitudes Jesus mentioned, discover their meanings, and clarify the promised blessings.

ATTITUDES IN THE BEATITUDES

Attitude to Be	Meaning	Promise to Be Given
Poor in spirit	Recognizes personal sin	Receive eternal life
Able to mourn	Is deeply saddened over sin	Be comforted
Meek	Is strong, yet submits to God	Inherit the earth
Desires righteousness	Craves the things of God	Be filled
Merciful	Extends compassion	Receive mercy
Pure in heart	Is in right standing with God	See God
Peacemaker	Holds no grudges; reconciles	Be called sons of God
Persecuted	Stands up for what is right	Possess heaven; be rewarded

Jesus' words were troubling to some who heard Him speak. Some rejected what He said. But for others, those who believed, He was their long-awaited Savior. His words represented a freedom that had been beyond their reach until then.

Prior to Jesus' public ministry, the Jews lived in a world of legalism. The sacrifices made on the altars of Israel pointed toward the Messiah who was to come, but legalistic adherence to extra-biblical rules predominated. Still, everyone understood the seriousness of personal sin. It had to be satisfied before a holy God. Then along came Jesus. He was telling them of a God to whom they could respond in faith and who would forgive them and even put His Spirit within them. He was telling people to examine their attitudes, to become pure in heart, and to expect persecution because they would be rewarded in heaven. This new knowledge brought mixed feelings.

Author Jerry Bridges clarifies the demands of the law and the final satisfaction of the law.

No One Is Declared Righteous Before God by Observing the Law (Romans 3:19–21)

The word righteous means exact and perfect conformity to the law of God. When I use the term "the law of God" here, I am not referring specifically to the law given to the nation of Israel through Moses. Rather, I am using the term in a more general sense to refer to the transcript of God's nature and the rule of obedience that He requires of all human beings. It includes all of the ethical commands scattered throughout the Bible.

The standard of obedience required by the law is absolute perfection, for James 2:10 tells us, "For whoever keeps the whole law and yet stumbles at just one point is guilty of breaking all of it."

There Is a Righteousness from God That Is Apart from Law (Verse 21)

. . . It is important to realize that our Lord Jesus Christ perfectly fulfilled the law of God, both in its requirements and its penalty. He did what Adam failed to do—render perfect obedience to the law of God. Then by His death He completely paid the penalty of a broken law. So, from the standpoint of obedience to the law and of paying the penalty for breaking the law, He perfectly fulfilled the law of God.

Therefore when God justifies us, or declares us righteous, He does not create some sort of legal fiction, calling something righteous that is not. Rather, He declares us righteous on the basis of the real, accomplished righteousness of Jesus Christ, which is imputed or credited to us through faith.[1]

This should not give us a flip attitude about the tablets Moses brought down from the mountain. New covenant teaching never speaks of neglecting the moral substance of the law. Instead, it speaks of satisfying the full requirements of the law through faith in what Jesus did on the cross. He substituted Himself for our sins. Our behaviors still matter.

The new covenant brought a new confidence. Instead of a "thou shalt not" list, there is now a more positive "blessed are" list. Because he has the assurance of being fully forgiven, fully loved, and fully in fellowship with the Lord, the beliver's biggest concern is no longer just salvation. It is acquiring the attitude of Christ. Through the passage of Scripture we just looked at Jesus gave us the basis for those like-minded thoughts. In a loving, yet direct way, He educated the people. He began by describing attitudes that are crucial to kingdom living. Since attitude becomes the heart of our Christian witness, we cannot ignore its importance.

HUMILITY

Some of us don't like the word *humble*. It makes us feel demoted, like eating a slice of humble pie or being a doormat. But that's not the true interpretation of the word *humble*. For the Christian, being humble is being fully confident of our abilities, yet respectful, polite, and unassuming in nature. Strength remains, but it is strength under the control of the Holy Spirit.

A humble person gives of himself to others. He willingly puts aside his own desires to meet the needs of others. This might mean having to postpone a fishing trip or not buying that new shirt. Being humble says, "I think less of myself, and more of others." That's what Jesus did.

Do nothing out of selfish ambition or vain conceit, but in humility consider others better than yourselves. Each of you should look not only to your own interests, but also to the interests of others. Your attitude should be the same as that of Christ Jesus: Who, being in very nature God, . . . made himself nothing, taking the very nature of a servant, being made in human likeness. And being found in appearance as a man, he humbled himself. (Philippians 2:3–8a)

Jesus was a giant example of humility. He cared so much for the welfare of mankind that He overlooked personal pain and willingly went to the cross. He gave all He could give. He gave His life that we might live. Andrew Murray wrote the Christian classic *Humility*. In this marvelous work, he helps us to grasp the necessity of living with this lowly, yet noble, attitude.

What a solemn thought, that our love to God will be measured by our everyday fellowship with men and the love it displays. How solemn that our love to God will be found to be a delusion, except as its truth is proved in standing the test of daily life with our fellow-men. It is even so with our humility. It is easy to think we humble ourselves before God. Yet, humility toward men will be the only sufficient proof that our humility before God is real. It will be the only proof that humility has taken up its abode in us, and become our very nature—that we actually, like Christ, have made ourselves of no reputation. When in the presence of God lowliness of heart has become, not a posture we assume for a time when we think of Him, or pray to Him, but the very spirit of our life, it will manifest itself in all our bearing toward our brethren.

The lesson is one of deep importance. The only humility that is really ours is not that which we try to show before God in prayer, but that which we carry with us, and carry out, in our ordinary conduct. The insignificances of daily life are the importances and the tests of eternity because they prove what spirit really possesses us. It is in our most unguarded moments that we really show and see what we are.[2]

To be enjoyable, all of life's relationships must have a core attitude of humility. Without humility of heart, we are serving the master of selfishness. And it is impossible to effectively serve others until we get selfish thoughts out of the way.

NEIGHBORLINESS AND GENEROSITY

A parent's attitude always affects the outcome of a child's life. When we feel good about giving to others, we model generosity before our children. That's how they catch the principle. Hopefully they will find pleasure in giving of their time and money as well.

When I was growing up, we didn't have very much money. But my dad still gave to anyone who had a need. If their cow was struggling to birth a calf, he would be the first one to help. If they had nothing to eat, he would find a way to get some meat to them. One family came often to catch small fish from our pond for their dinner. My dad didn't ask for anything in return. It was just the neighborly thing to do. This always made me feel good. And it gave me a desire to help others too. At his funeral many spoke of my father's generosity to them. He was well liked.

> A generous man will prosper; he who refreshes others will himself be refreshed. (Proverbs 11:25)

If we can do neighborly things, we can also find creative ways to bless those within the family too. Sometimes with family it's easier to feel more inconvenienced than with strangers. The family's needs are much more frequent. The interruptions never cease. It can seem like we never have enough time to care for the necessary things in our own lives, like exercise. But that's life. Interruptions won't stop, but our attitude can be one that takes the opportunity to bless instead of grumble.

I had just gotten into the car after finishing an aerobics class when my car phone rang. My youngest daughter was on the line.

"Mom, I need some milk. I'm making a recipe and there isn't any milk. Would you bring some home for me?"

The first thought I had was, *You've got to be kidding. I can't go in a store looking like this.* I was dripping with sweat. I had no makeup on. I didn't smell good, and I was wearing Lycra gym shorts. *What if someone sees me?* If I wanted an excuse, I definitely had a list to pick from! But on second thought, vanity aside, I replied, "Sure."

THE IMPORTANCE OF ENCOURAGEMENT

Jesus was also an encourager. Everywhere He went, He offered hope to the downcast. I like to think of Him as the God of the second chance. He's given me lots of second chances, and third, and fourth.

> But encourage one another daily, as long as it is called Today, so that none of you may be hardened by sin's deceitfulness. (Hebrews 3:13)

After divorce we all need encouragement to put our lives back together. Knowing someone believes in us spurs us on to try again.

"It seems like I don't know how to get over what's happened. All I do is cry," Kay said. "I must be a bad person. Otherwise I wouldn't be so unhappy. I just can't seem to understand why God let my husband leave me. What did I do that was so bad?"

"It will help if you can understand bad things happen to good people too," I said. "I'm sorry. But God doesn't think you are bad. He loves you. He even says He has a plan for you."

"How can God have a plan for me? I never worked outside the home in the twenty-six years we were married. I stayed home and raised my kids. I don't know how to do anything. So how can I get any work?"

"Well, let's think about that," I said. "Do you still enjoy being around children?"

"Well . . . yes. I watch my grandchildren all the time," Kay admitted.

"It seems like you have more skills than you realize," I said. "Since you enjoyed raising your children, you might try opening your home to do child care for others. Lots of working moms need help, and you spent years developing homemaking skills."

Kay was discovering two things. She was still loved by God, and she did know how to do some things very well. That little bit of encouragement lifted her spirits.

When we encourage others we bring value to them as a person. We make them feel good. Their otherwise cloudy day suddenly has a silver lining. Self-esteem always rises when we are encouraged.

GENTLE WORDS AND COMPASSION

We can learn the value of a gentle word as we reflect on the way Jesus dealt with the woman caught in adultery.

> The teachers of the law and the Pharisees brought in a woman caught in adultery. They made her stand before the group and said to Jesus, "Teacher, this woman was caught in the act of adultery. In the Law Moses commanded us to stone such women. Now what do you say?" They were using this question as a trap, in order to have a basis for accusing him.
>
> But Jesus bent down and started to write on the ground with his finger. When they kept on questioning him, he straightened up and said to them, "If any one of you is without sin, let him be the first to throw a stone at her." Again he stooped down and wrote on the ground.
>
> At this, those who heard began to go away one at a time, the older ones first, until only Jesus was left, with the woman still standing there. Jesus straightened up and asked her, "Woman, where are they? Has no one condemned you?"
>
> "No one, sir," she said.
>
> "Then neither do I condemn you," Jesus declared. "Go now and leave your life of sin." (John 8:3–11)

Did Jesus condone the woman's sin? Of course not. But to our surprise we don't find Him chewing her out either. Or, even worse, throwing stones at her. Instead, Jesus offered a better lifestyle to this woman. With compassion He gave her the opportunity to "go . . . and leave [her] life of sin." This is very different from what her accusers had in mind. As she stood before Him, I can only imagine her surprise at feeling loved.

Shouldn't we be able to offer this type of compassion to our own family members? We will if we have the attitude of Christ. Those who encourage as Jesus did say to others, "Why don't you try again? I believe you can make a better choice next time."

DISCOURAGING WORDS

Do not let any unwholesome talk come out of your mouths, but only what is helpful for building others up according to their needs, that it may benefit those who listen. (Ephesians 4:29)

On the flip side, discouraging words take the wind right out of our sails. Rather than feeling good, we feel sick inside. Words of discouragement are critical of a person's worth. They hurt. Often they are spoken in anger and leave a wounded spirit behind. Like a punctured tire, these harsh words leave us feeling deflated.

I was visiting a friend's home a few months ago. His teenage son, Jim, and I were visiting at the table after dinner. Suddenly an outburst came from his father.

"Jim! Get up and get these dishes done now," the father shouted, his demeanor one of unnecessary anger. "Why are you so lazy? You'll never amount to anything."

The young man's face fell. His pleasant conversation with me ended. He got up and walked to the sink, anger in his eyes.

Isn't it interesting that the attitude of our heart is expressed through the mouth? That's why it is so important to understand the power of the spoken word. It can be so deadly. With our mouths, we are able to wield more destruction than a physical blow. There was no need for harsh words that night. It was cruel to humiliate this young man in such a way, especially in front of a guest. But Jim is only one of many children who are spoken to with unkind words every day. Words that don't edify always hurt. They do not represent the attitude of Christ.

SELFISHNESS AND JEALOUSY

In most blended families two attitudes in particular pop up repeatedly. They are the attitudes of selfishness and jealousy. A sour attitude can prevent us from attaining the very things others want to give to us.

> Jealousy is a destructive attitude that poisons the way you view life. It is so harmful that God condemned coveting in two of the Ten Commandments. . . . Jealousy is an abomination in the life of a Christian. God has made us His children. None of us deserves to be God's child, so there is no need to compare our blessings with those of other children of God. Jealousy is self-centeredness at its worst. Jealousy robs us of joy and chokes out contentment. Jealousy hardens the heart and stifles gratitude. Jealousy assumes that God's resources are too limited for Him to bless another and still bless us. . . . Watch over your heart! If you find yourself unable to rejoice in the success of others, beware![3]

Sidonna, a friend of mine, admits to struggling with selfishness and jealousy. With her permission, let's look at how she feels.

"Even though we are adults now, we still struggle with our attitudes," Sidonna said with passion. "My mom has been remarried for ten years, and my sisters and brothers and I still resent sharing her with her stepkids."

"Why do you find that so difficult?" I asked.

"She's *our* mom, not *theirs*. My sisters and I are her real daughters, not her stepdaughters. It's just not fair that we can't plan the holidays with her. I admit we're being brats. We are making it very difficult for Mom to feel comfortable going to be with her husband's family this Christmas, even though we know she is part of that family too."

Sidonna's story is a classic case in point: selfishness mixed with jealousy over sharing their mother with another family. Most of us find selfish feelings heighten during the holidays. That's when we want to be closest to our family members. It is easy to feel slighted.

> Nobody should seek his own good, but the good of others. (1 Corinthians 10:24)

For now, my friend wants what will make her feel happy. But to be unselfish and to put away jealousy, Sidonna and her siblings will need to consider the additional family obligations a blended family has placed on their mother. In love, they could show understanding rather than begging for a change of plans.

A jealous spirit eats away at the very core of who we are. Christian men and women must recognize this deadly poison and put it out of their lives. The best antidote for the spirit of jealousy is a thankful attitude.

SELFISHNESS IN SHEPHERDS

What happens when our homes are headed by persons who are blind to selfish habits? What if their own needs make them insensitive to the needs of other family members? What are they teaching their children by their actions?

It's easy to become blinded by selfishness, just like Israel's watchmen. History has a way of shedding light on today if we will only take the time to learn from it. These watchmen had a serious problem with selfishness. The era of history may have changed, but unfortunately these men are representative of the spiritual leadership in many homes today. Selfishness still reigns.

> Israel's watchmen are blind, they all lack knowledge; they are all mute dogs, they cannot bark; they lie around and dream, they love to sleep. They are dogs with mighty appetites; they never have enough. They are shepherds who lack understanding; they all turn to their own way, each seeks his own gain. "Come," each one cries, "let me get wine! Let us drink our fill of beer! And tomorrow will be like today, or even far better." (Isaiah 56:10–12)

Doesn't this sound like the world we live in? The wording is a little different. We don't go around calling husbands or wives shepherds. But they are shepherds (guides) of their family flock. God has set forth certain qualities that define a good shepherd. A shepherd, above all, is a protector, a nurturer, and a provider. He is trustworthy and gives sacrificially of himself.

But today my heart breaks as I listen to story after story of homes headed by men and women with selfish interests. When money is needed to pay the bills, why are these husbands (or wives) looking for a beer party or a bingo parlor to gamble their hard-earned dollars away? Like mute dogs, they cannot even be alarmed at the harm being inflicted on their family. They just don't get it. Because they are blinded by self they can't see the bigger family picture. Instead of modeling a real concern for the family's well-being, they are demanding others meet their needs.

What we are seeing is a reenactment of Israel's watchmen. A true shepherd doesn't live that way. He guards against the spirit of selfishness by putting others first. He takes pleasure in being selfless.

WHAT'S SO BAD ABOUT PRIDE?

Jesus had every reason to be proud. He created the world and everything in it. He fed five thousand people with a couple of fish. He calmed stormy seas. He healed the leprous man, withered the fig tree, and cast out evil spirits. He was the Son of God Most High. He knew who He was. He didn't have to pound His chest to elevate Himself to greatness. He had nothing to prove. His position as a Son was to honor the Father. That would be accomplished in humility, and not by pride.

Often as a spouse or a parent, we want our position of authority to be recognized and respected. When that doesn't happen, our pride gets in the way and we can get out of sorts very quickly. The sulkier our attitude gets, the more our relationships begin to flounder.

Larry and Donna have been married a little over a year. They are both in their third marriage. Larry has a child he has not seen for fifteen years. Donna's seventeen-year-old son Nick, the apple of her eye, lives with them. The thought of being a stepparent is exciting to Larry. He really wants to do the parenting thing just right. But his insistence on getting to the bottom of every issue and making sure he fixes things as the man of the house should, only make Donna and Nick uncomfortable. Rather than winning their approval, he is seen as the antagonist of the family. Larry decided to seek counsel.

"I don't feel like I'm number one to Donna," Larry said with frustration. "I feel Nick is. I'm her husband, so I'm supposed to be her priority as well as the head of the house. Everything I read in the Bible tells me this is the proper order for our family."

"To begin with," Charlie said, "you need to understand that Donna and her son have had a relationship for seventeen years. You have only been in their lives for a short time. It won't pay for you to covet the bond they have as mother and son."

"But when it comes to her son," Larry added, "she won't even see that he lied to her last week when he skipped school. I just want her to let me hold him accountable for his actions."

"What difference does it make if you are 100 percent right, win the battle, and lose the war?" Charlie asked. "Whether you are right is not always what is important. Having to prove your point only displays your need to elevate yourself above her son. Let Nick take his own consequences for his actions. Do you remember when you were a teen? Did you ever skip school?"

"Well, yeah," Larry remarked sheepishly. "I guess I did stuff like that too."

"The outside world is difficult enough for today's teen. By demanding answers to Nick's behavior, you are trying to make him look small in his mother's eyes. Why don't you share your own past with him and try to understand? Nick needs a home and a dad who are a refuge for him to come to. By lightening up, you can reduce family friction and focus on relationship building."

"That makes sense," Larry said. "Thanks for hearing me out. I think God would like me to go home and ask my family to forgive me."

That's what Larry did. The next time we saw them, Donna had a testimony to share.

"You can't believe the difference in Larry's attitude," Donna shared as she held her husband's hand. "I suddenly feel Nick is safe with Larry. When my son is loved, I feel loved. Until now I couldn't get Larry to understand this."

Larry admitted he wanted to be the greatest in Donna's eyes. Being number one was his expectation. But, if a haughty spirit prevails, we don't have the attitude of Christ. When questioned as to who was the greatest, Jesus gave an interesting reply.

"Whoever wants to become great among you must be your servant, and whoever wants to be first must be your slave—just as the Son of Man did not come to be served, but to serve, and to give his life as a ransom for many." (Matthew 20:26–28)

This servant concept is difficult to swallow for those who don't understand kingdom living. In the world, getting to the top means pushing and shoving to gain a position of importance. Not so, according to God. He sees great leadership, whether as the head of a family, a government official, or in business, as *servant* leadership. Great leaders are first great servants. Like Jesus, they will give of themselves. They will wash feet.

PRAYER: AN IMPORTANT PLACE TO START

The best place to start forming a Christlike attitude is to begin adopting Christlike habits. One of the most important habits Jesus demonstrated was the habit of prayer.

Very early in the morning, while it was still dark, Jesus got up, left the house and went off to a solitary place, where he prayed. (Mark 1:35)

It sounds a little silly that the Son of God would need to pray. But He did. To Jesus prayer was communication with the Father. He looked forward to the intimate moments He and the Father shared each day. In these times Jesus poured out His thoughts, reaffirmed His work assignment, and found strength to move ahead with the daily struggle. Because He prayed, His focus remained on the Father's agenda. He had no doubt as to His purpose, nor was He tempted to form a different plan of His own.

Like us, Jesus had a busy life. His days were full of demanding, needy, people. By praying first, these demands become opportunities to serve. Prayer took the drudgery out of the work. By following Jesus' example, we can have the same confidence He had. A lot of us don't experience this confidence because we don't take the time to "clutter" our busy schedule with prayer. What a shame. That might be the reason many of us are so exhausted when we come home from work. We do it all in our own strength. But we don't have to.

An acquaintance at church returned from a work and witness trip to Papua New Guinea with an interesting testimony.

"I did forty surgeries in the few days I was in Papua New Guinea," Dr. Bert said. "The strangest thing of all, I wasn't tired. When I'm home, doing six or seven in a similar period of time leaves me exhausted. The presence of the Lord was with us in such a powerful way. We just knew He was there. If we felt the need, we'd even stop in the middle of an operation and pray."

That's the kind of energy the Lord gives to those who take time to meet with Him. We may be going to church because it is the "right" thing to do. But the Lord is more than going to church. His relationship to us is personal, not a religious habit reserved for Sunday. And nurturing a relationship takes time.

Prayer should be a daily attitude of the heart. Moment by moment we have the ability to communicate with the Lord. But it's our choice. Corporate worship is great for encouragement of one another, but personal time with the Lord is of far more benefit. It's in those times alone with God we find balance to live by.

In 1982 I began a daily time of prayer. I admit it wasn't an easy habit to start. Luckily I am a morning person, so half the battle was already won. But I still needed to get up at least thirty minutes earlier than usual to begin this new habit. To accomplish this I made an agreement with the Lord. If He would wake me up earlier, I would get up and have a quiet time each morning. I was amazed as morning after morning I awoke thirty minutes early. And I was alert! The Lord was so faithful. It wasn't long before I understood why Jesus enjoyed the early morning. It was so quiet, so uninterrupted, so alone with God.

As I tried to figure out how to structure my prayer time, I discovered God didn't leave me wondering how to begin. He gave me the how-to and the why-to of prayer, with step-by-step instructions.

"But when you pray, go into your room, close the door and pray to your Father, who is unseen. Then your Father, who sees what is done in secret, will reward you." (Matthew 6:6)

1. *When?* Set aside a routine time for daily prayer.
2. *Where?* Select a quiet place to pray (even the bathroom!).
3. *How?* Begin by shutting the mind's door to interruptions.
4. *What?* Speak praises and petitions to my Father; it is personal.
5. *Why?* God promises to reward me for time spent in prayer.

This sounds a little strange, but my very first, specially selected secret place for prayer was the bathroom. I knew that was the one room where I would be given uninterrupted private time. So, morning after morning, I began to meet the Lord there. At first I found it difficult to keep my mind from wandering to the concerns of the day. To stay focused, I wrote out a list of prayer concerns I wanted to take to the Lord. With that list, my Bible, and a notepad, I was equipped to make the most of my time with the Lord.

I began with only fifteen minutes a day. This was an achievable goal. It wasn't long before I found an attitude of prayer to be my secret weapon for life. The time I spent with the Lord began to lengthen. Now my daily time with the Lord is like a welcome visit with an old friend.

Oswald Chambers found great value in spending time in "the secret place":

> When we truly live in "the secret place," it becomes impossible for us to doubt God. We become more sure of Him than of anyone or anything else. Enter into "the secret place," and you will find that God was right in the middle of your everyday circumstances all the time. . . . If you will swing the door of your life fully open and "pray to your Father who is in the secret place," every public thing in your life will be marked with the lasting imprint of the presence of God.[4]

Chambers was right. Spending time with the Lord brings us the assurance of God's presence. Others will sense something different about us. We will leave an imprint of the Father wherever we go.

Quick bedtime prayers are nice, but for me they are not as effective. One prayer many of us learned when we were children went like this: "Now I lay me down to sleep. I pray the Lord my soul to keep. Watch and guard me through the night, and wake me with the morning light." This prayer only concerns itself with the fears of the night, not the giants of the day. It's during the waking hours when our attitudes are prevalent to exposure and most easily drawn astray by Satan's schemes. We don't make poor choices while we're asleep. That's why following Christ's example with early morning prayer makes life more manageable.

ATTITUDE: A MATTER OF CHOICE

Modeling the attitude of Christ is a daily, moment-by-moment choice we make. Charles Swindoll, Christian author, pastor, and the president of Dallas Theological Seminary, once made an interesting observance about attitude. And he's right. We all can make attitude a matter of choice.

> The longer I live, the more I realize the impact of attitude on life. Attitude, to me, is more important than facts. It is more important than the past, than education, than money, than circumstances, than failures, than successes, than what other people think or say or do. It is more important than appearance, giftedness or skill. It will make or break a company . . . a church . . . a home. The remarkable thing is we have a choice every day regarding the attitude we will embrace for that day. We cannot change our past. . . . We cannot change the fact that people will act in a certain way. We cannot change the inevitable. The only thing we can do is play on the one string we have, and that is our attitude. . . . I am convinced that life is 10 percent what happens to me and 90 percent how I react to it. And so it is with you . . . we are in charge of our attitudes![5]

Growth and Application

Commit to memory Philippians 2:3–4.

1. Think of a circumstance of the past week where your choice of
   attitude played a significant role in the outcome. Describe the
   circumstance and the attitude you chose.

   Did your attitude reflect the attitude Christ would have used?
   If not, what were the differences?

   What would the outcome have been if another attitude had
   been chosen?

2. Do you believe it is possible to attain the attitude of
   Christ?_____ Why or why not?

   Do you sense the necessity to possess this attitude for the sake
   of blending in your home? _____ How could this make a
   difference?

   How is the attitude of humility evident in your family now?

3. Do you think attitudes are chosen or imposed upon us? Why or why not?

In this chapter there is a quote by Chuck Swindoll. Do you agree with his statement: "I am convinced that life is 10 percent what happens to me and 90 percent how I react to it"? Why or why not?

If you were to change just one attitude, what would that be?

4. Read Mark 1:35. Jesus demonstrates His attitude toward prayer. When does He meet with the Father? _____ What is His purpose?

How could beginning your day in prayer, as Jesus did, contribute to healthy attitude choices?

Prayer of Application

*Lord, You have given us a high calling—to possess the very attitude
You demonstrated while here on Earth. But You haven't left us to do
this in our own strength. You have equipped us with Your power and
the written Word to follow. Because of that we know it is possible to
achieve healthy attitudes. Cause us to think often of our need for
prayer, to desire a daily time to meet with You. At times we have been
full of pride, selfishness, and the use of words that lack encouragement toward others. Please forgive us. Help us daily to demonstrate
godly attitudes of humility, selflessness, and encouragement, especially to all those You have placed in our family. Each one is special.
Thank You for all the blessings that follow right attitudes. May our
attitudes become a pleasant aroma back to You. Amen.*

NOTES

1. Jerry Bridges, *The Discipline of Grace* (Colorado Springs: NavPress, 1994), 47, 49.

2. Andrew Murray, *Humility* (Springdale, Pa.: Whitaker, 1982), 43–44.

3. Henry T. Blackaby and Richard Blackaby, *Experiencing God Day-by-Day: A Devotional* (Nashville: Broadman & Holman, 1997), 326.

4. Oswald Chambers, *My Utmost for His Highest: An Updated Edition in Today's Language* (Grand Rapids: Radio Bible Class, Discovery House, 1992), reading for August 23.

5. Charles Swindoll, quoted at the 1993 Mayor's Prayer Breakfast in Medford, Oreg., sponsored by Priority Living.

Chapter Eleven

ONE
MORE
BLESSING

Have you ever been awakened in the night by thoughts you didn't think you had on your mind? I have. And some of them really get my attention.

On one occasion, I had gone to Tucson to celebrate my mother's eightieth birthday. Along with my brother's family, we planned to make this a special party night for her. We made reservations at a restaurant she loved and plans for a wheelchair van to escort her back and forth from the nursing home.

It was a real treat for my mother to get out for an evening. She was like a kid in a candy store. She loved to be fussed over and prettied up. But it was also quite a chore for everyone else. Physically she was very fragile and unable to help with most of her basic needs. So it took a definite plan to pull the event off. But it was worth the effort to see how happy she was being the center of attention for a few hours.

We spoke with the nurses and they arranged to have her dolled up extraspecial. Her hair looked really pretty. A soft touch of makeup brought a fresh glow to her face, and she was wearing a new pink-and-gray dress. It had a nice V-neck collar with a delicate lace edge. The perfect dress to wear with the soft pink sweater I'd brought along as a gift.

Mother's eyes lit up as the Handi-Car driver escorted her into the restaurant and she saw the family waiting. Her five-year-old grandson David looked at her like she was the most special lady in the whole wide world. He wanted to push the wheelchair to the table. With his mother's help he managed not to bang her feet into too many things.

It was a fun party with all of us around the table, talking and laughing and feeding Mom lasagna. She still had quite an appetite! Then the moment came when the waiters brought out the cake and sang "Happy Birthday." And with a little help she even blew out the candles.

Reminding Mom of all the family connections was a little difficult because the relatives had gotten quite fuzzy in her mind. It became a game of show-and-tell. We'd show pictures and she'd think. Then we would tell. This became quite a funny game. Since my mother's mother had done the same thing, it wasn't devastating to any of us. We knew she couldn't help herself. So it was more enjoyable to reincorporate her into the family with photos. Humor helped. Then we would all laugh, and nobody cried. Mother was always so amazed at how large the family had become. "I did all that!" she exclaimed with amusement to those gathered around the room. We would point back the comment, saying, "Yes. It's your fault. Because of *you* we are all here today." Everyone smiled.

After lengthy good-byes at the nursing home, I went back to the hotel. Exhausted from the day's activities, I soon fell asleep. But within a couple of hours I was awake. It was so frustrating. To make matters even more peculiar, I had someone very unusual on my mind. It was Deborah. Why her? Why now? How did these thoughts squeeze in at a time when I was so preoccupied with my immediate family? How did they squeeze in at all?

My husband's first marriage over thirty-eight years ago had never really impacted our marriage. It was a short marriage, lasting approximately three years. As I lay in bed, I began to recollect the facts as I remembered hearing them. A child was born six months after Charlie's divorce was final. She had been named Deborah. At the time of his divorce, Charlie hadn't known of the pregnancy. He doubted that he was Deborah's father. And it was even more puzzling when he learned that no father was named on the child's birth certificate.

After the divorce, my husband's life took a different direction—a stint in the army, another marriage, three children, another divorce, and yet one more marriage—ours! Rather than living on the East Coast, he was now living on the West Coast. At best, there were a few vacation trips to Boston, but none that included meeting Deborah. Once in a while curiosity peaked when we heard a rumor that Deborah might be his child. Yet Charlie was convinced that at best the issue was extremely questionable.

Sometimes I've found middle-of-the-night awakenings are like middle-of-the-night phone calls. They're really important. More than once these awakenings have prepared me for a future event. This felt like one of those nights. Since I wouldn't have chosen to have Deborah on my mind, I felt sure God had placed her there. And I was just as sure this would be one of those "big" things. So there I was, alone in the darkness, with all these strange thoughts and unanswered questions in my mind. I began to pray for understanding. The promise of Romans 8:28 settled into my heart: "All things will work out for good; just trust Me. I have a purpose for this." I fell back to sleep weighing the importance of all these things.

Two days later I returned home and was once again caught up in life's busy pace. Then a phone call came for Charlie. A young woman named Deborah began to awkwardly introduce herself to him.

"I think we are related to one another," Deborah began. "I'm Judy's daughter. Maybe I'm your daughter too. When I was six, my grandmother got angry with me. She said I wasn't really her granddaughter. That's when I learned the man I called Daddy wasn't really my father. And my mother wouldn't answer my questions. She just got mad. But now she says you are my father."

"What makes you think that could be true?" Charlie asked.

"From pictures I've seen, I think I look like you," Deborah replied. "My eyes are green, my skin is olive-toned, just like yours. I really look like a 'Guinea' (slang for Italian). So I think I could be your daughter."

"When your mother and I divorced I didn't even know she was pregnant. I don't think I can be your father. We weren't seeing much of each other, and she was dating other men."

"My mother seems certain about this," Deborah said. "She even showed me the house where I was conceived. Do you remember a night in February with her?"

"I'm sorry," Charlie answered. "That was a very difficult time in my life. My father was dying in the hospital. Your mother and I were not getting along. I was extremely upset and angry. Thinking back, I do recall we saw each other once, but I don't remember the details. I'm just not convinced that I could be your father."

"I still think it's possible," Deborah insisted. "My mother wouldn't lie about something that important."

"If it means that much to you, I'm willing to do whatever it takes to find out the truth. The only way we will know for sure is if we have DNA tests done. Would you like to do that?"

"Yes," Deborah answered. "I really need to know who I am."

The decision was made. Charlie and I agreed to pursue paternity testing. It didn't feel right to let something this important go unresolved. The truth remained that Charlie and Deborah's mother did have a relationship. That couldn't be denied, so we knew the truth needed to be discovered.

We began making phone calls to gather information about DNA testing. We had heard from news broadcasts about people who went through the Red Cross to verify paternity issues. So we started by contacting them. But they were not equipped to do the tests for us. They told us it would be better to contact our local hospital lab. Bingo! They gave us the name of the only lab in our state designed for such special testing. Until now, it had never occurred to us that so few labs did this type of work. We were learning lots of things along the way. The nearest lab where samples could be analyzed for us was three hundred miles away.

We called and the lab technician was very helpful. She carefully explained the whole procedure. DNA testing typically takes three weeks before the results are known and it costs approximately seven hundred dollars. Both parties have to submit to blood tests, have photos taken, and complete an extensive questionnaire. Everything had to be synchronized.

A lab on the East Coast was contacted. Appointments were made for Deborah and Charlie to have their blood drawn on the same day. As scheduled, Deborah went ahead with her part of the test. Charlie did the same at our local hospital's lab. Polaroid photos were taken, and the lengthy personal questionnaires were filled out. Then both labs carefully packaged everything in special envelopes and shipped them via overnight delivery to the authorized lab in Portland, Oregon. We had officially moved into the wait-and-see stage.

Not a day went by that we didn't wonder what the tests would reveal. How would we feel if we received positive paternity results? That kind of knowledge would change our lives forever. In our desire to bless Deborah with answers, we were saying yes to adding even greater blending issues to our family. I'll admit some of the possibilities made us uneasy. If the tests were positive, what would our other six children think about the news of another sister? Would they be angry? Would they want to meet her?

At the same time, other thoughts caused us to look ahead with anticipation. It could be fun having one more daughter. Especially one who seemed so eager to know her father. There would be so many gaps to fill in, so many years to catch up on.

But a positive test didn't automatically mean a relationship would begin. What if Charlie wanted to build a relationship and she didn't? Maybe Deborah wouldn't accept a father who hadn't been there all those years. Did Charlie need another dose of rejection if she didn't? Lots of questions raced through our minds. It was such a time of mixed emotions. Our prayers became very focused as we waited.

The day finally arrived. The envelope was in our hands. Our hearts were pounding as Charlie tore it open. He began to read:

Regarding Parentage Testing Case #_____: All of the DNA data are completely consistent with you being the true biological father. The probability of you being the biological father is greater than 99%. You are the alleged father of Deborah _____.

We stood motionless, leaning on the kitchen counter. Then Charlie looked at me. I looked at him. The printed page stared back at us. All doubt was gone. Charlie and Deborah really were father and daughter.

Uncovering hidden things brings very strange feelings. For us there was apprehension mingled with an amazing sense of peace. It was like being caught between "Okay, I like this" and the opposite feelings of "How do we begin to live with what we've just discovered?"

I thought back to that night in Tucson when I had awakened in the middle of the night. All those thoughts had meaning now. God had brought everything into focus. I was thankful He had prepared me for this day. I took a deep breath.

"You have another daughter," I said, breaking the silence.

"That's what the paper says. Are you all right with that?" Charlie asked cautiously.

"Yes. It feels strange, but I think God prepared me to accept this news a few months ago," I answered. "The bigger question is —how do you feel knowing you are Deborah's father?"

"I guess I'm glad to know the truth. Thanks for being so supportive through all this. A lot of wives would have been angry."

"What affects you affects me. I want our life to be real," I answered. "That means I need to know the things that are a part of your life. You need to know them as well. Only then will we be fully honest about who we are. Especially when it comes to children. They deserve answers to their heritage and the assurance of knowing they are accepted. I feel God has given us a very unusual blessing."

"I think so too," Charlie admitted. "But I feel really bad that I didn't look into this sooner. I've let her down all these years."

"We can't change that," I said. "We can only go forward with where we are today."

"Would you mind if I invited her out for a few days? If Deborah's willing, I'd like to get to know her," Charlie said as he moved toward the phone.

"I think that's a great idea."

OUR FIRST MEETING

"We'd better leave now. Deborah's plane will be landing in less than half an hour," Charlie said, as he grabbed the keys in one hand and a vase of flowers in the other.

"You're right. That will give us enough time to park and get inside before she arrives."

Nervous excitement had built throughout the day. Deborah hadn't sent a photo because she wanted to see if her birth father could pick her out in the crowd. Soon the plane landed and the terminal was filling with people. Which one would she be? Would Charlie be able to pick her out? Fortunately, my husband is tall, so that made it easier for him to see above all the heads.

"I think I see her," he said, pointing to the doorway in the terminal. "That has to be her. She looks Italian."

God is so good. He allowed Charlie to pick Deborah out of all those people. It was a little eerie. As the young woman drew nearer, Charlie walked toward her. In that moment, eyes focused on each other, they embraced for the first time.

We were astonished at the resemblance Deborah had to her father. Although she had a much slighter build, the Italian heritage was evident. As we waited for the luggage to arrive, I quickly took a photo of their father-daughter moment.

It didn't take the two of them long to start comparing their features with one another. That was fun. And Deborah was right. Their eyes were the same color and even their cheekbones were the same bone structure. Upon arriving at our home, she became very interested in the photographs of the other children that hung upon the walls.

"I look more like you than all your other children!" was her delighted response as she and her father talked nonstop.

The missing pieces of her life were finally fitting together.

Charlie was having a wonderful time. He went to get the box of old family photos and important papers. The box held death certificates and rosary beads and lots of family treasures. He began to share these with Deborah. Looking on, I felt there was a real compatibility between them.

Deborah's gestures, features, and voice reminded us of her grandmother. When she spoke, speech patterns from Charlie's mother rang in our ears. Since Charlie and Deborah had never met, genetics was the only explanation. Old photos continued to confirm the family resemblance. Deborah's face assured us she was enjoying her night of discovery.

We couldn't have asked for a more enjoyable evening. We both felt a real bonding had begun—especially when Charlie received an extra nice set of hugs upon taking her back to the hotel that evening. Our apprehension had given way to a comfortable feeling. This was nice.

Looking into Deborah's face that night, I sensed the same feelings poet Lonnie Hull Dupont penned upon meeting her biological father for the first time. It was a *finding* time, and a *closure* time, and a time to *fit* the missing pieces of a life together.

HOW IT IS TO LOOK LIKE SOMEONE

In my twentieth spring, I first met my father,
saw him through his diner's window,
that big curly-haired Greek
counting his money, cigar clamped in his teeth,
smoke rising, coiling around him.
March rain carried odors of onions and starch,
his heavy-lidded eyes looked like mine,
his hands like mine, the Mediterranean nose,
the tilt of his head, his scowl.[1]

For Lonnie, many questions were answered just by looking at this man. A sense of knowing her roots was finally established. No longer would she wonder about the face of her father or why she looked like she did. Something within her soul had been quieted. She knew where the nose and even the scowl on her own face had come from. She truly was a reflection of her father. And now I felt Deborah had found the same thing.

The night passed quickly. The early morning brought a fresh breeze into the room. Still enjoying memories of the night before, we eagerly awaited Deborah's call. We had plans to take her on a scenic river trip later that day. At nine o'clock the phone rang. As Deborah began to speak, our feelings of joy were dashed. She explained that her purpose for coming to meet her father was only for "closure."

"I don't need two dads in my life. The man who raised me is my dad. He's been good to me, and I love him. You can't expect me to think of you as my dad when you have never been a part of my life. 'Dad' is a title representing a relationship. And we don't have that."

Deborah made it plain that her childhood home was where her loyalties and father-daughter relationship would remain. She was making plans to return to the East Coast immediately. A planned four-day weekend had been reduced to a four-hour visit! There was so much more we wanted to say, so much more we wanted to learn of Deborah. It wasn't to be.

WHAT HAPPENED?

To begin with, Charlie and Deborah probably held different expectations for this meeting. He was hopeful a new beginning would be established. Deborah wanted to bring closure to the uncertainty surrounding her birth. That remained her agenda even after she met her father. Charlie and I could have misread her interest in the family as more encouraging than she intended it to be. And it's possible the whole situation was much more complicated than we realized.

Blended families always bring with them a very complex picture. Our household was not the only one being affected by such big news. It would be perfectly understandable for Deborah to feel caught between feelings of pleasing those related to her childhood family unit and wanting to open her life up to include a new relationship with the father she'd found.

But sometimes closure is all that is sought. People don't necessarily want to deal with the added issues of building new relationships. They simply want truth. That knowledge is enough to free them from the questions that have troubled them. Like finally reading the last chapter of a good book, these people now have a real sense of moving on. They have put to rest the uncertainty that overshadowed their lives.

If this was Deborah's desire, her goal was accomplished. And her excitement was a natural part of the euphoria she felt by solving her own personal mystery. Closure did take place. And that is important.

An article printed on-line in the May 1997 issue of *Well Said* reveals wisdom concerning closure.

> Closure is important and necessary for you to experience a smooth transition from then to now or from the present to the future. . . .
>
> *What is the reality of closure?* Closure helps you to recognize experiences and others' contributions. You can examine your progress in life. It is important to take a closer look at your relationships and decide where to go with them. Resolve specific issues that may be left as unfinished business. You don't need extra baggage.
>
> *Why is closure important?* Closure is an event of great importance. Without closure, you may experience some emotionally taxing times that could have been avoided. Closure may be somewhat time consuming, but with some simple planning, communicating, and thinking, you can keep it short and simple.[2]

Two years have passed and Deborah has not initiated any in-depth contact with Charlie. We can't make that decision for her. Until she requests more communication, we will respect her wish to leave the matter closed. We have told our other children about a sister named Deborah. We even gave them her photo. For now, that is the best we can do to give her a rightful position within our family.

Our family isn't that unusual. More and more individuals are seeking out missing pieces of their family puzzle. In fact, there is a computer Web site called "Find People Fast." It's that important. I was fascinated by what I found through this organization.

> Fred, of Montana, found two brothers and a cousin after 52 years apart. Fred says, "I would like to say that this has been without a doubt, the most wonderful event of my life."
>
> Betty, of Connecticut, says, "I got the best Christmas present in the world. I found my father after 29 years."
>
> Kathy, of Washington State, says, "I would like to thank you very much for the fast efficient service that we received through your service. I am so happy that we gave you a call. Now the void is gone from the children's lives and they finally have a father."[3]

Most of us are like these people. Finding family is important to us. Even if we aren't impressed by what we find, we are driven to know to whom we belong. Something deep within the human spirit requires answers.

Ann was born to an unwed mother during the midfifties. Months later she was adopted, and the files surrounding her adoption were sealed. Eighteen years later, a letter from Aunt Doris, her birth mother's sister, was passed through the agency's hands to the family that had adopted Ann.

Aunt Doris wrote: "Has she lived? Is she happy? Does she need anything? Life plays tricks on us all. If this young woman is alone and needs help, I want to help."

"I decided that if this woman cared enough about me to wonder how I was eighteen years after I was born, then I owed it to myself and to her to try and find her," Ann said.

"It wasn't easy. My adopted mom wrote the agency a letter so they would give me the information they had in my file. She felt if two adults wanted to find each other, they should be allowed to. Even then, the agency wasn't eager to do this for us. Finally a caring social worker took my side and went all the way to her higher-ups and then to the state. That's when I got my aunt's last name and last address. But it proved to be a dead end. She didn't live there any longer. Then one day I called a friend. He was a detective. I asked him to run a DMV report to see what came up.

This time I had luck. The people at that address knew where she was and put me in contact with her."

"Did you and Aunt Doris build a friendship?" I asked.

"Yes, we did," Ann said. "It was a special relationship for both of us. Her health was failing, but we visited each week until her death. Those visits filled in a lot of the missing pieces of my life. One of my biggest concerns had been that I might not find Aunt Doris soon enough—that she would die before I could find her. Then I would never have the information I wanted. I had questions about my mother, even though I was pretty certain she was dead from the information I already had. Was I like her? What medical concerns were in the family?

"I was more concerned with finding out who my father was. I didn't even know my father's name. The only piece of information I had about him was that he had worked near Forest Lawn. So I thought maybe he could be buried there as well, since my adopted father worked for Forest Lawn. I spent many times up there wondering if one of the graves could belong to my birth father. Maybe it was one with pretty flowers on it. But mostly I was troubled by the graves that had nothing on them or no one to visit them. Did one of those belong to my father?"

"How did finding your aunt help you?" I asked.

"She was able to answer my questions," Ann replied. "I confirmed my birth mother had died years ago. And my birth father was also dead. Thanks to Aunt Doris I now knew his name. After her death, I checked out what she had told me with the coroner's office and found out more than I wanted to know."

"You were given a wonderful opportunity to pull together your personal history," I said. "Did Aunt Doris reveal anything else to you?"

"Yes," Ann said. "I learned that Aunt Doris had wanted to adopt me, but the family was not supportive of her idea. I'm glad she wanted me, but after hearing all about the family and their problems, I'm very glad that I got the parents I did.

"Then she did a very unusual thing. She changed her will and left much of her estate to me. That was totally unexpected."

The heritage of bloodlines is important to all of us. It makes us feel connected to a particular group of people. Most of us know our roots. And we take them for granted. But for those who don't, there is a mystery to be discovered. The pieces of life need to be found. When that search is successful, like it was for Ann, the web of unanswered questions is finally untangled.

Sometimes finding answers doesn't lead to a happy time or even a reunion. Some people who wish to keep their past locked away just don't want to be discovered. In 1998 the Associated Press released a touching story entitled "No Reunion for This Long-Lost Pair."

A woman who had given up her child over thirty-five years ago was awakened very early one morning by an individual asking "if the date April 22, 1963, rang a bell."

Before she could form a groggy answer, she was told, "The daughter you gave up for adoption has been looking for you, and now you're found."

"The guilt was immediate and overwhelming," the woman said. To her surprise, she was told information she thought had been sealed in court documents, never to be opened. Instead of being happy about a daughter she had been told wanted to meet her, she was feeling threatened and angry. Angry enough to file a lawsuit against the private investigators hired by her daughter to find her, alleging invasion of privacy and intentional infliction of emotional distress. She had no desire to be reunited with the child she had given up years earlier. The fact that she had been a pregnant unwed student was a secret she wished to keep to herself.

"The 35-year-old woman at the center of the case says she never meant to hurt her birth mother. 'I just wanted to know something about my history.'"[4]

This case and many others across the country raise a serious question. Is it more important to be concerned with privacy or to give our adopted children a right to their ancestry?

There is the real possibility that children wanting to make discoveries about their own personal history won't find a parent who welcomes them. Instead they could find rejection at the end of their search. Those who have kept a past truth hidden are not always overjoyed at being found. They want the past to remain in the past. Most of them have established families of their own who don't have a clue about their past. Why should they welcome such an intrusion? They never thought they would have to explain all that to their spouse or children.

LIVING WITH FAMILIAR ROLES

People are creatures of habit. We become familiar with the knowledge of who we are in the same way that we habitually sit in the same pew each week, tune in to watch the same weekly television program, or wake up at the same time each morning. We like what feels comfortable. But we can feel comfortable with unhealthy patterns too.

When we feel life has dealt us a raw deal, we tend to live as victims. Those who want to find a missing parent can easily label themselves as victims of abandonment. This sense of being a victim becomes a part of their personal image. And they feel it diminishes their worth. Because of that, these people sometimes overlook the fact that they are precious blessings to the families who have raised them.

Since God formed each of us in the womb, none of us is born a victim. We are only victims by choice. Tough things happen to everybody. Many people are born into less-than-ideal circumstances. Some people make the most of it. But for people who see themselves as victims, things are out of focus. And they become comfortable with their less-than-favorable status by gathering sympathy for their pitiful existence. It's not easy to change the mind-set of a victim. Even though he wants love, he doesn't move forward to accept it from estranged family members. If he did that his personal story would have to be rewritten. He would have to forgive and offer love in return. Withholding love is his way of reaffirming his role as a victim and evening the score for past hurts.

Life isn't fair. Nor does it always make sense. It is not a neat little package with a bow on top. But all of us have choices to make. We can choose to accept what God has allowed to develop in our lives. Those who know the Lord always have victory over life's circumstances, even those that brought about their birth.

Our prayer is that Deborah does not feel like a victim. But if she does, I would say, "You are here. God has, on purpose, given you life. It was not a parental decision but a decision of God! Your heavenly Father chose that you would not be a miscarriage! He gave you life. You are very special. In fact, the Bible refers to you as the 'apple' of God's eye."

> For this is what the Lord Almighty says: . . . "For whoever touches you touches the apple of his eye." (Zechariah 2:8)

A BITTERSWEET PERSPECTIVE

God had more than one reason for allowing us to discover our other daughter. Finding answers for Deborah was only part of the story. My husband's life was changing. At that time he had made a big career move into the ministry. The church had issued him a District License, and within weeks he would be taking a position as an associate pastor. The timing was incredible. This was the final piece of missing information from his own history. God wanted Charlie to be a clean vessel through which he could minister to others. Without a doubt we believe this was God's handiwork. It was His way of bringing the last piece of unfinished business from Charlie's past into place.

Our human understanding is so limited, but God's wisdom is perfect. Even if finding the truth brings us embarrassment, we need to appreciate the work of truth. Truth paves a straight path.

> Trust in the Lord with all your heart and lean not on your own understanding; in all your ways acknowledge him, and he will make your paths straight. (Proverbs 3:5–6)

We will fondly remember the joy we felt upon meeting Deborah. Yes, my husband's heart was broken afterwards—and mine was too. Life is often strewn with broken hearts, especially when there are broken homes. This is very sad. We have termed this meeting "bittersweet" and have chosen to be thankful for the hours of blessing God allowed.

Growth and Application

Commit to memory John 8:32.

1. We discovered another daughter. Have you encountered any surprise change to your blended family?

   Are you thankful when truth is revealed, or are you defensive, perhaps embarrassed?

   How can you cultivate a thankful heart for unexpected events?

2. From John 8:32, why is truth so freeing?

3. "Grace and truth came through Jesus Christ" (John 1:17). Why do you think God speaks of grace and truth in the same Scripture?

How does it make you feel to know God's grace acts as a buffer for difficult truth?

4. Read Job 28:11: "He searches the sources . . . and brings hidden things to light."

How has God brought hidden things to light in your life?

Did this knowledge result in a blessing for your life? In what way?

Prayer of Application

Lord, You are so loving in the way You expose truth in our lives. Even when we don't seek it, You find quiet ways to introduce us to truth. But sometimes looking at ourselves as fully "real" brings feelings of uneasiness. Thank You for the grace that accompanies truth and makes it bearable. We pray that You will grant us a greater understanding to view new circumstances, even those that expose us, as blessings from You. Help us to be convinced of Your hand at work in our lives. May we always cherish Your wisdom and timing above our own. Amen.

NOTES

1. Lonnie Hull DuPont, *Child of the Left Hand* (San Francisco: Eyelet, 1996), 15.
2. Karen Kramer, "Promise You'll Never Forget Me, Ever," *Well Said* 14, no. 8 (May 1997), http://wellness.uwsp.edu/Health_Service/Staff/hoffman/wellsaids/may.html.
3. Find People Fast, http://www.fpf.com/quotes.html.
4. Karen Testa, *Mail Tribune,* (Medford, Oreg.) © 1998 The Associated Press.

Chapter Twelve

MAKING
THE BEST
OF IT

I began to hate traveling to Portland. That's where my husband's three children live. The hours in the car would drag on. The conversation would go nowhere. It was always the same. Why don't the children make us feel more welcomed?

Although they say they forgive their father for divorcing their mother, they do little to express a desire for a close relationship with him. There are no invitations from any of them to share holiday times. And they never entertain the thought of coming to Dad's for special occasions. If Charlie fails to meet their expectations, it takes very little to bring on another bout of anger toward him. For the most part, our relationship with my stepchildren has been a lot like a roller-coaster ride. One day we feel "up," sensing progress is taking place, and the next we plummet down from the hope that had begun. Twenty-four years later we are still on the same ride. It's exhausting.

I saw a wonderful T-shirt in a store window one day. A woman, her hair in disarray, hands on hips, was imprinted on the shirt.

(I think it was a self-portrait!) Beneath the picture were the words, "Get Over It." I loved it! The humor was so right on. I should have bought a shirt for each of these kids. But I restrained myself.

The more I thought about those words, the more I liked their message. Why do so many people have trouble "getting over it"? Maybe we don't think it's possible. Or maybe we believe letting someone off the hook for the pain they've caused us is not acceptable.

These words make us laugh when we see them printed on shirts and greeting cards. And they are perfect for over-the-hill birthday gags. But since they pack so much truth, maybe we should take them more seriously. They hold the secret to healing a wounded heart. They fit well under the heading of "tough love." Love at this level is not insensitive, although it may be interpreted as such. Tough love cares enough to be candidly honest in the hopes of jolting the recipient toward change.

It was a great day when I figured out I couldn't thank God and feel sorry for myself at the same time. That's when I "got over it." "It" meaning my divorce, its aftermath, and the first few years of emotional upsets in my second marriage. My life is not picture-perfect. But it is still my life. God wants me to make the best of it.

> All this is for your benefit, so that the grace that is reaching more and more people may cause thanksgiving to overflow to the glory of God.
>
> Therefore we do not lose heart. . . . For our light and momentary troubles are achieving for us an eternal glory that far outweighs them all. (2 Corinthians 4:15–17)

Why is it important that we get over it? Because there is a lot at stake: the well-being of our children and our own mental health. We must not let our feelings set the pace for our lives. But a lot of us do. We don't get over it. Our families suffer, and our life's purpose is hindered. The past holds us in an ever-tightening grip until we realize we can be thankful for where we are today. God has not left us. We owe it to our present family structure to shake the dust from our feet and move on. God has not told us to spend our days in constant longing for relationships to be reestablished when the effort is primarily one-sided. God has told us to put His purposes ahead of others, even our sons and daughters. Time is precious. We must make the most of the moments we are given.

> "Anyone who wants to be my follower must love me far more than he does his own father, mother, wife, children, brothers, or sisters —yes, more than his own life—otherwise he cannot be my disciple." (Luke 14:26 TLB)

TODAY'S EFFECTS

An article by Maggie Gallagher in the December 1, 1998, issue of *The Wall Street Journal* brought to the nation's attention a study undertaken to find out why the number of juveniles arrested for homicides had risen by an alarming 87% between 1980 and 1990.[1] There was interest in finding out if the rise in divorce and remarriage could be a contributing factor. The study, conducted by Cynthia Harper of the University of California, San Francisco, and Sara McLanahan, of Princeton University, showed that child support was not a crucial factor in a child's becoming a criminal, though remarriage and poverty "[made] it more likely that a boy [would] be incarcerated as an adult."[2] But "family structure was more important than income," Harper noted. Gallagher believes that while "the structural advantages" of growing up in a home where the biological parents are married make things much better for boys, "the attachment between father and son [is the] key. Fathers teach their sons lessons, directly and indirectly, about what it means to be a man. When boys identify with fathers who are loving and available, the likelihood lessens that they will define their masculinity in terms of rebellion and antisocial aggression."[3]

With the reported rise in juvenile homicidal arrests, and the results of this study, we are now able to come up with a sobering fact. Nationwide averages confirm that a large number of stepfathers are not stepping into the role of a loving and available father with their stepchildren. Perhaps they do not understand their significance in the structure of the stepfamily. Because of this fact a portion of our young people are feeling emotionally abandoned and turning to violent means to make a statement. It is sad to turn on the news and hear of one more teen who has been part of a premeditated killing spree, or another senseless school shooting.

These findings are very serious. Some people might say, "That's not happening in my family." And that's great. You have reason to be thankful. But it would be foolish to stick our heads in the sand and not care about the impact of troubled youth on the nation as a whole. A lot of blended families aren't faring well. And that should matter to the rest of us. Troubled youth, like those evidenced in the survey, are in our schools, churches, and neighborhoods. They have value. But they may not feel valuable unless someone takes the time to tell them.

WHAT CAN I DO?

There is a lot we can do. Four things come to mind.

1. We can start by taking to heart the results of the survey. We can believe that disrupted families are in greater need of reassurance than we realized. Each one of us can decide to make a difference.
2. This study points dramatically to the results that follow when there is a lack of relationship between children and their fathers. It proves our youth aren't suffering nearly as much from financial problems as they are from the loss of a father's nurturing. This is a fixable problem. It takes more time than money. It takes an investment of time from a father or a male role model. Keeping promises, giving a hug, taking time to listen, throwing a ball, showing up for a school performance, and praying together are more precious than the things money can buy. They are priceless. They build memories as well as trust.

3. Understand that God sees everything that touches our lives. This fact gives life a healthy perspective. With this outlook there is space for life to become a journey of greater purpose than just making it through each day. Since divorce has occurred and we are remarried—with children—we should each include a simple question in our morning prayers: "What can I do today to make my family a better, more happily adjusted group of people?"

4. We can do our best to keep frustration at a minimum. People don't marry again thinking they are going to mess up their children's lives. New beginnings are full of optimism. That's what makes them so exciting. But in blended homes so much can be going on in so many lives that the home front resembles a field of land mines. Frustration creeps in easily when parents don't know how to make "happy" happen. That's why I get excited when I see couples going the extra mile to create a happy home after divorce. These people are focused on giving sacrificially of themselves to preserve a sense of natural family for their children.

TWO COUPLES

In December 1998, *48 Hours* aired a program titled "Surviving Divorce: A Family Affair." Dan Rather introduced us to the stories of Chip and Bess, and Don and Leslie. Each couple had one child and later divorced. Today, Chip and Leslie are together, while Bess and Don have not found other partners. Because of Chip and Leslie's relationship, these four people and their two children, Niko (Don and Leslie's son) and Jen (Chip and Bess's daughter), have become a modern-day family. Their lives are forever intertwined.

Dan Rather: Somewhere out there you believe you'll find a partner for life, and when it happens, you'll have only the best of intentions. You expect to be together forever. But, unfortunately, it doesn't always work out that way. . . . The statistics are staggering. Nearly half of all marriages in this country end in divorce. Every year over one million couples go their separate ways. Every year more than one million children watch as their parents split up. Tonight: A look at how American families are surviving divorce.

We begin . . . with Harold Dow, and with two couples (Chip and Bess, and Don and Leslie) who once had imagined their lives as endless love.

Dow: With Don's knowledge, Leslie took Niko, then four years old, and moved into Chip's apartment in a San Francisco suburb.

Don: We took him out of a family. We took him out of a school. We took him away from his friends, put him in a whole new environment, and his father wasn't around.

Dow: Don followed Leslie to the West Coast, taking a marketing job in Los Angeles so he could be closer to Niko.

Leslie: It was hard on Niko. It was confusing. He—he got very insecure for a period of time.
Dow: So how does this scattered, newly blended family manage?

Dow: Well, these days Leslie and Niko live with Chip . . . and a lot of the time they also live with Jen, Chip's daughter from his marriage to Bess.

So you got divorced but your family's gotten bigger?

Chip: Absolutely. I—I feel like all we did is blended more people into our family.

Chip: We describe what we have as a blended family.

Dow: Jen spends half her time with her mother, Bess, who edits a newsletter out of her home office.

Dow: . . . Don moved again from L. A. to the San Francisco suburbs where everyone lives now.

Don: My intent is to not let Niko grow up without his dad.

Dow: All four parents live within a mile of each other and see one another regularly.

Dow: Both Jen and Niko are in the same first-grade class.[4]

Notice the interesting solutions these couples have come up with. To begin with, they are still communicating effectively. Don and Leslie put what was best for their son into a workable plan. Don took a new job and relocated in California. Bess rose above her feelings of betrayal and also made a plan with Chip to put their daughter's interests first. They do their best to coparent Jen with fifty-fifty time. All four parents chose to live in the same neighborhood! So what do the children think of all this?

Dow: Do you understand what divorce means?

Jen: It means you're separated and you don't live in the same houses.

Niko: I don't like the two parents who are fake parents very [much]—as much as I like my mom and dad taking care of me.

These four adults continued to mature in their ability to work things out for the sake of the children. They want the children to feel a constant sense of love and connectedness to each birth parent.

Bess: I'll get angry, you know, and it's like why am I angry now? It's been so long, I should be over this, you know?

Dow: And she knows their daughter Jen, now six years old, also feels the pain.

Bess: I don't like watching my daughter have to go back and forth.

Chip: She understands that I don't want to live with Bess. She doesn't really understand why.

Bess: And we make it work OK for her, but it's not what she wants. She wants her parents in the same house.

Don: I didn't lose Leslie, I lost my family as well.

Dow: Don understands all too well what Bess is going through. How do you feel about Chip today?

Don: He seems to be taking good care of Leslie and he seems to be very cognizant of my son's needs.

Dow: But deep down inside, don't you hate him a little bit?

Don: You know, no, I don't. I don't hate him.

Dow: Don, how has all of this affected Niko?

Don: I think he really wants all of us to get back together. I think it—there's a hole for him that I can't fix.

Dow: Perhaps few people would be surprised if Bess and Don hated Chip and Leslie, but instead of holding on to all that anger and all that bitterness, these four adults decided to focus on the glue that holds them together, their two young children.

Bess: You might as well make it a big happy family, because you don't have a choice. You're still in the same family.

Dow: You get along?

Bess: Yeah, we get along. We get along fine. . . . We make it work.

Dow: For the children?

Bess: For the kids, and for us, too.

Dow: When you have kids, divorce, unlike marriage, is forever.

Bess: He's always going to be in my life. He's always going to be my kid's dad.

Dow: We asked Bess, Chip, Don and Leslie to come together . . . to tell us how they make divorce work so well.

Chip: We four have never actually sat and talked about how we do this. We just do it.

Dow: Their golden rule, they say, is to put the children first.

Chip: The kids didn't make this problem. The kids should not be suffering unnecessarily because of these problems.
  . . . What our kids get is four loving adults in various combinations and permutations. And if nothing else, it has them feel much more secure in the world because they got three different households where they get nothing but love.

The four of them exemplify "getting over it." They should be commended for the incredible effort they have put forth. Rather than building a war zone, they have surrendered to the circumstances they find themselves in. For the good of everyone involved, they have chosen to work together. This should send a message to the rest of us. Divorce doesn't have to mean hatred.

"THE FAMILY"

"We started with very little understanding of what we had gotten ourselves into," Susan said. "We didn't have a clue that we were facing such a magnitude of family issues until we were living them out. To make matters worse, the construction business, my husband Phil's work, was at an all-time low. And we had a lot of debt. So we were living hand-to-mouth. Here were all these kids and not enough bedrooms to go around. It seemed impossible at times. But we were determined to make it work."

"How many children did you bring together when you and Phil married?" I asked. "And what kind of challenges did that present?"

"I had two. He had five. But Phil's oldest child was already married with two children. Every child in our home was affected in some way by alcohol or substance abuse, just like I had been. I didn't feel qualified to make good choices for all these people. I felt like a victim myself!"

"So how did you begin to cope with so many needy people under the same roof?"

"Without the Lord's help, I couldn't have made it," Susan answered. "In fact, on more than one occasion, I told God I couldn't do all this. I felt like God sent me to Africa when all I wanted was an everyday life. But God kept telling me I *could* do it. So I started praying and believing Him. I hung onto the promise found in Joel where God said He would replace the years the locusts had eaten. Because of that promise, I had the courage to face the pain that had begun in my childhood. I knew I had to be the first one to get well."

"What was your life like before you married Phil?" I asked.

"I grew up in a large family. We had lots of fun times. My parents were good people, but my dad had a problem with alcohol. During my junior high years, he began drinking heavier and became more and more verbally abusive. My mother would make excuses for his behavior.

"When I was older I married a man whose social drinking turned to alcoholism as well. He was more verbally abusive than even my father had been. It would have been easier to be hit than to bear the hurt of all those words. After sixteen years we divorced, but by then I was also using alcohol to cope with life. I was an alcoholic. I had learned how to behave as an alcoholic from the time I was a child. I could lie and make excuses really well. There were lots of bad times. I didn't feel good about myself. After the divorce, I began counseling. The first six months I went every day. Just to make it through the day."

"Looking at you today, it's obvious your healing has been very successful. How have the changes in your own life affected your family?"

"I felt so responsible for the children. God has allowed my own mistakes and my own healing to become a testimony to change in their lives. I never made any of them feel condemned or unwelcome. I made sure they knew they were loved and could be forgiven. After all, God forgave me and gave me a whole new life."

"Tell me more about your husband," I said. "How did he support you during this time?"

"Phil hadn't given his heart to the Lord at the time we married, but he was very supportive. His accepting Christ came a while later. He knew all too well what I was coming out of with my alcoholism. His ex-wife also abused alcohol. Phil had attended many Al-Anon meetings in an attempt to understand her sickness. So he was very familiar with the issues in my life. And he was so kind. I wasn't used to that. As a husband he fulfilled things in me I had never experienced before, like unconditional love and encouragement. Phil worked very closely with my counselor in my healing. I began to feel special. Like I could do good things. I no longer wanted to die."

"Did you attempt suicide at one time?" I asked.

"Yes," Susan responded. "After that attempt I questioned God. I asked Him why He had let me live. I came to understand He knew something I didn't. I had a problem, but I was still valuable. He saw who I was becoming, not who I'd been. God already knew my heart would be softened and useful for His purposes."

"With as many children as the two of you have, there must

have been lots of issues to resolve," I said. "In what way have you and your husband approached family difficulties together?"

"Phil said a profound thing to me one day," Susan said. "He told me, we don't have to judge our children. All we have to do is love them. This was so freeing to me. I could look beyond their performance to see their potential. So that is what we were able to do with my son, Randy. He struggled a lot with drugs. He was in jail several times, but they always released him within a few days. So getting caught wasn't any big deal to him.

"The rest of us could see the devastation he was bringing upon himself and his wife. The family decided to go to him and attempt a family intervention. He was so angry, and he wouldn't listen. So life didn't get any better for him. It got worse. A while later Randy was picked up on more serious charges. This time he wasn't getting out so quickly. Phil and I confronted him together. By the time we reached the jail's visitation room, my son's spirit was already broken. He said, 'Mother you must be so disappointed in me.'

"I simply said, 'No. This isn't who you really are. I am hurting over what you are doing to yourself. God has such a wonderful plan for you.'

"My husband and I began to pray right in front of him. He asked us to forgive him. I love to watch God break down the walls, just like He did with me," Susan declared with passion. "I've cried with my children, and I've shed tears through the night. But it's worth all of that when they find Jesus and the victory begins to show. Seeing my son submissive to the Lord is the most wonderful thing. I know it's a miracle! He was in lots of trouble. But even though Randy faced felony charges for dealing drugs, he only received ninety days jail time. Only God could have kept him from going to the state penitentiary. There is so much to be thankful for."

"If my people, who are called by my name, will humble themselves and pray and seek my face and turn from their wicked ways, then will I hear from heaven and will forgive their sin and will heal their land." (2 Chronicles 7:14)

"You are obviously having a great impact on your children," I said.

"My family all know where I am coming from," Susan replied. "I give advice from the Word, not from me. I'm always honest with them. And I touch them because I care. Hugs are important. The anger seems to dissolve, and they begin feeling better."

"You are a remarkable woman," I said. "You have given hope to your children, but you didn't stop there. I understand you have touched the lives of many more young people. How did that come about?"

"As Phil and I built our nucleus with the Lord, I began to see so many young people at loose ends," Susan replied. "It seemed like the Lord wanted us to do something beyond our own family. Something that would make a difference. That's when I realized my life's dream to be a princess would have to be put on hold. God was equipping me to be a servant.

"We took in three girls from a crisis pregnancy center. I found I was able to teach them manners, parenting skills, and even how to cook and do dishes. They began watching me and learning practical things for life. This felt good. One of the girls asked me, 'Why do you have all the answers?' I simply said, 'Because I have made so many mistakes, I learned.' It was during those days I realized God had brought me through my own pain so I could share hope with others. These young people were a reflection of who I had been. I knew God had something better for their lives. I felt I could help them see who they could become."

"You have given love in such tangible ways," I said. "But how do so many people with such dysfunctional histories feel about one another?"

"We pull together well. Perhaps better than some families," Susan said. "Everyone gathers if one is hurt, or in need of food, or ill. They all do for each other. We clean together, paint together, and even help each other with yard work. The kids who were once misfits now feel connected because we are all available to help each other out. Each of us is accountable to the others. We are family."

Susan's troubled past didn't stop God from using her in some pretty amazing ways. And it felt good. She'd found purpose. She and her husband have become surrogate parents to lots of misfits. Their own family quit trying to sort out who's who. And friends refer to them as "The Family," not knowing when another member might join the ranks.

GROWING AND PRUNING

As Susan allowed God to prune away the pain of her own alcoholism, she found herself bearing the fruit of patience with others. We can grow godly fruit just like Susan did—by eating the Word of God and then living it out it in practical actions. It's similar to the digestive process for the physical body. We get hunger pangs every day. Otherwise we would starve to death. Spiritually we have the same needs. The soul's hunger cries out to be fed on a daily basis.

> "Why spend money on what is not bread, and your labor on what does not satisfy? Listen, listen to me, and eat what is good, and your soul will delight in the richest of fare. Give ear and come to me; hear me, that your soul may live." (Isaiah 55:2–3a)

Why do people live with a malnourished spirit when God is willing to fill us with abundance? We wouldn't do that with our physical needs. We'd dig in the cupboards or ask others for a bag of groceries. But when it comes to feeding our soul the richest of fare, we don't even see our need. Maybe we can't perceive the ears and the eyes in the same way we can the mouth—as vessels to receive nourishment.

The fruit of the Spirit isn't the normal kind of fruit we put in our grocery basket. In fact, it's curious that the Bible defines this fruit as behaviors and attitudes. But it does. When these behaviors and attitudes are "eaten" they seem to bring more nourishment to life than apples and oranges. So what are they?

> But the fruit of the Spirit is love, joy, peace, patience, kindness, goodness, faithfulness, gentleness and self-control. Against such things there is no law. (Galatians 5:22–23)

God's fruit basket is filled with nine special fruits. First there is the fruit of love. Without love, there will be no pleasure in eating. Pleasure over a good meal can be called joy. Spiritually speaking, joy is the presence of God. Joy brings the assurance that we've tasted the best of the Chef's creations. After tasting joy, we find peace, because peace is the essence of being satisfied. With satisfaction comes a sense of well-being.

Love, joy, and peace are the appetizers that prepare our heart's palette to digest the remaining fruits of patience, kindness, goodness, faithfulness, gentleness, and—the strangest of all fruit —self-control. Self-control tops the meal off, like a sinfully rich seven-layer chocolate decadence cake. It brings the touch of excellence. Dining at the King's table is quite an experience. And we don't need reservations!

I remember a time when my husband and I were discussing this passage of Scripture. It had been a very difficult day. The smell of rotting spiritual fruit was in the air. And I was very frustrated. After looking at this list and then reading it aloud, I knew we weren't living like God wanted us to.

"If I were God, I'd spit us out of my mouth," I said. "Why aren't we able to have fruit like this in our own lives?"

"Because *I* don't have any of these," Charlie said with little expectation of gaining them. "Look at this list. I don't have even one of these fruits."

"If God said we should have these, He must have given us a way to get them," I responded, pointing to the passage of Scripture. "God wouldn't tell us to possess something He didn't have the ability to deliver."

Fortunately, Charlie respects the Word of God. Even though he wasn't always applying it well, he still looked at it as the plumb line of truth. His religious training as a child had taught him to fear God but not really how to live a godly life. Growing up as a young boy in Catholicism, he wasn't allowed to read the Bible himself. At that time it was considered a sin for the common people to read Scripture. And not just a venial sin, but a mortal sin. They might not interpret what they read correctly. Only the priests and nuns were capable of proper understanding when it came to God's Word.

But now Charlie knew differently. He was no longer afraid to open the Bible. So seeing this list of the fruit of the Spirit got him to thinking. He agreed to pray about it. Again, we found God faithful. His Word did not return void. The promise of Isaiah 55:11 was true. The Word began to plow up the hardened soil in my husband's life. There were new signs of self-control. A lot of issues in our lives hadn't changed, but I realized Charlie was acting differently. He wasn't getting mad about stuff like he had before. Patience and gentleness were noticeable. And he had a lot more peace. Charlie had discovered the fruit of the Spirit was for him too.

Life is a lot like a fruit tree. No matter how long we walk with the Lord, we will be in need of pruning. All of nature has a rhythm to its existence. In the early spring new growth comes. Then the fruit buds. The summer months bring a sweetness, ripening the fruit as it matures on the tree. Fall represents harvesttime as we gather the fruit at its peak of perfection. And then come the winter months. A time for pruning and resting to prepare the tree for an abundant harvest the following year.

Most of the time, pruning takes place as the people around us rub us the wrong way. They give us ample opportunity to exhibit the fruit of the Spirit. If that is not our reaction to personal confrontation, then we need a little more pruning. The best fruit comes from the branches that are cut back. Fruitful lives keep bearing fruit, pruning branches, bearing more fruit, and pruning more branches—all the time.

EXAMINING THE FRUIT

God made it plain that good fruit and bad fruit cannot grow on the same tree. They are not compatible with one another. An internal battle will rage until one wins over the other.

"Make a tree good and its fruit will be good, or make a tree bad and its fruit will be bad, for a tree is recognized by its fruit." (Matthew 12:33)

Take note of the word *make*. This word says we play an active part in what we become. That means we will also be held accountable for the end result. Then look at the word *recognized*. This word tells us that other people have formed an image of who we are by the fruit they see in our lives.

Because our fruit is on display, let's consider what it might be like. Does it have the sweet aroma of freshly cut melon or the sun-ripened flavor of a large Forty-Niner peach taken fresh from the tree? These fruits contribute to the joy of summer. Many a picnic is graced with their presence. So why do they taste so good? They don't argue with God about what is best for them. They are not resentful of the rain that falls upon them. Instead they drink it in, using it for their own advantage. Neither do they resent the heat of the sun. Its intensity is useful in making them sweet. They simply conform to God's will for optimum growth, whatever the weather brings. Those who are scrumptious fruitbearers encourage a warm family feeling within their homes. Pleasant memories are being made. Insecurities are at a minimum.

But bad fruit is another story. It is very self-centered. Consider the Sour Grape. He stews over past hurts and expects others to comfort him in his time of need, which is most of the time. He is always in need of better conditions in which to grow. We are also familiar with the Prickly Pear. He is foulmouthed, critical, and perhaps physically abusive. Getting too close could be painful.

And some could be referred to as Choke Cherries. You just can't stomach being around them. They are like time bombs. They are argumentative and they always have to be right. It's only a matter of time before they explode, leaving shrapnel behind.

Which one of the above fruits best describes your heart's condition? What would your family say? It matters to God. And it will determine whether you receive a heavenly inheritance or be cut off from God's blessings.

"The ax is already at the root of the trees, and every tree that does not produce good fruit will be cut down and thrown into the fire." (Luke 3:9)

John's preaching accented the radical nearness of the coming kingdom. He stressed that the kingdom of God was "at hand," at the point of breakthrough. . . . [He] declared that "the ax is laid to the root of the trees." This was a symbol of imminent judgment. The coming of the Messiah would be a time of crisis for the people.

We notice that the image John used was that of the ax reaching the root or the core of the trees. He was not merely in the process of sharpening the ax. He had not merely begun to chip away at the outer bark of the trees. The ax had already penetrated to the core. The image suggests that one more strike from the ax will bring the tree crashing down.[5]

Two years ago the pear orchard near our home began to change. Many rows of pear trees were cut down. It made me sad. I didn't understand what the workers were doing. Like dead men, the trees lay in heaps along the orchard road. Later I learned that the trees were diseased and no longer producing enough quality fruit.

These trees brought home the message of Luke 3:9 so clearly. A day really is coming when the tree of our life will be examined. What will the Master find? Will He be able to say, "Well done," or will we feel the woodsman's ax? This question will not go unanswered.

Growth and Application

Commit to memory Galatians 5:22–23.

1. What are the nine elements of the fruit of the Spirit? Give a brief description of each.

   1.
   2.
   3.
   4.
   5.
   6.
   7.

8.

9.

Beside each of the above fruits write a number from 0–10 representing the measure of that fruit in your life. 0 = none; 10 = abundantly

2. John 15:2 speaks of God's pruning process. What is the benefit of pruning?

Pruning can be uncomfortable. Have you allowed God to prune away your unproductive vines (i.e., cursing, self-pity, unforgiveness, harsh words, etc.)?

How has this been evident in your life?

3. Read 2 Chronicles 7:14. Four key elements are mentioned: humble, pray, seek, and turn. What do each of these words mean to you?

In what way could applying this verse result in healing in your life?

4. Do you struggle with "getting over it," or do you "get over it" and move ahead with a positive mind-set? Explain.

Prayer of Application

Lord, forgive us for the pity parties we have held. They are sin before You. Your Word tells us to be thankful in all things. Sometimes that is so hard to do. But we want to please You in this matter. So please help us to get over past hurts that are common to divorce and blended families. We want to create happy homes for our children to grow in. It is our desire that the fruit of the Spirit would be seen in our lives. If there is pruning to be done, You have permission to take away the things that are harmful to us. We trust in Your Word. All of it is beneficial to us. Thank You for being such a loving Gardener of Your children's lives. Amen.

NOTES

1. Maggie Gallagher, "Fatherless Boys Grow Up into Dangerous Men," *Wall Street Journal*, 1 December 1998.
2. Ibid.
3. Ibid.
4. "Surviving Divorce: A Family Affair," *48 Hours*, CBS News, 3 December 1998. Transcript produced by Burrelle's Information Services, Livingston, N.J.
5. R. C. Sproul, *The Glory of Christ*, Logos Library System (Wheaton, Ill.: Tyndale, 1990).

Epilogue

A CLOSING PERSPECTIVE

Families like ours bear a resemblance to a favorite nursery rhyme. Like Humpty Dumpty, we've had a great fall. Divorce has left us with lots of broken relationships. And sometimes all the king's men and all the king's horses can't put us back together again.

Some parent-to-child relationships are still fragmented for us. Our hopes were high when we agreed to help one of our sons financially with a career move. When the idea didn't work out, a lot of bitter feelings erupted from him. Once again, we found ourselves on the outside looking in and our hopes at an all-time low.

"I am so tired of the anger that is thrown on us at the drop of a hat," I said in disgust. "There is no reason for the lack of respect we are given. He was singing a different tune a few months ago when we wrote out the check."

"I feel like one of those eight greyhound dogs," Charlie said. "I'm in the gate, ready to run the race. The starting bell sounds! The race has begun. But my door doesn't open. There's no way I can win. I'm not allowed onto the track."

And he's right. We have tried very hard to pull a sense of family together with all of our children. But seesaw relationships continue: progress-setback, progress-setback. . . . Repeated attempts to heal wounds from the past and build new family memories have not brought about solid change with some of our children. Their acceptance of us is very conditional. When we give it's not enough. And if we don't give when it's expected, we are labeled uncaring. So year after year the scarlet letter remains upon our lives. It feels like a no-win situation.

What can we do? We can face our limitations squarely. Even though it hurts, we have to accept the fact that some of our children are choosing not to reconcile. There is no way we can make anyone else put away their black book with its list of accounts against us. That is up to them.

When we know we have done our best to rectify a relationship, it's time to let go and leave the matter in God's hands. God has not left us. He knows our hearts. He also knows the work that needs to be done in the lives of our children to bring them to desire reconciliation: first with God, and then with us.

Relationships are a two-way street. When one side of the street is blocked, we will have to choose an alternate route. For us, it is the road of prayer. Our prayers will do more for our children than our continual pleas to be a part of their lives.

> So he said to me, "This is the word of the Lord . . . : 'Not by might nor by power, but by my Spirit,'" says the Lord Almighty.
> "What are you, O mighty mountain? Before Zerubbabel you will become level ground. Then he will bring out the capstone to shouts of 'God bless it! God bless it!'" (Zechariah 4:6–7)

God does not want us to live with discouragement. He has given us hope. But the end results of our parent-child relationships are in the Lord's hands. Only by His Spirit will the mountain of disappointments become the level ground of new beginnings. And if God tarries in accomplishing our desires for reconciliation and the hole in our heart remains, that is also for our good. We are His to do with as He chooses. When we are yielded to God's will, everything has a purpose.

THOUGHTS TO REMEMBER

1. *All of us share a common truth regarding our ancestry.* We are related to one another in a Genesis fashion through the breath of God. "In the beginning . . . God created man in his own image, in the image of God he created him; male and female" (Genesis 1:1, 27). That fact makes our stepchildren as significant as our natural children. Parents can determine to create genuine heart space, like God does, for each child.

> The Lord appeared to us in the past, saying: "I have loved you with an everlasting love; I have drawn you with loving-kindness." (Jeremiah 31:3)

2. *Honor the personhood of another.* Demanding respect is an abuse of authority. It establishes a militant environment within the home. It will result in fearful obedience or outright rebellion, but not genuine respect.

> You, my brothers, were called to be free. But do not use your freedom to indulge the sinful nature; rather, serve one another in love. The entire law is summed up in a single command: "Love your neighbor as yourself." If you keep on biting and devouring each other, watch out or you will be destroyed by each other. (Galatians 5:13–15)

3. *Take time for self-examination.* Be willing to admit wrongs. What worked for David in Psalm 51 has the same value for us today! We must know who we are and have a hunger to be clean from sin. This makes it possible for us to be a godly example in our homes.

> Wash away all my iniquity and cleanse me from my sin. For I know my transgressions, and my sin is always before me. . . . Create in me a pure heart, O God, and renew a steadfast spirit within me. (Psalm 51:2–3, 10)

4. *Avoid performance-based love.* Godly love is unconditional. Love like this undergirds all healthy relationships.

> If I speak in the tongues of men and of angels, but have not love, I am only a resounding gong or a clanging cymbal. If I have the gift of prophecy and can fathom all mysteries and all knowledge, and if I have a faith that can move mountains, but have not love, I am nothing. If I give all I possess to the poor and surrender my body to the flames, but have not love, I gain nothing. Love is patient, love is kind. It does not envy, it does not boast, it is not proud. It is not rude, it is not self-seeking, it is not easily angered, it keeps no record of wrongs. Love does not delight in evil but rejoices with the truth. It always protects, always trusts, always hopes, always perseveres. Love never fails. But where there are prophecies, they will cease; where there are tongues, they will be stilled; where there is knowledge, it will pass away. For we know in part and we prophesy in part, but when perfection comes, the imperfect disappears. (1 Corinthians 13:1–10)

5. *Hold no grudges.* Reconciliation is God's plan for our lives. This happens as we extend forgiveness to others, especially those in our own household. Forgiveness is a big part of the healing process.

> Therefore, if anyone is in Christ, he is a new creation; the old has gone, the new has come! All this is from God, who reconciled us to himself through Christ and gave us the ministry of reconciliation. (2 Corinthians 5:17–18)

6. *Realize it's OK to be part of a blended home.* We cannot relive yesterday or make it any different. Live in today. A true believer understands the price Jesus paid to buy his freedom from guilt.

> Let us draw near to God with a sincere heart in full assurance of faith, having our hearts sprinkled to cleanse us from a guilty conscience and having our bodies washed with pure water. (Hebrews 10:22)

7. *Develop a consistent prayer life.* This will be life changing. Pray in your secret place. Pray with your family. Pray in corporate

worship within a church body. With prayer, anxiety is replaced with peace and wisdom. It puts God in the driver's seat. If we take time to pray we will never doubt God's desire to bless us.

> Do not be anxious about anything, but in *everything,* by prayer and petition, with thanksgiving, present your requests to God. (Philippians 4:6, italics added)

8. *Show compassion toward one another.* Take time to walk in the shoes of other family members. This simple act says, "I value you and want to understand what you are feeling."

> Carry each other's burdens, and in this way you will fulfill the law of Christ. (Galatians 6:2)

9. *Remember that we need each other because we are different.* We are all designer originals, not carbon copies. God has created each of us with distinct gifts. And there is something good to be contributed by everyone. Enjoy discovering the gifts within your family.

> The eye cannot say to the hand, "I don't need you!" And the head cannot say to the feet, "I don't need you!" On the contrary, those parts of the body that seem to be weaker are indispensable, and the parts that we think are less honorable we treat with special honor. And the parts that are unpresentable are treated with special modesty, while our presentable parts need no special treatment. But God has combined the members of the body and has given greater honor to the parts that lacked it, so that there should be no division in the body, but that its parts should have equal concern for each other. If one part suffers, every part suffers with it; if one part is honored, every part rejoices with it. (1 Corinthians 12:21–26)

10. *Guard your mouth.* Words can bring a smile or a tear. They can encourage or bring despair. Verbal abuse leaves scars that go much deeper than those inflicted by physical blows. Once they are let go, words deliver a message. Will it be a positive message or one we will regret?

Pleasant words are a honeycomb, sweet to the soul and healing to the bones. (Proverbs 16:24)

The tongue also is a fire, a world of evil among the parts of the body. It corrupts the whole person, sets the whole course of his life on fire, and is itself set on fire by hell. . . . With the tongue we praise our Lord and Father, and with it we curse men, who have been made in God's likeness. Out of the same mouth come praise and cursing. My brothers, this should not be. Can both fresh water and salt water flow from the same spring? (James 3:6, 9–11)

11. *Live a life of integrity.* Children mourn the loss of a birth parent who is no longer with them on a daily basis. We can do our best to avoid criticism of that father or mother. And we can honor the visitation and monetary agreements that were made with an ex.

"I know, my God, that you test the heart and are pleased with integrity." (1 Chronicles 29:17a)

12. *Set financial goals for your family.* Diffuse the money monster. There are many godly tools and counselors available today. Just learning how to implement a simple budget will lighten the stress associated with money.

Plans fail for lack of counsel, but with many advisers they succeed. (Proverbs 15:22)

13. *Come to agreement about discipline.* Don't be too hasty for change to occur. Continue as much as possible to discipline in ways that the children are already accustomed to. And allow the birth parent to be the primary disciplinarian. As a stepparent, place more emphasis on relationship building. Time will eventually level out the power base within the home in a more congenial fashion without unreasonable demands and a spirit of anger taking over.

Fathers, do not exasperate your children; instead, bring them up in the training and instruction of the Lord. (Ephesians 6:4)

14. *Establish family meetings that include the children.* Their world has changed dramatically. Not only does this give them a voice, but it also cuts the frustration level down.

> And let us consider how we may spur one another on toward love and good deeds. Let us not give up meeting together, as some are in the habit of doing, but let us encourage one another—and all the more as you see the Day approaching. (Hebrews 10:24–25)

15. *Honor your partner.* Resolve to have a "one flesh" marriage. A past failed marriage is the past. This is the time, this is the marriage, that can come under the scriptural context of oneness.

> Then the Lord God made a woman from the rib he had taken out of the man, and he brought her to the man.
>
> The man said, "This is now bone of my bones and flesh of my flesh; she shall be called 'woman,' for she was taken out of man."
>
> For this reason a man will leave his father and mother and be united to his wife, and they will become one flesh. The man and his wife were both naked, and they felt no shame. (Genesis 2:22–25)

16. *Remember that attitude plays a big role.* My attitude is my choice. It will either fall in line with God's will and reflect Christ, or it will satisfy Satan's desires. Either way, my demeanor will affect others.

> You were taught, with regard to your former way of life, to put off your old self, which is being corrupted by its deceitful desires; to be made new in the attitude of your minds; and to put on the new self, created to be like God in true righteousness and holiness. (Ephesians 4:22–24)

17. *Life will bring pain. Expect it.* But God has a purpose for our suffering. Through the valley of affliction we learn valuable lessons. Those who suffer much are often the ones who also for-

give much. Because of our own pain we grow in character, in grace, and in appreciation for the Word of God.

> Before I was afflicted I went astray, but now I obey your word. . . . It was good for me to be afflicted so that I might learn your decrees. The law from your mouth is more precious to me than thousands of pieces of silver and gold. . . . I know, O Lord, that your laws are righteous, and in faithfulness you have afflicted me. (Psalm 119:67, 71–72, 75)

18. *Don't fear exposure.* We all need it. Sometimes surprise findings reveal things we really need to know. It is God's workmanship. He is opening up another area of growth in our lives. Exposure helps us face who we really are.

> And we know that in all things God works for the good of those who love him, who have been called according to his purpose. (Romans 8:28)

19. *Take heart. Don't become discouraged when others don't meet our expectations.* God has told us to love them, not change them. That's His job. The only one we are responsible to change is self.

> And he said: "I tell you the truth, unless you change and become like little children, you will never enter the kingdom of heaven." (Matthew 18:3)

20. *Realize the blending process is continual.* Don't become impatient. With so many personalities there will be issues of jealousy and money and who has to dump the garbage for years to come. It is a natural part of our lifestyle. We will be "forever blending!"

> Be completely humble and gentle; be patient, bearing with one another in love. (Ephesians 4:2)

Evaluation

Your input is valuable to us. *Please give this page (or a copy) to your group leader after your last class.*

1. What three insights from the concluding thoughts impacted you the most? Why?

    1.

    2.

    3.

2. What has been the most significant truth learned in the past twelve weeks?

3. As a result of this study how has your family grown? Did you make progress toward your goal?

4. Would you recommend this study for other blended families? Why or why not?

5. Do you have suggestions that would make the study better? What are they?

Get your family headed in the right direction with other helpful family titles from Moody Press.

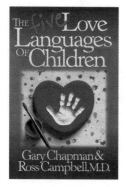